ARTHURIAN STUDIES LXXXIII

EMOTIONS IN MEDIEVAL ARTHURIAN LITERATURE

ARTHURIAN STUDIES

ISSN 0261-9814

General Editor: Norris J. Lacy

Previously published volumes in the series
are listed at the back of this book

EMOTIONS IN MEDIEVAL ARTHURIAN LITERATURE
BODY, MIND, VOICE

Edited by
Frank Brandsma, Carolyne Larrington and
Corinne Saunders

D. S. BREWER

© Contributors 2015

All rights reserved. Except as permitted under current legislation
no part of this work may be photocopied, stored in a retrieval system,
published, performed in public, adapted, broadcast,
transmitted, recorded or reproduced in any form or by any means,
without the prior permission of the copyright owner

First published 2015
D. S. Brewer, Cambridge
Paperback edition 2018

ISBN 978 1 84384 421 1 hardback
ISBN 978 1 84384 500 3 paperback

D. S. Brewer is an imprint of Boydell & Brewer Ltd
PO Box 9, Woodbridge, Suffolk IP12 3DF, UK
and of Boydell & Brewer Inc.
668 Mt Hope Avenue, Rochester, NY 14620–2731, USA
website: www.boydellandbrewer.com

The publisher has no responsibility for the continued existence or accuracy of
URLs for external or third-party internet websites referred to in this book,
and does not guarantee that any content on such websites is,
or will remain, accurate or appropriate

A CIP catalogue record for this book is available
from the British Library

This publication is printed on acid-free paper

Contents

Acknowledgements — vii
Contributors — viii

Introduction — 1
FRANK BRANDSMA, CAROLYNE LARRINGTON AND CORINNE SAUNDERS

Part I Thinking about Emotions in Arthurian Literature

1 Being-in-the-Arthurian-World: Emotion, Affect and Magic in the Prose *Lancelot*, Sartre and Jay — 13
JANE GILBERT

2 Mind, Body and Affect in Medieval English Arthurian Romance — 31
CORINNE SAUNDERS

3 'What cheer?' Emotion and Action in the Arthurian World — 47
ANDREW LYNCH

Part II Bodies, Minds and Voices: Investigating Emotion in Arthurian Texts

4 *Ire*, *Peor* and their Somatic Correlates in Chrétien's *Chevalier de la Charrette* — 67
ANATOLE PIERRE FUKSAS

5 Kingship and the Intimacy of Grief in the Alliterative *Morte Arthure* — 87
ANNE BADEN-DAINTREE

6 Tears and Lies: Emotions and the Ideals of Malory's Arthurian World — 105
RALUCA L. RADULESCU

7 Mourning Gawein: Cognition and Affect in *Diu Crône* and some French Gauvain-Texts — 123
CAROLYNE LARRINGTON

8 Emotion and Voice: 'Ay' in Middle Dutch Arthurian Romances — 143
FRANK BRANDSMA

| 9 | Translating Emotion: Vocalisation and Embodiment in *Yvain* and *Ívens Saga*
SIF RIKHARDSDOTTIR | 161 |

Afterword: Malory's Enigmatic Smiles   181
HELEN COOPER

Bibliography   189

Index   205

Acknowledgements

The editors would like to thank the many scholars, students, colleagues and friends who have contributed towards the project of which this book represents one outcome. We owe a particular debt of thanks to Elizabeth Archibald, Ad Putter and the other organisers of the XXIIIrd International Arthurian Congress, held in Bristol in July 2011, who allowed us to mount three sessions on Arthurian emotions. The thought-provoking papers presented in these sessions are the basis for the chapters in this book. The Congress also permitted us to hold a Round Table on Emotions; discussion at this productive encounter fed into the thinking of all the participants, and we thank Johnny McFadyen, Laura Jose, Jacqueline Wessel, Miriam Muth, Jan de Putter, John Petrus, Jessica Quinlan, Stefka Eriksen and Gina Psaki for their interventions at the Round Table. The Arthurian Emotions project also organised a morning devoted to 'Positive Arthurian Emotion' at the XXIVth International Arthurian Congress, in Bucharest in July 2014, thanks to Catalina Girbea; many of the book's authors took part in this, and we were also joined by Andreea Boboc, Brindusa Ciubotaru-Grigoriu, Stefka Eriksen and Gioia Paradisi for fruitful and lively engagement with the topic of emotions.

Thanks also go to our contributors, and especially to Helen Cooper, both for her support at the 2011 Round Table and for kindly agreeing to write an afterword. And we also wish to thank Caroline Palmer and the production staff at Boydell and Brewer for their enthusiasm and patience. The editors express individual thanks to Tim Bourns and Anna Dow for their assistance in reading, formatting and finalising the text, and to the Wellcome Trust for their support for Corinne Saunders' research. Financial support for the publication of this book was provided by the Utrecht Stichting voor Literatuurwetenschappelijk Onderzoek (USLO).

Contributors

Anne Baden-Daintree is a Teaching Fellow in English at the University of Bristol.

Frank Brandsma is Associate Professor in Comparative Literature (Middle Ages) at Utrecht University.

Helen Cooper is Emeritus Professor of Medieval and Renaissance English at the University of Cambridge, and a Life Fellow of Magdalene College, Cambridge.

Anatole Pierre Fuksas is Associate Professor of Romance Philology at the University of Cassino, Italy.

Jane Gilbert is Senior Lecturer in French at University College London.

Carolyne Larrington is Official Fellow and Tutor in Medieval English Literature at St John's College, University of Oxford.

Andrew Lynch is Professor in English and Cultural Studies at The University of Western Australia and Director of the Australian Research Council Centre of Excellence for the History of Emotions.

Raluca L. Radulescu is Reader in Medieval Literature at Bangor University and Co-Director, the Institute for Medieval and Early Modern Studies, Bangor University and Aberystwyth University.

Sif Rikhardsdottir is Associate Professor and Chair of Comparative Literature at the University of Iceland.

Corinne Saunders is Professor in Medieval English Literature and Co-Director of the Centre for Medical Humanities at Durham University

Introduction

FRANK BRANDSMA, CAROLYNE LARRINGTON
AND CORINNE SAUNDERS

Feeling the Fear

As Gawain rides towards the Green Chapel, the sound of someone grinding a huge axe rings through the silent snowy landscape and signals that this is where he may expect to be beheaded. The Green Knight welcomes him, praises him for keeping his promise to receive in his turn the blow he dealt his opponent a year ago in Arthur's court, yet also urges Gawain not to struggle or argue. With a wisecrack – once *his* head is off he can't restore it – the hero promises to stand still and bares his neck: 'And lette as he noȝt dutte / For drede he wolde not dare' (He behaved as if he did not fear at all, he would not cower for dread).[1] Gawain, it is suggested, dreads the axe, even if he will not show it. As the Green Knight swings the huge blade, Gawain sees it coming:

> Bot Gawayn on þat giserne glyfte hym bysyde,
> As hit com glydande adoun on glode hym to schende,
> And schranke a lytel with þe schulderes for þe scharp yrne.
> (ll. 2265–7)

> (But Gawain glanced sideways at the axe
> As it came hurtling down in a flash to shatter him,
> And he shrank a little with his shoulders from the sharp edge.)

And who wouldn't shrink from a blow like this? Even today, a modern reader can share Gawain's anxiety, the tension in the shoulders, and perhaps even his instinctive movement. The text builds up the suspense in this scene in a simple yet very effective way, unobtrusively presenting the emotions of the hero, moving the audience from feeling curious about what will happen next to sharing Gawain's fear.

---

[1] All translations are the editors'. All citations from *Sir Gawain and the Green Knight* are from the edition in *The Poems of the Pearl Manuscript 'Pearl', 'Cleanness', 'Patience', 'Sir Gawain and the Green Knight'*, ed. M. Andrew and R. Waldron, 5th edn (Exeter, 2007). Here ll. 2257–8.

When this story is told to children, they very much enjoy the scariness of the beheading. It is never hard to find a volunteer Gawain when the beheading scene (two near misses and one soft touch) is enacted in the classroom; in one session, the tale-teller actually spent quite some time after the performance 'beheading' a whole line of young spectators, all of whom wanted to see and feel the axe swooshing towards their necks, just like Gawain. The emotions in play with the children (and their play-emotions) were easy to recognize and study: both empathy and aesthetic responses to terror were at stake. To explore medieval emotional responses to the scene of Gawain's near-beheading is much more complicated. For, as this book will demonstrate time and again, we have only the text to work with. The only available resources for discovering and understanding emotions of the past are the texts (and images) that have come down to us. Working with these sources, in this book specifically Arthurian romances, raises all kinds of issues: of methodology, of medieval conceptions of and terminology for feelings, of the gap between modern and medieval emotional regimes and communities, of the constructed nature of the emotions in literary texts, to name just a few of the obvious challenges. Before turning to medieval literature within its culture, however, we need to recognise the larger philosophical formulations of emotion that have developed since the medieval period.

Emotion and Philosophy

How do we express the feeling of a feeling? What is emotion? How do mind, body and affect connect? Philosophers have returned to such questions again and again over centuries, with some vastly different conclusions; but they have often focused on the opposition of mind and body, stated memorably by Thomas Hardy: 'Why should a man's mind have been thrown into such close, sad, sensational, inexplicable relations with such a precarious object as his own body!'[2] Hardy's question makes clear how far such Cartesian dualism is fuelled by ancient notions of the body as fragile, flawed and unstable, though Descartes was unforgiving in his view of earlier theories. Descartes's theory of the emotions, expounded in his late treatise *Les Passions de l'âme* (1649), laid the ground for much twentieth-century philosophy and psychology of the emotions. Emotions, Descartes argued, were felt in the mind rather than the heart: they had physical causes, occurring as a result of agitation of the 'animal' (lower or material) spirits, but were *felt* in the soul, the term used by Descartes to signify the mind (consciousness), and perceived precisely at the point where he imagined the soul as joined to the body, the 'pineal

---

[2] *The Life and Work of Thomas Hardy*, ed. M. Millgate (London, 1984), p. 265.

gland'.³ Emotions were contingent, dependent on sensory circumstances; they had physical causes, and they led to physical effects, but the experience of the emotions was mental, a private event. Emotions and sensations were as much aspects of mental experience as volitions – mental actions. Descartes's theory is considerably more complex than Cartesian caricatures of the 'mindful body' or body as machine suggest – but it also clearly reifies the mind–body distinction. These ideas underpinned later explorations of emotion. Spinoza extended Descartes's naturalistic emphasis in his exploration of human psychology, placing 'affects' or emotions, principally desire, joy and pain, as both modifications of the body and the ideas of such modifications.⁴ Locke adopted Descartes's notions of sensation and reflection in the mind. Hume emphasised the causal connections of emotions and distinguished between impressions and ideas of emotions: the mind was a perceiver or observer.⁵ The idea of contingency – the link between physical cause and manifestation – was most famously taken up by the nineteenth-century psychologist William James, who opposed the Cartesian mind–body split in identifying emotions as perceptions of bodily processes; assessments of physical experience:

> Our natural way of thinking about these standard emotions is that the mental perception of some fact excites the mental affection called the emotion, and that this latter state of mind gives rise to the bodily expression. My thesis on the contrary is that *the bodily changes follow directly the PERCEPTION of the exciting fact and that our feeling of the same changes as they occur IS the emotion.*⁶

Since James, Descartes's conception of emotion as mental event has been variously questioned and refined, most often with a continuing emphasis on mind. Thinkers such as Martha Nussbaum have focused on the cognitive aspects of emotions: her approach reiterates Cartesian mind–body dualism, but opposes the traditional contrast drawn between emotions

---

3   R. Descartes, *Passions of the Soul*, in *The Philosophical Writings of Descartes*, trans. J. Cottingham, R. Stoothoff and D. Murdoch, 3 vols (Cambridge, 1985), I: 325–404; see especially Part 1, articles 25–9 on feeling in the soul, and articles 30–32 on the pineal gland.
4   B. Spinoza, *Ethics* (1677), ed. and trans. G. H. R. Parkinson, Oxford Philosophical Texts (Oxford, 2000), part 3, 'On the Origin and Nature of the Affects'.
5   J. Locke, *An Essay Concerning Human Understanding* (1689), ed. P. Nidditch, in *The Clarendon Edition of the Works of John Locke* (Oxford, 1975): see especially Book 2, chapters 1–7, on simple ideas, exploring sensation and reflection, and chapters 9–11, on faculties of the mind; D. Hume, 'An Enquiry Concerning Human Understanding', in *Enquiries Concerning Human Understanding and Concerning the Principles of Morals* (1777), ed. L. A. Selby-Bigge (Oxford, 1975): see especially Part 2; this work revises *A Treatise of Human Nature* (1739), ed. L. A. Selby-Bigge (Oxford, 1978): see especially Book 2 on the passions. Hume also published this material separately as one of four Dissertations, 'Of the Passions' (1757).
6   W. James, 'What is an emotion?', *Mind* 9 (1884), 188–205, at pp. 189–90 (emphasis in the original).

and rational thoughts, emphasising the role of judgement or appraisal in emotions.[7] This perspective finds its opposite in the behaviourist understanding of emotions as purely bodily, made up of stimuli and learned response.

Recent philosophy, drawing on the phenomenological approaches of Husserl, Heidegger and Merleau-Ponty, has to some extent turned back to the work of James, to develop his radical emphasis on the bodiliness of emotions:

> The structure of our relationship with the world cannot be adequately conveyed in terms of any account that imposes a clear boundary between self and non-self or bodily and non-bodily upon all experience.[8]

Philosophers have drawn on contemporary neuroscience to employ the idea of the 'affect program', the neural circuit that initiates emotional response. The term 'affect' brings back the body: it signals an instinctual reaction to some kind of stimulation before cognitive processes produce a more complex emotion.[9] Affect may, of course, be produced through cognitive processes, or may stimulate cognition that produces further affect. Affects, emotional and visceral concerns, have come to be seen as crucial in shaping human responses. The writing of Gilles Deleuze, particularly his work with Félix Guattari, has promoted this 'affective turn': Deleuze takes up and develops Spinoza's concept of affects, particularly as elaborated in Henri Bergson's work on the relation of body and spirit, which emphasised the physical quality of affection. For Deleuze, the distinction between affect and emotion becomes crucial in marking the corporeal, instinctive aspects of the former, which is dependent on an individual's particular place in space and time: the concatenation of social and cultural influences on individual experience.[10]

---

[7] See M. Nussbaum, *Upheavals of Thought: The Intelligence of Emotions* (Cambridge, 2001). Nussbaum takes a long cultural perspective, spanning disciplines from classical and medieval philosophy to contemporary neuroscience, and draws on a wide range of literary and artistic examples to argue for the ethical power of emotions, particularly compassion and love, as 'intelligent responses to the perception of value' (p. 1).

[8] M. Ratcliffe, *Feelings of Being: Phenomenology, Psychiatry and the Sense of Reality* (Oxford, 2008), p. 94. The phenomenological approach is underpinned by the work of Maurice Merleau-Ponty: see especially Merleau-Ponty, *Phenomenology of Perception*, trans. C. Smith (London, 1962); see also P. Goldie, *The Emotions: A Philosophical Exploration* (Oxford, 2000), and R. C. Solomon, *The Passions: Emotions and the Meaning of Life* (Indianapolis, 1993).

[9] Affect program theory is developed by P. Griffiths, *What Emotions Really Are: The Problem of Psychological Categories* (Chicago, 1997); see also Griffiths, 'Is emotion a natural kind?', in *Thinking about Feeling: Contemporary Philosophers on Emotions*, ed. R. C. Solomon (Oxford, 2004), pp. 233–49.

[10] See G. Deleuze and F. Guattari, in *A Thousand Plateaus: Capitalism and Schizophrenia*, trans. B. Massumi, vol. 2 (Minneapolis, 1987; first published as *Mille plateaux, capitalisme et schizophrénie*, vol. 2 [Paris, 1980]), and H. Bergson, *Matter and Memory*, trans. N. M. Paul and W. Scott Palmer, Library of Philosophy (London and New York, 1911), first published as *Matière et mémoire* (Paris, 1896).

Especially striking are the recent theories of cognitive neuroscientists, in particular, Antonio Damasio, who has argued that emotion is essential to cognition and moral judgement, and that brain and body are closely and inextricably linked.[11] Whereas cognition – non-emotional processes of memory, perception, action, attention, problem-solving – was traditionally the focus of neuroscience, affect has more recently come to the fore. Until quite recently, emotion was associated with the lower neural strata of the brain, seen as primitive and non-cognitive, but, while the subcortical parts of the brain are indeed involved in emotion, it is now known that the situation is more complex, and that emotional and cognitive circuits work together. Emotions can be stimulated by sensory experience or by the flow of mental images in the memory. This leads in turn to chemical changes in the brain systems, sending commands to other parts of the brain and to the body, both through the bloodstream and through neuron pathways, leading to feelings and to the consciousness of them, the feeling of a feeling. Damasio looks back to James to argue that the body is the theatre of the emotions – but to add that the brain also plays a key role:

> Regardless of the mechanism by which emotions are induced, the body is the main stage for emotions, either directly or via its representation in somatosensory structures of the brain.[12]

Though Damasio's notion of 'Descartes's error' is reductive, his theory is crucially different from Descartes's notion of emotions as private mental events. Most exciting is Damasio's exploration of emotion – body and brain – as enabling cognition and playing a key role in rational/intellective processes – a radical new idea of the embodied mind:

> [T]he comprehensive understanding of the human mind requires an organismic perspective ... not only must the mind move from a nonphysical cogitum to the realm of biological tissue, but it must also be related to a whole organism possessed of integrated body proper and brain and fully interactive with a physical and social environment.[13]

Research in neuroscience such as Damasio's is beginning to show sound physiological bases for emotional reactions: for example, the possible existence of 'mirror cells' in the brain, which react not only to directly experienced emotional triggers but also to representations of emotional reactions.

---

[11] See A. Damasio, *The Feeling of What Happens: Body, Emotion and the Making of Consciousness* (London, 2000).
[12] Damasio, *The Feeling of What Happens*, p. 287.
[13] A. Damasio, *Descartes' Error: Emotion, Reason and the Human Brain* (New York, 1994; repr. London, 2006), p. 252. The book in fact scarcely mentions Descartes, but is written against the notion of a simplistic mind–body split.

Medieval thought offers remarkable parallels to contemporary theories, parallels that are only beginning to be explored, as Saunders' chapter in this book makes clear. The theory of the four humours current in the Middle Ages underpins a concept of a mind–body continuum that resonates with current conceptions of the embodied mind. Within the fallen world, emotion was both a bodily passion and a mental experience, and affect was understood to play a significant role in thought, moral judgement, intention and the shaping of the self. The interrelation of voice, mind and body was recognized and explored long ago, within the very different thought-world of the Middle Ages. These three conceptual domains have informed and structured the chapters that follow.

The Affective Turn in Medieval Studies

With the work of medieval historians such as Barbara Rosenwein, Piroska Nagy and others, the study of medieval societies has followed the 'affective turn' which had already become apparent in wider Western cultural contexts.[14] Rosenwein coined the influential term 'emotional communities' to describe 'groups in which people adhere to the same norms of emotional expression and value – or devalue – the same or related emotions'.[15] Rosenwein's test cases, drawn from the sixth and seventh centuries, were predicated on the idea of 'textual communities', evidenced through individual dossiers of materials comprising 'conciliar legislation, charters, hagiography, letters, histories, and chronicles'.[16] Rosenwein fully acknowledges that 'texts may be insincere, make things up, mislead and even lie' (p. 28), but argues that emotion is always a matter of interpretation, by the person who is feeling and by the one observing.[17] Nevertheless, some degree of distrust in the 'made-upness' of literary texts remains among medieval historians. Although historians have often made use of literary texts in their investigation of emotion, they have also tended to regard the presentation of emotion in highly fictional texts with suspicion, as bearing an exaggerated – or at least unverifiable – relation to actual historical behaviours.[18] And it is certainly true that literary texts complicate our understanding of medieval emotions at the same time

---

[14] See, for example, B. Rosenwein, *Emotional Communities in the Early Middle Ages* (Ithaca, NY, 2007), *Le sujet des émotions au moyen âge*, ed. P. Nagy and D. Boquet (Paris, 2009), *La chair des émotions*, *Médiévales* 61, ed. D. Boquet, P. Nagy and L. Moulinier-Brogi (2011), and, dealing with the eighteenth century and later, W. Reddy, *The Navigation of Feeling: A Framework for the History of Emotions* (Cambridge, 2001).

[15] Rosenwein, *Emotional Communities*, p. 2.

[16] Rosenwein, *Emotional Communities*, p. 26.

[17] Rosenwein, *Emotional Communities*, pp. 27–8; quotation from p. 28.

[18] See, for example, *Anger's Past: The Social Uses of an Emotion in the Middle Ages*, ed. B. Rosenwein (Ithaca, NY, 1998) and special issue of the journal *Early Medieval Europe* 10 (2001).

as they mediate emotion in very different ways from non-literary texts. In particular, the genre of romance attends closely to the private and the individual, rather than the public and political, subject matter of epic and *chanson de geste*. Literary texts draw attention to normative behaviours, often modelling appropriate reactions within the text to guide the audiences' responses, and they comment on bizarre or inappropriate reactions. In the *Travels of Sir John Mandeville*, for example, the fictive 'Sir John' visits the exotic island of Dodyn in the Far East, where, when a man seems to be on the point of death, his family kill him, and then:

> And after that thei choppen all the body in smale peces and preyen alle his frendes to comen and eten of him that is ded ... And alle tho that ben of his kyn or pretenden hem to ben his frendes, and thei come not to that feste, thei ben repreued for eueremore and schamed and maken gret doel, for neuere after schulle thei be holden as frendes.[19]

> (And after that they chop the body all into little pieces, and invite all his friends to come and eat the dead man ... And all those of his kindred or who claim to be his friends, if they do not come to that feast, they are disgraced for evermore and are shamed, and they who were not there to eat him, are greatly disgraced, and they lament a great deal, for never again afterward shall they be regarded as friends.)

This behaviour, the social context, the consequences for those who fail to participate in the normative ritual conform to very different norms from those current in medieval western Europe; the narrative problematizes, but also relativizes, human feelings and actions. The Mandeville-narrative in part takes its cue from the accounts of Franciscan travellers to the Far East, such as Odoric of Pordenone, and from the encyclopaedic writings of Vincent of Beauvais, but at the same time the author gestures at European norms by inventing a systematically converse praxis. For, through the cannibal funeral feast, the dead man's family celebrate his life and invite his friends to participate in the mourning process; to miss the funeral feast is as shameful as failing to do due honour to the dead in Western culture, an observation that the Mandeville-author adds to the ethnography of Odoric of Pordenone at this point.

Literature, then, if read with appropriate methodological orientations, can tell us much about emotional norms within different medieval societies at different times: the courtly, the learned, the bourgeois, from the twelfth to the fifteenth centuries, and all across Europe, participate in ever-changing, intersecting and differentiated emotional communities. Literary texts, in particular romance texts, not only represented characters as experiencing emotion and reacting emotionally to the behaviour of others within the text, but they also, intentionally, evoked and played upon emotion in the audiences who heard and saw them performed or

---

[19] *Mandeville's Travels*, ed. M. C. Seymour (Oxford, 1967), pp. 146–7.

read. The so-called 'basic emotions' of anger, disgust, happiness, fear and surprise, the events and perceptions that elicit them, the somatic responses and the behaviour that results from them, the social contexts which allow us to read and interpret them, are all well evidenced in romance and other literary texts. And a whole range of subtler emotions such as resentment, *Schadenfreude*, vicarious shame, or nostalgia may also be delineated or suggested in literary contexts, more often perhaps than in other kinds of documentary source.

Arthurian Literature and the Comparative Study of Emotion

As early as Ælred of Rievaulx, stories about King Arthur were closely associated with emotional responses in their audience. Ælred's *Speculum caritatis* was written five or so years before Geoffrey of Monmouth's *Historia Regum Britanniae*, the first surviving biography of Arthur, appeared. In Book II.17, Ælred notes how the hardships of attractive and admirable characters (*amabilis ... mirabilis*) in tragedy or epic can move the audience to the point of weeping, though this response is not to be equated with a genuinely felt love for the fictitious character (*hinc fabulosum illum*).[20] This discussion leads into the famous anecdote in which the novice whom Ælred is addressing admits that he too remembers having been moved to the point of tears (*memini me nonnunquam usque ad effusionem lacrymarum fuisse permotum*) by stories of King Arthur.[21]

Arthurian literature, then, in its fixed points of love and loss, its emphasis on enchantment and the supernatural, and its emotional extremes, offers a remarkably fruitful corpus for the study of medieval emotion in literature; the stories of Arthur, his queen and his knights are transmitted and translated across the major European languages, offering unparalleled opportunities for comparison and contrast, for variation and local innovation, and for reconfiguration of emotional behaviours and responses, both within texts and on the part of audiences. Emotion, as Andrew Lynch notes, is not a medieval word; medieval languages map the domain through such terms such as 'felyng' or through precise words for particular emotional experiences. 'What were the consequences, for instance, of having *Middle English* feelings, as distinct from Anglo-Norman, Welsh, French or Latin ones?', asks Sarah McNamer in a recent essay, a question which this book seeks to unpack in a range of Arthurian contexts.[22] Which are the words that mediate emotions in the languages

---

[20] Ælred of Rievaulx, *Speculum caritatis*, PL 195, cols. 565B–565C.
[21] See J. Tahkokallio, 'Fables of King Arthur: Ælred of Rievaulx and Secular Pastimes', *Mirator* 9.1 (2008), 19–35, for insightful discussion into Ælred's arguments here.
[22] S. McNamer, 'Feeling', in Oxford Twenty-First Century Approaches to Literature: Middle English, ed. P. Strohm (Oxford, 2007), pp. 241–57, at p. 248. See also McNamer's book *Affective Meditation and the Invention of Medieval Compassion* (Philadelphia, 2009).

of medieval western Europe, and how can we comprehend them? Lexical analysis, as Anatole Pierre Fuksas argues in his essay in this book, is a crucial first stage for the understanding of emotion in its contexts.[23]

Emotions in Medieval Arthurian Literature explores three interrelated aspects of emotion: body, mind and voice. The book offers a dialogue between medieval and modern, theoretical and experiential. While modern concepts are often employed to analyse and interpret medieval depictions of emotion, medieval theories are also illuminated and probed; one focus of the book is the conflict, outlined above, between pre- and post-Cartesian attitudes to emotion, and the resolution of this through contemporary theories of embodiment and recent neuroscientific and psychological theories. A wide range of modern and contemporary theoretical perspectives, relevant to the study of Arthurian emotion, is explicitly drawn upon by the contributors to this volume. As well as neuroscience and psychology, our contributors also employ different philosophical, social and anthropological theories. Neuroscience opens up the workings of the brain and the ways in which affect, felt in the body, is made sense of by the brain, how it is translated into 'emotion', which combines affective and cognitive responses. Psychology provides other ways of understanding the mind, including, for example, the concept of emotional intelligence, and it emphasizes the importance of integrating processes of perception and cognition in intra-texual and audience affective responses. Social theories have shown the goal-oriented quality of emotion, and the strategic role it may play in society: the power of affect has recently become a major concern of cultural geographers. Theories of mind are also central to anthropology, which has highlighted the importance of ritual and repetition in emotional response. The medieval texts considered in these essays are opened up in illuminating new ways through these various insights; but the texts can also call into question and oppose the sometimes limiting models of contemporary disciplinary theories of mind, body and affect.

Body, Mind, Voice

The subtitle of this volume, *Body, Mind, Voice*, signals the special significance of embodiment in medieval understandings and representations of emotion, the affective quality of the construction of mind, and the intermediary role of voice as both embodied and consciously articulating emotion. Emotion is physically written on the body – tears, illness, madness – as well as displayed in conscious gestures, while the medi-

---

[23] See also C. Larrington, 'Learning to Feel in the Old Norse Camelot?' *Scandinavian Studies*, special issue on 'Arthur of the North: Histories, Emotions, and Imaginations', ed. B. Bandlien, S. G. Eriksen and S. Rikhardsdottir, 87.1 (2015), 74–94.

eval mind is understood to be shaped by feeling, and is represented as both brain and heart. Emotion reflects the conjunction of affective and cognitive responses, and is expressed both consciously and instinctively. The essays here probe the precise lexis of emotion (Fuksas) and treat the primary emotions of love and grief, and their physical manifestation – in tears, trembling and blood (Fuksas, Baden-Daintree, Radulescu, Lynch). They engage explicitly too with cognitive aspects of emotion: the relation between trauma and memory and between desire and intention (Saunders, Gilbert, Larrington). The connection between emotion and action (or inaction) is a key theme, and many essays probe the role of affect in motivating action and directing the will. While the thinking and feeling individual is a particular focus, the book also explores the social, public contexts and role of emotion: the affective force of ritual and gesture; the political and strategic powers of affect (Radulescu, Lynch, Baden-Daintree); and the possibilities of emotional deception (Larrington). Emotion may be both performative, in the sense of achieving change within and external to the text, and performance: a strategic display of emotional signs which do not necessarily correspond to internal affect.

The title flags up too the importance of voices both within and external to the texts: the voice of the narrator/author, of the performer of the text on any one occasion, and of the characters within the text (Brandsma, Rikhardsdottir). Literary genres depict the workings of affect and play on their audiences in different ways, and so the book explores the distinctiveness of Arthurian romance in its treatment of emotion. Jean-Paul Sartre's concept of emotion as transformative or 'magical' has a special resonance for this genre, where emotion is shaped through a distinctive nexus of magic, consciousness and ethics (Gilbert). Finally, the essays explore the gaps between expressed and suppressed emotions within texts, the cues given by medieval writers to help the audience to respond to them, and the ways in which bodiless characters, consisting only of linguistic signs, can produce physical reactions in the men and women who hear and read narratives about them (Brandsma, Fuksas, Larrington).

Emotions in Medieval Arthurian Literature breaks new ground in inviting comparative and highly focused analysis of texts composed in English, French, Dutch, German and Norwegian milieux. The questions it raises, about methodologies, semantics, lexis, interpretation, social contexts and somatic responses, are both urgent and complicated, and the answers the book offers may often be tentative, provisional or provocative. It represents, however, a beginning, an opening move in the literary study of emotion in the medieval period, and the editors hope that it will stimulate debate, suggest new applications, and awaken new interest in emotions, their history, and the rich literature of the Arthurian legend.

PART I

THINKING ABOUT EMOTIONS IN ARTHURIAN LITERATURE

1

*Being-in-the-Arthurian-World: Emotion, Affect and Magic in the Prose Lancelot, Sartre and Jay**

JANE GILBERT

Jean-Paul Sartre's 1939 *Esquisse d'une théorie des émotions* (translated as *Sketch for a Theory of the Emotions*) emerges from his engagement with Edmund Husserl's phenomenology, which studies consciousness from the point of view of the first-person subject interrelating with objects.[1] The *Sketch* outlines what a phenomenological theory of the emotions might look like. I quote Sartre's conclusions at length, as they will structure my discussion throughout:

> Thus consciousness can 'be-in-the-world' in two different ways. The world may appear before it as an organized complex of utilizable things, such that, if one wants to produce a predetermined effect, one must act upon the determinate elements of that complex. As one does so, each 'utensil' refers one to other utensils and to the totality of utensils; there is no absolute action, no radical change that one can introduce immediately into this world. We have to modify one particular utensil, and this by means of another which refers in its turn to yet another, and so on to infinity. But the world may also confront us as one non-utilizable whole; that is, as only modifiable without intermediation and by great masses. In that case, the categories of the world act immediately upon the consciousness, they are present to it *at no distance* (for example, the face that frightens us through the window acts upon us *without* any means; there is no need for the window to open, for a man to leap into the *room* or to walk across the *floor*). And, conversely, the consciousness tries to combat these dangers or to modify these objects at no distance and without means, by some absolute, massive modification of the world. This aspect of the world is an entirely coherent one; this is the *magical* world. Emotion may be called a sudden fall of consciousness

---

* I am grateful to Marilynn Desmond for drawing the *Esquisse* to my attention, to Andrew Leak for guiding my reading on Sartre, and to Katherine Ibbett for generous guidance and discussion on the subject of affect, and for her suggestions on an early draft of this essay. I am also grateful to the editors for their help in improving it.

[1] J.-P. Sartre, *Esquisse d'une théorie des émotions*, 2nd edn (Paris, 1948). Translated by P. Mairet as *Sketch for a Theory of the Emotions* (London, 1962). Further references to the English translation will be given in parentheses in the text.

into magic; or, if you will, emotion arises when the world of the utilizable vanishes abruptly and the world of magic appears in its place.

(*Sketch*, pp. 90–91)

According to Sartre, when I am being emotional, I am living in a world that is immediate – without instruments, distance or deferral. These latter characterize the utilizable, instrumental world. Emotion is therefore a species of magical thinking.

What I shall call the 'emotion-magic trope' is an old one, present in medieval literature as in modern philosophy.[2] In the first section of this essay, I shall ask how Sartre uses magic in order to think about the topic of emotion, and shall look at what light his essay may cast on the emotion-magic trope in the early thirteenth-century French cyclic prose *Lancelot*.[3] The second section will explore how the prose romance claims to re-enchant the Arthurian world and Arthurian literature through its use of powerful emotion and of names. Here I shall experiment with following the example of recent theoretical writings about affect and about visual art in discussing subjects that are difficult to articulate. In my view, the prose *Lancelot* is engaging in similar adventures through its use of the emotion-magic trope. The rhetoric of new, improved modes of expression and of being does not necessarily lead in politically desirable directions, and needs to be approached with an analytic eye as well as celebrated for its revolutionary qualities.

'Magical Thinking'

Sartre's essay in fact offers two distinct accounts of emotion; although both present it as magical thinking, they offer contrasting evaluations of both magic and emotion.[4] The quotation above refers to the second, on which I shall comment further below. In his first, more conventional account, Sartre presents the 'fall of consciousness into magic' under the power of emotion as an inferior kind of action, so limited in scope as to be practically ineffectual and even harmful. To take an Arthurian example: at the beginning of the prose *Lancelot*, Lancelot's father, Ban of Benoïc, is on his way to ask Arthur, his overlord, to come to his aid against Claudas, who has been ravaging Ban's lands. On the journey, Ban witnesses from

---

[2] Medieval literary magic itself is not my topic, only its tropic relation to emotion. For an overview of the scholarship, see C. Saunders, 'Introduction', in *Magic and the Supernatural in Medieval English Romance* (Cambridge, 2010), pp. 1–12. Saunders' book is itself a significant contribution to the field.

[3] References will be to *Lancelot: Roman en prose du XIIIe siècle*, ed. A. Micha, 9 vols (Geneva, 1978–83). English translations are quoted from *Lancelot-Grail: The Old French Arthurian Vulgate and Post-Vulgate in Translation*, trans. N. Lacy et al., 5 vols (New York, 1995) (hereafter *L-G*).

[4] In treating these as separate but related accounts, I follow S. Richmond, 'Magic in Sartre's Early Philosophy', in *Reading Sartre*, ed. J. Webber (London, 2010), pp. 145–61.

afar his one remaining castle go up in flames, and with it, his only hope of recovering his kingdom. Impotent to prevent this loss, he envisages the consequences:

> Si a pitié de che qu'il convendra son fil issir de France en povreté et en dolor et sa feme estre en autrui dangier que el sien et en avoeries de maintes gens, et lui meisme covendra estre povre et vielg et en grant soufraite user sa vie le remenant de son eage, qui tant a esté doutés et riches et qui tant a amei bele compaignie de gent et joieuse mainie en sa jonece.
>
> Toutes ches coses recorde li rois Bans et met devant ses iex, et li touches si grant dolor au cuer que les lermes li sont estoupees et li cuers serrés el ventre et se pasme. [...] Grant pieche a jeu li rois Bans en teil maniere.
>
> (He was distressed to think that his son would have to leave France in poverty and sorrow and his wife fall under some authority other than his own and pass from one protector to another; and distressed that he himself, old and poor, would have to scrape through the rest of his days in dire need, he who had been so feared and powerful and had in his youth so loved fine company and a joy-filled house.
>
> King Ban recalled all these things and could see them with his mind's eye, and there was such great pain in his heart that his tears could not even flow. He felt a spasm in his chest and fainted. [...] For a long while King Ban lay senseless.)[5]

Ban recovers from his swoon only to die a pious death. Compare Sartre's analysis of what he calls 'passive fear':

> I see a ferocious beast coming towards me: my legs give way under me, my heart beats more feebly, I turn pale, fall down and faint away. [...] [B]eing unable to escape the danger by normal means and deterministic procedures, I have denied existence to it. I have tried to annihilate it. [...] And, in the event, I have annihilated it so far as was in my power. Such are the limitations of my magical power over the world: I can suppress it as an object of consciousness, but only by suppressing consciousness itself.
>
> (*Sketch*, pp. 66–7)

Sartre implies a distinction between a fantasy way of being-in-the-world, in which I incorrectly project my own emotions onto unresponsive things, and a realistic one, in which the world will continue coldly on its path unless I intervene in it in an instrumental manner to change the course of events. By swooning, Ban does not modify the situation that threatens him, 'only' his experience of that situation. The instrumental way of being-in-the-world is ethically, existentially and practically superior. Sartre's scorn for both magic and emotion here is unmistakable.

We can advance various objections to this first analysis of emotion. On historical grounds, firstly: for instance, Barbara Rosenwein's edited volume shows that anger has not always been an inferior and impotent

---

[5] *Lancelot*, ed. Micha, VII, 23–4; *L-G*, II, 8.

response, but can be appropriate and instrumental. A literary example is the *chanson de geste* or Old French epic genre, where anger is a political instrument fully integrated into the feudal system.[6] Secondly, for theoretical reasons: the distinction between an ineffectual world of emotion and an effectual one of tools is unsustainable as soon as we consider the realities of human interaction. A burst of anger, tears or laughter can succeed where careful manoeuvring fails. In the prose *Lancelot*, Ban's pitiful death and Arthur's failure to help him will motivate a number of events later in the narrative. Finally, Sartre's first view is limited in its phenomenological development. Phenomenology sets out to challenge the dualism that would split the conscious human subject off from the world it encounters, conceiving them instead as profoundly interdependent. A strength of phenomenology is that it allows us to think about the relations between self and world, and between subject and object, dynamically and without privileging either term: the subjectivity that phenomenology proposes is not isolated, the objectivity not unresponsive. For someone in search of a phenomenological account of emotion, then, this first account is unsatisfactory.

Appearing towards the end of his essay and answering the objections just raised, Sartre's second account of emotion is much more innovative. In his summary (see pp. 13–14, above), Sartre referred to his own earlier example of how we can be 'frozen with terror' when 'a grimacing face suddenly appears pressed against the outside of the window'. If the first account presents emotion as an ineffectual and illusory agent of instrumentality, this second version insists on its immediacy, converting lack of finality into an indication of its power: 'one is not even tempted to flee.' This is no longer the mind's evasion of the nature of the world, its bad faith. 'Sometimes,' Sartre comments, 'it is this world that reveals itself to consciousness as magical just where we expect it to be deterministic' (*Sketch*, p. 84). The face at the window represents my startled apprehension that others truly exist, and are the centres of their worlds as I am of mine; an inassimilable proposition, of which I need to be repeatedly reminded. In this alternative account, emotion is associated not with withdrawal into my own little world, but with the shocking face-to-face encounter with another consciousness, necessarily experienced as alien and threatening. Central here is the idea that we feel emotion only in relation to what we perceive to be another psyche. I curse and threaten my computer when it refuses to comply with my commands. This is 'magical thinking' insofar as it anthropomorphizes and ascribes subjectivity to the machine, but the point is not so much the comical error as the truth thus uncovered about human being. For according to Sartre,

---

[6] B. Rosenwein, ed., *Anger's Past: The Social Uses of an Emotion in the Middle Ages* (Ithaca, NY, 1998); on *chansons de geste*, see especially S. D. White, 'The Politics of Anger', pp. 127–52.

[T]he category of 'magic' governs the interpsychic relations between men in society and, more precisely, our perception of others ['d'autrui']. [...] It follows that man is always a sorcerer to man and the social world is primarily magical. (*Sketch*, pp. 84–5)

Sartre now calls upon 'magic' to express an ethically, phenomenologically and ontologically powerful idea: '[t]here is an existential structure of the world which is magical' (*Sketch*, p. 84). This entails a notable revision in value for both magic and emotion.

This alignment of the social domain with emotion and with the magical might be taken to support the idea that emotions such as pathos or anger are fully socialized and indeed politicized in certain art forms and in certain societies. Sartre, however, maintains the conceptual distinction between emotions as immediate and social order as instrumental. When confronted starkly with the reality of other beings, he argues, the instrumental and deterministic world appears merely a set of evasive rationalizations:

> Not that it is impossible to take a deterministic view of the inter-psychological world or to build rational superstructures upon it. But then it is those structures that are ephemeral and unstable, it is they that crumble away as soon as the magical aspect of faces, gestures and human situations becomes too vivid. (*Sketch*, p. 85)

In Sartre's second account, magic as a figure is no longer unreal but exceptionally real, capable of dissolving seemingly solid rational and instrumental structures. Sartre now compares emotion to magic in order to emphasize that its sphere of influence is not merely ordered society but something much more radical and dynamic, extending beyond our normal apprehension of 'the human'. He wants us to feel how our selves are at a profound level open to other selfhoods as to something radically foreign, and conversely, how our being a foreign object to others at once jars with and plays a constituent role in our own personhood. In this view, the human subject is sited beyond as well as within such distinctions as 'me' and 'you', 'subject' and 'object', 'self' and 'world', 'active' and 'passive'. Where this is most obvious and most true is in privileged emotional moments such as that produced by the sudden, uncanny manifestation of the face at the window. These emotions cannot be omitted from our discussions of the social, but they remain at odds with society as such: spontaneous, disruptive and disorderly, non-instrumental and irrational.

In this second, more phenomenological account, emotion and magic represent not solipsistic withdrawals from the real world, but an engagement with human being in its most proper and intimate form. Emotion is no longer about my (effective or ineffective) activity in the world, as in the first account, but about how something-someone comes over me. I suffer the world, via the other's psyche. I therefore experience emotion as what

Sartre calls an 'irrational synthesis of spontaneity and passivity' (*Sketch*, p. 85), reflecting how my sense of self is penetrated by my sense of other people. The term 'passion' carries some of the sense at which he aims.[7]

These ideas may be explored in relation to the protagonist of the prose *Lancelot*, to whom Christological overtones often cling. Lancelot's heart is utterly possessed by his love for Guinevere – that mighty heart which is his defining feature in the prose *Lancelot*.[8] He is living (fictional) proof of the overwhelming objective reality of interpsychic relations and of its devastating effect on normality. Guinevere's impact on him translates into his on the world around him as, in the face of Lancelot's unrealistic and excessive *joie*, supposedly insurmountable obstacles crumble away:

> [E] disoit maintes fois, quant il estoit en sa grant joie, que riens nule ses cuers n'oseroit emprendre que ses cors ne peust mener a fin, tant se fioit en la joie, qui de mainte grant besoigne le fist puis au desus venir. Et par che qu'il em parloit si seurement, li fu il atornei a mal de mainte gent qui quidoient que il le deist par beuban et par vantise, mais non faisoit, ains le disoit par la grant seurté qu'il avoit en che dont toute sa joie venoit.

> (And he often said, when he was full of joy, that there was nothing his heart dared undertake that his body could not accomplish, so much did he trust in the joy which let him meet many a great challenge with success. But such self-confident words were taken the wrong way by many people, who believed that he was speaking out of arrogance and boastfulness. That was not the case, however, and he was rather expressing the great assurance that he found in the very source of his joy.)[9]

Instead of footling around in the instrumental world, Lancelot acts directly and immediately, and cannot be withstood. His love and its behavioural expressions, his prowess and nobility, belong to the magical mode of existence and they carry the Arthurian world out of its rational paths. The non-instrumentality and irrationality of his love are emphasized when, in flagrant disregard of the chivalry topos, he embraces dishonour for love's sake, or when that love repeatedly induces a recklessness that almost kills

---

[7] For this and later discussions of terminology, I draw on S. Trigg, 'Introduction: Emotional Histories – Beyond the Personalization of the Past and the Abstraction of Affect Theory', *Exemplaria* 26 (2014), 3–15 (a special number on Pre-Modern Emotions), and on R. Terada, 'Introduction: Emotion after the "Death of the Subject"', in *Feeling in Theory: Emotion after the 'Death of the Subject'* (Cambridge, MA, 2001), pp. 1–15. Terada is concerned throughout with the passions.

[8] The heart represents the total person, 'une unité d'esprit et de corps indissociablement associés' (a unity of spirit and body indissociably associated); M. de Combarieu du Grès, '"Un cœur gros comme ça" (Le cœur dans le *Lancelot-Graal*)', in *Le 'Cuer' au moyen âge: réalité et 'sénéfiance'*, *Sénéfiance* 30 (Aix-en-Provence, 1991), pp. 77–105; http://books.openedition.org/pup/3104, para. 14 of 144 [consulted 23 July 2014]. For C. R. Dover, Lancelot's heart is the defining figure of both the *Lancelot* proper and the *Lancelot-Grail* cycle; 'From Non-Cyclic to Cyclic *Lancelot*: Recycling the Heart', in *Transtextualities: Of Cycles and Cyclicity in Medieval French Literature*, ed. S. Sturm-Maddox and D. Maddox (Binghamton, NY, 1996), pp. 53–70.

[9] *Lancelot*, ed. Micha, VII, 74; L-G, II, 19.

its host.[10] Other characters distinguish this aspect of Lancelot's behaviour from his superlative achievement of a more comprehensible prowess and high-mindedness. When fighting to save the queen's life in the false Guinevere episode, for instance, his supporters have to dissuade him from what they consider a suicidal combat against three knights at once in favour of the lesser though still supreme feat of fighting them one after another (the text leaves us in no doubt that he could have defeated them all together).[11] Lancelot's highly emotional mode of action is anything but ineffectual, exceeding and exploding the instrumental world of reason and social order. Indeed, the central subject of the prose *Lancelot* may be said to be the Lancelot-effect, amplified by both narrative and narration as a constant source of wonder and attraction.

Although there is no consensus on the subject, several recent thinkers take 'emotion' to connote such ideas as interiority, personality and subjectivity, thus implying a traditional 'humanist subject'. Those interested in developments of phenomenology that challenge distinctions between subject and object, self and other, inside and outside, active and passive or human and non-human, often prefer the term 'affect', which has consequently acquired political edge. As I shall use the terms here, however, 'emotion' designates something relatively identifiable and self-contained, while 'affect' proclaims the overwhelming of containment and identity and a move beyond the actual, and even normally heroic human. By presenting a named and recognizable emotion such as *ire*, we evoke an ordered system for classifying and analysing; rationality places this treatment on the side of the instrumental. Contrastingly, affect theory aims to describe phenomena that overwhelm and overspill the familiar categories which allow us to grasp the world and bend it to usable form. Thus, a focus on Arthurian 'affect' would emphasize that it is not Guinevere but *joie* that impresses itself upon Lancelot, entering him as (not 'like') something alien. *Joie* is here an *abstractum agens*, on the path perhaps to personification, but interrupted at an intermediate stage. Although an agent, it is not presented as a human subject, and its strange influence over his heart causes the knight to do things which carry him outside the chivalric remit. Neither subject nor object in the normal sense, Lancelot possessed by *joie* is mysterious and transcendent. The Lancelot-effect detailed above may therefore be better thought of as a Lancelot-affect, since it unites Lancelot's alien love with his extraordinary nobility and prowess on the one hand and, on the other, with characters', readers', and writers' curiosity about, desire for and susceptibility to him. No one in or out of the text is indifferent to Lancelot. It is possible, of course, to

---

[10] Most notably in the Charrette episode; *Lancelot*, ed. Micha, II, 2–108; *L-G*, III, 3–32. For a comparison between its treatment in Chrétien and in the prose *Lancelot*, see M. T. Bruckner, 'Redefining the Center: Verse and Prose *Charrette*', in *A Companion to the 'Lancelot-Grail' Cycle*, ed. C. Dover (Cambridge, 2003), pp. 95–105.

[11] *Lancelot*, ed. Micha, I, 132–3; *L-G*, III, 270.

analyse his charm: Lancelot attracts and overcomes through his peerless 'vertus del cuer et cheles del cors' (powers of the heart and those of the body), which are corroborated by and reflected in his love for Guinevere.[12] Such a dissection, however, differentiates between aspects which are actually intimately confluent. The term 'affect' allows us to name that confluence, which seems to be what the text aims at. In the prose *Lancelot*, whereas the emotion-magic trope plays down the significance of both the milder emotions and conventionally digestible magic, a corresponding affect-magic trope creates a new *merveilleux* around strong, unfamiliar emotional experiences which impel characters into (what are presented as) new *chemins* (paths) and ever greater adventures.

As in Sartre's account, then, the *Lancelot* uses magic as a kind of yardstick to evaluate emotional quality. There are, however, significant differences. Sartre treats emotion and magic as having equal status. Thus, in his first account, both magic and emotion are axiomatically false, misleading and inadequate. When in his second view he wants to describe the strong emotions aroused by the mysterious reality of human interpsychic relations, he turns to a reconceived magic to express how counter-intuitive and problematic is the interrelation of subject and object in such cases. The prose *Lancelot*, on the other hand, typically treats magic as efficacious but limits its efficacy to the instrumental world.[13] Associated with *clergie* and with *engin*, magic in the prose romance maps the potential extents and limitations of technology. Its restricted powers ambiguously celebrate human ingenuity while also qualifying its status relative to a superior world of immediacy and affect that reach outside the familiar human domain – an irrational world of chivalric nobility, above that of the cleric. Thus his or her susceptibility to magical activity measures a character's proximity to immediacy and to authenticity on this noble scale. Potions can make someone 'love' only if they are not already deeply in love and therefore beyond manipulation; Arthur can be enchanted to love another, Lancelot only tricked into thinking Guinevere is where she is not.[14] This marks a qualitative difference between the two men's loves. Arthur's is a tame emotion, its manipulability reflecting its failure to engage broader issues of human interconnectivity, and its disappointing predictability; Lancelot's ethically greater and more challenging love is something wild, a full 'affect'.

It is well established that the metaphorical relation between emotion and magic in medieval works often works to credit the former and discredit the latter, 'displacing wonder from magic to emotion', as Helen

---

[12] *Lancelot*, ed. Micha, VII, 248; *L-G*, II, 58.
[13] On belief in magic's efficaciousness, see R. Kieckhefer, 'The Specific Rationality of Medieval Magic', *American Historical Review* 99 (1994), 813–36, at p. 814.
[14] *Lancelot*, ed. Micha, IV, 209–10; *L-G*, III, 164.

Cooper puts it.[15] However, their less discussed metonymic relation opens up a space for us to see the overwhelming, truly interpsychic emotional dimension as magical because possessing the immediacy and impact that Sartre evokes in his second account. For there is in the prose *Lancelot* a persistent, positive but indirect association between magical phenomena and emotional intensity. Most obviously, the hero's superlative capacity for love exists alongside the magical Lake that claims him as a baby and that he bears lifelong in his name. Among a host of further examples, Claudas's powerful lament for his dead son is connected narratively with the enchantment that makes his court mistake Lionel and Bors for two greyhounds.[16] Ban's proximity to the magical Lake may lead us to revise our view of his death, the pathos of which, as noted above, is far from ineffectual in the narrative. The prose *Lancelot* seems careful to steer us away from considering that these magical elements might play a determining causal role in the great emotional events, thereby avoiding instrumentality. Nor does magic here appear as the false currency that allows the coin of true emotion to shine out. On the contrary, the oblique association with magic encourages us to perceive such powerful experiences and their expression as immediate and *merveilleux*: outlandish, even fantastical, and flouting reason, order and convention, holding the potential to transform those things *en masse* into some as yet unrealized alternative. The truly magical resides in affect.

Thus in the prose *Lancelot* there are two ways of being-in-the-Arthurian-world. Through its protagonist and his distinctive effect, the text manages patterned shifts between, on the one hand, a realm that, following Sartre, I have been calling 'instrumental': a world conceived as 'an organized complex of utilizable things' (p. 13, above), characterized by relatively distinct subjects and objects, ordered social structures, strategic thinking and deferred gratification; and on the other, an 'immediate' world in which overriding interpsychic realities create eerie linkages and transitivities, and whose power, though intermittent and unpredictable, dissolves every element of the instrumental world with which it comes into contact, promising 'some absolute, massive modification of the world' (ibid.) which is at once feared and priceless.

Re-Enchanting the Arthurian World

In the first section I drew parallels between the ways in which Sartre and the prose *Lancelot* use the emotion-magic trope. In both texts, a first move demystifies and diminishes both magic and emotion, a position rendered

---

[15] H. Cooper, 'Magic That Doesn't Work', in *The English Romance in Time: Transforming Motifs from Geoffrey of Monmouth to the Death of Shakespeare* (Oxford, 2004), pp. 137–72, at p. 156.

[16] *Lancelot*, ed. Micha, VII, 119–29; L-G, II, 29–32.

largely rhetorical in both cases: postulated only so as to be superseded by new, greater enchantments, a compelling and immediate *merveilleux* in which the texts invest.

In this second section, I shall argue that the prose *Lancelot*'s use of 'magical' affect aims to re-enchant the Arthurian literary world, thereby carving out a niche for Arthurian prose romance within the competitive literary field of early thirteenth-century French. This section is, frankly, experimental. I am inspired and intrigued by recent developments in affect theory, exemplified by the work of Eve Kosofsky Sedgwick and Adam Frank, who emphasize that, in order to approach affect, we need to find new ways of recording, understanding and expressing data. New, but also old: our normal 'digital (on/off)' mode needs to be supplemented with 'analog[ue] (graduated and/or multiply differentiated) representational models'.[17] They argue that since the mid-twentieth century, the 'digital' has dominated Western theorizing.[18] It captures well cleanly distinct states, especially binary contrasts; an 'analogue' account would lose in crisp definition but could register more subtle shades of phenomena and relationship, and could quantify both continuities and discontinuities. Sedgwick and Frank aspire to produce 'a complex, multilayered phyllo dough of the analog[ue] and the digital' in a rich account which will capture the complexity of affective phenomena.[19] Challenging though it is, their example is potentially very valuable. As I read it, Sedgwick and Frank's distinction recalls the one that Sartre makes between the rational and the immediate, but refuses to relegate the latter term to inarticulacy, mystery and magic. Writing about 'analogue' dimensions of experience and using 'analogue' representational models will require us to develop other ways of articulating: dividing, distinguishing, explaining, relating. Without claiming to have met this challenge, I want in this section to try layering the digital with the analogue in a description of how signification, the emotional and the magical combine in the prose *Lancelot*. In order to do so, I shall draw on contemporary philosopher Martin Jay's essay 'Magical Nominalism: Photography and the Re-Enchantment of the World', which addresses similar issues in the context of modern visual art; I hope to show how referring to visual art can aid our understanding of matters linguistic and emotional.[20]

---

[17] E. Kosofsky Sedgwick and A. Frank, 'Shame in the Cybernetic Fold: Reading Silvan Tomkins', *Critical Inquiry* 21 (1994–5), 496–522, at p. 505; see especially pp. 505–8.

[18] 'The cybernetic fold' is their term for the mid-twentieth-century intellectual movement which arose when computing, before its great technological developments, dominated intellectual imaginings in many fields, opening up the idea of calculating far more complex and various data than previously possible; 'Shame', pp. 508–11. An important strand of this movement was structuralism.

[19] 'Shame', pp. 517–18.

[20] M. Jay, 'Magical Nominalism: Photography and the Re-Enchantment of the World', *Culture, Theory & Critique* 50 (2009), 165–83. Further references will be given in parentheses in the text.

I start with a simple observation about Arthurian affect, which is that it is embodied in figures with personal names. This is such an obvious point that it is easily overlooked; but contrast Guillaume de Lorris's roughly contemporary *Roman de la Rose*, where personified emotions stalk an allegorical landscape while the only figure which might be construed as experiencing those emotions walks among them as Amans. The *Rose's* anonymous subject is embroiled in psychomachia, the plaything (or playground) of emotional impulses which, having taken the step from *abstractum agens* to full embodiment and social interaction, are as opaque as any human person would be. The Lover's encounters with these figures lack the numinous, interpsychic quality of the affective encounters described in the first section of this chapter. Although he is penetrated by the God of Love's arrows of Beauty, Company, and so on, his (?) emotions remain outside him.[21] I do not belittle Guillaume's *Rose*, which as a text projects a powerful sense of the mystery of interpsychic affectivity, and whose playful self-consciousness and irony, as well as the surprises that it pulls in its explorations of psychology and interaction, are no less disturbing than those of the *Lancelot*. The latter's discourse of character and affect are, however, quite different.

No named Arthurian character can be read as a walking instance of any single emotion. The reliably ruthless Brun sans Pitié may epitomize 'haine, cruauté et violence' (hatred, cruelty and violence), but he does so in a different way from that in which the *Rose's* Dangier personifies *dangier*.[22] Both figures exemplify their governing quality through repeated behaviour, but the effect when they act 'out of character' is different. Personifications in the *Rose* who depart from type present us with an intriguing paradox leading to an exploration of the fragmented state of the psyche and of the extents and limitations of allegorical writing and of signification *per se*, which is a major element in the work's literary legacy.[23] Contrastingly, in Brun's conduct we confront the problem of how human character exceeds rational analysis, classification or predictability, and the further mystery of how and why human relations may provoke and tolerate such comportment.[24] Brun's affect particularizes him; it is

---

[21] Guillaume de Lorris and Jean de Meun, *Le Roman de la Rose*, ed. F. Lecoy, 3 vols, CFMA 92, 95, 98 (Paris, 1965–70); vol. 1, ll. 1679–1878; *The Romance of the Rose*, trans. F. Horgan (Oxford, 1994), pp. 26–9.

[22] Brun appears in the prose *Lancelot* but grows fully into his epithet in the prose *Tristan*. See R. Trachsler, 'Brehus sans pitié: portrait-robot du criminel arthurien', in *La Violence dans le monde médiéval*, Sénéfiance 36 (Aix-en-Provence, 1994), pp. 525–54; http://books.openedition.org/pup/3180 [consulted 17 July 2014] (para. 20 of 31).

[23] Dangier (Rebuff – although the term is difficult to define or translate) is reproached for softening towards the Lover by Honte (Shame) and Peur (Fear); *Rose*, vol. 1, ll. 3651–3736; *Romance*, pp. 56–7. The playful stretching of the limits of personification allegory in both parts of the *Rose* is discussed by S. Kay, *The Romance of the Rose* (London, 1995), pp. 23–32.

[24] 'Brehus est le contraire de tout ce qui est stable, fiable, acquis. Le seul élément constant en lui – et c'est ce qui fait l'essence de son personage – c'est l'absence de pitié […]. Brehus l'insaisissable se situe en dehors de tout système' (Brehus is the opposite of everything

not interchangeable with that of Kay, another repeat infringer of chivalric codes. Both Brun and Kay can and do change, within or between texts (a pleasure of Arthurian discourse is character revision).[25] Nevertheless, in any text where it arises, the Arthurian proper name indicates a haecceity, an individuating 'thisness' which somehow conjures up the character whole and instantaneous. Thus the name 'Brun' represents a configuration of qualities, experiences and relations, behaviours, actions and effects, actors, opponents, beneficiaries and audiences, magical in its fused totality and in its immediacy: the Brun-affect.

Not that Arthurian prose romances lack an analytical or 'digital' process: characters in the prose *Lancelot* are possessed by *ire* or torn between *joie* and *dolor*; they may *avoir poor, estre esbahi* or *liez, faire duel* (see Fuksas, this volume). However, the inflections of rivalry, anxiety, jealousy, aggression, curiosity, desire, self-sacrifice, suppression and so on which colour the romances are not captured by this process. Where emotions are concerned, reasoning and logical language appear inadequate either to explain or to guide. Characters are a mystery to themselves as much as to others; human voluntarism has only a restricted and often ironic role. The very 'conte' that narrates prose romances emphasizes how the text draws upon an impersonal, inhuman resource that is less made than found.[26] In contrast to the *clergie* and *engin* that characterize the works of Chrétien and his admirers, and the (ironized) emphasis in their works on rationalism and on scholastic analysis, the prose *Lancelot* and works like it cultivate a mixture of stark declaration and equally stark inarticulacy:[27]

> Et la roine est venue en ses chambres et fu avec lui Galehout et Lionials et la dame de Malouat; si font trop grant duel ensamble et dist la roine a Galehout: 'Don ne m'a bien trahi vostre compains? Par foi ou il est mors ou il est mortels traïtres, kar je ne cuidaisse mie que nus peust mon anel avoir sanz lui. Mais s'il vit, il s'aparcevra de sa desloialté, que jamés m'amor n'avra; et s'il est mors, je le comperé plus assés k'il ne fera, si k'il ert seu par totes terres.' Longuement ont parlé de lor duel et Galehout dist que il movra ja après la damoisele ki s'en va ne jamés ne finera de chevalchier tant que il savra se Lancelos est mors ou vis. Et Lionials dist que il ira avec lui, kar autresi iroit il tot sanz, et Galehout dist k'il ne quiert ja autre compaignon avoir.
>
> (The queen went back to her rooms, accompanied by Galehaut and Lionel and the lady of Malehaut, and they were all sorrowing together. The queen

---

stable, reliable, accepted. His only consistent element – and the essence of his character – is the absence of pity. Brehus the elusive takes his place outside every system); Trachsler, 'Brehus sans pitié', paras 18–19.

[25] On Kay's characterization, see L. Gowans, *Cei and the Arthurian Legend*, Arthurian Studies XVIII (Cambridge, 1988).

[26] I refer to Jay's account of how conventionalist nominalism produces 'an order that is less found than made' (see below, p. 26); 'Magical Nominalism', p. 167.

[27] Among many discussions of irony and *clergie* in Chrétien, still useful is T. Hunt, *Chrétien de Troyes: Yvain* (London, 1986).

said to Galehaut, 'Your companion has betrayed me, hasn't he? I swear, he is either dead or a traitor in his heart, for I would never have thought anyone could get my ring from him. If he is alive, he'll pay for his disloyalty, never having my love anymore; and if he is dead, I'll pay for it much more than he, everyone everywhere knowing about it!' They talked at length about their grief, and Galehaut said that he would set out after the messenger and not stop riding until he found out from her whether Lancelot was dead or alive. Lionel said that he would go with him, indeed would go in any case, and Galehaut said that he did not care to have any other companion.)[28]

The dualities here do not work in the analytical manner we might expect in a twelfth-century verse romance. The juxtaposing of direct and indirect speech (Guinevere's expression of her pain and Galehaut's withholding of his) imparts to each a monumental quality which increases their affective charge and endows the characters with aesthetic and ethical grandeur. Read at length, the text's 'prosaic' qualities and lack of rhetorical adornment cast a spell over the reader, expressing much more than they articulate. Signalling understatement, the *Lancelot* eschews the self-conscious display of artifice which is part of the disenchantment and rationalization operated by the Arthurian verse tradition, emphasizing instead the power of a mysterious 'world' over the human domain. The move into prose is generally held to signify a greater and different truth-value from that of verse romances: prose was previously associated with historiography, wills, contracts, sermons and Bible translation. Thanks to such official or officious texts, prose is held to bestow 'l'illusion mimétique' (the mimetic illusion).[29] Prose romances aspire at once to a greater realism than in verse, and to a higher truthfulness. 'The Arthurian world' here denotes not only the characters' everyday culture and society but also something that in special moments surges up from elsewhere to demand a different way of being, ethically and ontologically more powerful because more difficult. Through the power of affect (and relatedly, of names), the prose *Lancelot* makes psychology and rationalism act only as a foundation above which we rise to intuition of a higher, magical sphere. Beyond the familiar, conventional or clever, this supra-human sphere is posited as most truly Arthurian. Thus being-in-the-Arthurian-world takes the two distinct forms that Sartre describes: one relatively commonplace and instrumental, designed to be mastered; the other aspirational, disturbing and magical, defying mastery. As in Sartre's assessment, the virtue of this latter way of being is ascribed to the magical world itself, and not primarily to human agency.[30] Subjects who are-in-the-Arthurian-world in

---

[28] *Lancelot*, ed. Micha, I, 354; *L-G*, II, 325.

[29] E. Baumgartner, 'Le Choix de la prose', *Cahiers de recherches médiévales et humanistes* 5 (1998), 7–13, online at http://crm.revues.org/1322 [consulted 28 July 2014] (para. 10 of 16). See also M. R. Warren, 'Prose Romance', in *The Cambridge History of French Literature*, ed. W. Burgwinkle, N. Hammond and E. Wilson (Cambridge, 2011), pp. 153–63.

[30] 'Thus there are two forms of emotion, according to whether it is we who constitute

this way conduct its virtue (in the sense that certain substances conduct lightning) but do not own it. Their activity testifies at least as much to the power and authenticity of the noble ideology they serve as to their personal qualities.

In describing the power of names and relating them to affect and to the magical, I have been influenced by Jay's account of what he calls 'magical nominalism'; an exposition will clarify the wide implications with which he is concerned. Jay begins his essay by outlining how nominalist philosophy aspires to 'rid thought of collective conceptual entities, such as substance, essence or intelligible form, understood as superfluous fictions which hamper the straightforward cognition of the world in all its individual uniqueness' (p. 166). Names and concepts are mere conventions bestowed by groups of people for convenience's sake. Jay emphasizes how in medieval thinking such scepticism towards universals opened onto two kinds of agency: on the one hand the absolute potency of God, and on the other the relative creativity of his creature, man, who, 'deprived by God's hiddenness of metaphysical guarantees of the world, [...] constructs for himself a counterworld of elementary rationality and manipulability'.[31] The sense of God's participation having receded, Jay argues, nominalism has increasingly celebrated a heroic human inventiveness which exercises itself upon a malleable nature. Sartre's 'instrumental' world could be this myth's sovereign fiction, testifying to man's quasi-divine powers.

Jay tracks efforts to re-enchant modern Western culture, although not by reintroducing a divinity. He returns to the basic nominalist tenets which assert that all objects are particular and concrete, and charts their development through certain strands of modernist visual art, exemplified by Marcel Duchamp's readymades. The readymade is a given object, only found and not made by the artist; as such it rejects the 'voluntarist moment of self-assertion *ex nihilo*' (p. 171) conventionally associated with nominalism. By re-labelling an object in a way which indicates that it is 'art', the artist strips that object of its usual function and context and forces us to confront the thing itself, in all its particularity. This activity sets itself against general categories, which in art include genres, forms and types, and against the conventions on which they rely. Jay insists that the nominalism invoked here implies no triumph of human mind and will, but instead draws attention to the irreducible specificity of the thing. Demonstrating 'the assertion of the world against the domination of the subject' (p. 165), readymades are anti-humanist.

the magic of the world to replace a deterministic activity which cannot be realized, or whether the world itself is unrealizable and reveals itself suddenly as a magical environment' (*Sketch*, p. 86).

[31] H. Blumenberg, *The Legitimacy of the Modern Age*, trans. R. M. Wallace (Cambridge, MA, 1983); quoted by Jay, 'Magical Nominalism', p. 167. Hereafter, page references to 'Magical Nominalism' are given in the text.

Jay wants us to consider the possibility that everyday names may work in the same way. Stripped of the dimensions of conventionality and arbitrariness, even an ordinary noun re-labels; it may be considered not as something that catalogues or categorizes, but as something that 'rigidly designates [a thing] as a unique entity' (p. 171). This revised nominalism is 'magical' for several reasons. Jay refers to Charles Sanders Peirce's 'indexes', linked to things by 'brute, existential fact', and cites Walter Benjamin's Adamic account of language, according to which all names recall and restore the primordial naming of creation (pp. 174–5).[32] Tinged with Benjaminian 'aura', names become one with the unique things they name, resonant with a 'realism of particulars' (p. 181);[33] by using its proper name, I access the thing itself. Jay's 'magical nominalism' posits names as immediate and effectual emanations of a powerfully real world beyond artifice and what we would normally consider instrumentality.

Jay operates a number of shifts in connecting this theorising about names to the visual domain (his principal concern, but helpful to me mainly as an analogy to explain the working of names). He alludes to Benjamin's allegation that our raw, visual experience of colour is non-conceptual and sharply opposed to its articulation in language, which divides, identifies and classifies what is experienced as – and what in actual fact is – intense, 'infinitely nuanced' and 'manifold' (p. 174). A child's pre-linguistic apprehension of a rainbow is phenomenally truer than its expression in the sequence of words 'red', 'orange, 'yellow', and so on. For Benjamin, this experience does not detract from the power of ordinary language but, on the contrary, endows it with aura: the rainbow's true, Adamic name, though inaccessible, at once exceeds, haunts and underpins everyday linguistic use.[34] Names truly understood are like colours; they 'resist the conceptual imposition of generic categories on the world' (p. 175), thus rejecting instrumentality in favour of immediacy, the magical and an other reality. Building on these observations, and elaborating on the work of visual theorist W. J. T. Mitchell and modern nominalist Nelson Goodman, Jay mobilizes a distinction between two kinds of sign system. One operates 'via discontinuous gaps and differentiations' such that meaning is defined relationally and differentially, while the other posits that signs hold meaning thanks to systems that are 'dense, replete

---

[32] The phrase 'brute, existential fact' comes from A. Atkin, 'Peirce's Theory of Signs', *The Stanford Encyclopedia of Philosophy* (Stanford, CA, 2013), ed. E. N. Zalta, http://plato.stanford.edu/archives/sum2013/entries/peirce-semiotics/ [consulted 28 July 2014], Section 2: 'Peirce's Early Account: 1867–8', para. 2 of 3.

[33] On the circulation in the thirteenth century of the idea that words might be 'natural' and therefore have benign magic power, see C. Fanger, 'Things Done Wisely by a Wise Enchanter: Negotiating the Power of Words in the Thirteenth Century', *Esoterica* 1 (1999), 97–132.

[34] Jay summarizes: 'Ironically, without the conventional linguistic name for a color, [the child] is able to experience something like the individual proper name of the hue it sees along a spectrum of infinite graduations' ('Magical Nominalism', p. 175).

and continuous' (p. 177), essentially holistic.³⁵ Texts are usually assigned to the former, images to the latter camp; however, Jay follows Benjamin to affirm that names depend not on 'crisply defined digital oppositions' but on 'dense, replete, nuanced symbolic systems' that are better considered to be 'analogue' (p. 178). The meaning of a truly numinous name would therefore be experienced like a colour, saturated with shade, resistant to analysis and irreducibly specific (note that specificity is here on the side of the holistic, not the analytic). Jay insists on the magical qualities of this variety of signification, which embodies the excess of world over our ability to make sense of or to instrumentalize it (pp. 179–80). Adamic names want something of us, calling upon us to experience 'awe, wonder and humility' in the face of the non-human world.³⁶

I find Jay's depiction of the 'digital' and the 'analogue' as distinct symbolic systems helpful in elaborating a 'multi-layered' account of the way in which names, affect and ethics work in the prose *Lancelot*. The clearest example is Lancelot himself. What constitutes the Lancelot-affect, the charisma of his name and his superiority, is not a measurable difference of Lancelot's emotions and abilities from those of other knights. Galehaut is notably similar in these respects, yet his affect is quite different. The affect of any character, while being absolutely particular, resists measurement, analysis or restatement; for the major figures at least, we are called to marvel at its plenitude and concentration. Lancelot is ... Lancelot, Morgain ... Morgain, Guinevere ... *la reine* and so on, and the narratives only uncover further the rich intensity of each's being. As with the colours of Benjamin's rainbow, these names conjure up each character's fullest dimensions as something to be experienced holistically, forcefully and specifically, transcending familiar categories. This 'analogue' mode extends to the romance's ethical dimension, since ethical quality manifests itself as and through affect. Chivalry and love, *courtoisie* and kingship, loyalty, enmity and betrayal, are presented as densely replete wholes that exceed rational or instrumental analysis. Lancelot's chivalric pre-eminence and his extraordinary, noble love are intertwined in his superlative prowess.³⁷ The magical functioning of his name and affect endows the hero with an intensely real being-in-the-Arthurian-world: that superior Arthurian

---

³⁵ The former account, of course, recalls structuralism.

³⁶ Jay explores Mitchell's half-rhetorical claim that pictures (for Jay, especially photographs), 'grab us and demand our attention, telling us to stop the flow of time and pause in our rush into the future'; 'Magical Nominalism', pp. 179–80, at p. 180. The 'complex relation to temporality' (ibid.) which Jay ascribes to photographs is also a feature of Arthurian prose-writing and especially of the Grail; see E. Baumgartner, 'Le Graal, le temps: les enjeux d'un motif', in *Le Temps, sa mesure et sa perception au Moyen Âge*, ed. B. Ribémont (Caen, 1992), pp. 9–17.

³⁷ All diminish significantly as the Grail enters the narrative horizon and alters the ethical parameters. The *Queste del saint Graal* is notably more 'digital' than the other texts in the *Lancelot-Grail* cycle: there, the primary element implied by the name 'Lancelot' is 'not-Galahad'.

world which embodies the pre-eminence of noble over clerical ideology, and which more 'digital' literary conventions cannot conduct. Change to the established order becomes not only possible but unstoppable. Thus the prose *Lancelot* brings into being a series of figures who both renew and foreclose Arthurian discourse.

Since agency and virtue are ascribed to the Arthurian world rather than to the individual, the transformative power of affect can attach to many figures, regardless of their personality or of their position within the established order. This feeds an endless critique which both nourishes and undermines the Arthurian order. Galehaut's pain over Lancelot challenges the romance's conception of chivalry. The paternal sorrows of Claudas and Ban feed into a complex questioning of the role and duties of a king. Pelles' daughter's love for Lancelot, while in many ways wrong under the system's own terms, leads to the conception of Galahad and the definitive connection to a truer world via the Grail. It is affect, and not heroic action, which is at once ideal and fatal for the Arthurian order, and it may be channelled by those who are neither great nor good. On the other hand, names work also to differentiate classes of character; and here we return to the discriminations of the 'digital' mode. For there is a whole cast of figures who never achieve proper nomination and to whom affect and the creative, troubling way of being-in-the-Arthurian-world appear unavailable. The characteristic doubling strategies of Arthurian romance clarify the distinction. The existence of a false Guinevere only enhances the original's affect, while a minor knight such as Yvain li Avoutres can be sacrificed (in the *Queste del saint Graal*) because he is not the legitimate Yvain.[38] Confined to an instrumental way of being-in-the-world, such figures are mere plot devices in other people's stories. Contrast their inadequate nomination with those privileged characters who adventure incognito or in ignorance of their own names. *Pace* the usual description, such characters find rather than make their names, which gesture towards a truth already present in the world and independent of human action. Even when anonymous and placeless, Lancelot nevertheless has immediate and total impact; he is not without the name 'Lancelot' even before he encounters it. *Beaux inconnus* (Fair Unknowns) naturally turn out to be of a rank commensurate with their talents; merit is invoked only to comfort caste.[39] Names, when they arrive, cannot but place their bearers within a stratified social system. However, I do not imply that names' magical qualities and characters' superior affect are only ideological obfuscation. Layering the 'digital' with the 'analogue', we can

---

[38] *La Queste del saint Graal*, ed. A. Pauphilet (Paris, 1923), p. 153; L-G, IV, 49.
[39] E. Kennedy, 'The Quest for Identity and the Importance of Lineage in Thirteenth-Century French Prose Romance', in *The Ideals and Practice of Medieval Knighthood, II: Papers from the Third Strawberry Hill Conference*, ed. C. Harper-Bill and R. Harvey (Woodbridge, 1988), pp. 70–86.

register how such deployments of the emotion-magic trope fuel both social elitism and a more valid way of being-in-the-world.

To summarize my arguments in this section: recent writings building on phenomenological tradition help develop our understanding of the transformative powers of affect in ways that illuminate the working of the emotion-magic trope in the prose *Lancelot*. The instrumental magic ever-present in the romance (and in other romances) is stripped of numen and meaningful explanatory power, accompanied in this discrediting by a scholastic approach to emotion and by narratorial *engin* and *clergie*. Magical power is attached instead to names and to 'affect', presented not as instances of human making or mastery but as indices of an ontologically and ethically better way of being-in-the-world, beyond normal human ken. The implied narrative of the re-enchantment of an Arthurian world which earlier verse romance had disenchanted is a literary-historical myth elaborated by the prose romance to delineate and advertise the specificity of its own discourse. Its force is proleptic and even prophetic, since it posits that a truly Arthurian way of being-in-the-world may, in a reformed present and future, revitalize such crucial concepts as chivalry, love and alliance. The romance itself holds out the possibility of taking an active part in that renewal to readers who will assent to what it presents as its new modes.

Conclusion: Being-in-the-Arthurian-World

In an essay on 'Modernity and Enchantment', Michael Saler looks forward to the 'reconciliation of modern disenchantment [with] a form of enchantment that delights but does not delude'.[40] The prose *Lancelot* similarly contrasts an older and misleading approach to magic and emotion with new, progressive variants. To suggest that new versions cannot lead us astray, however, is to show too much faith in the resources of the present. Being-in-the-Arthurian-world at its best means being open to the shocking reality of others' existence and to the unforeseen demands on us of unexpected others: to the grief of the reprehensible Claudas, to the unreciprocated love of Pelles' daughter or of Galehaut. But the text works also to moralize and control. Directing sympathies along ideological lines, it turns away from the traumatic and potentially revolutionary interpsychic dimension and towards a known, deterministic social order. Names not only communicate affect but also contain its ethical potential by means and to the benefit of social hierarchy. Nevertheless, the layers are always there: magic, like emotion and affect, remains something which cannot be fully controlled.

---

[40] M. Saler, 'Modernity and Enchantment: A Historiographic Review', *American Historical Review* 111 (2006), 692–716, at p. 708.

2

Mind, Body and Affect in Medieval English Arthurian Romance

CORINNE SAUNDERS

Literary studies have recently been marked by an affective turn – a new interest in and emphasis on the workings of affect that reflects a broader academic trend.[1] The later twentieth century saw an influential shift away from ideas of Cartesian dualism, towards phenomenology: the connections between body and mind, self and world, thinking and feeling all came to the fore in the disciplines of philosophy, psychology and neuroscience. Affect became a prominent subject across the humanities and social sciences. Yet this seemingly radical 'turn', like so many, was also a turn to the past: medieval thinkers, using very different models, took for granted many of these ideas. This essay traces the understandings of mind, body and affect that underpin medieval notions of psychology, and the ways that these ideas inform and are explored in medieval English romance. For all their emphasis on action, the intensity of these works is rooted in their affective power and their psychological acuteness. Romance treatments of emotion are dependent on the intimate connections made between minds and bodies within the medieval thought world. Writers rely on and creatively adapt conventional notions of love and grief, exploring how these are felt in hearts and minds, and probing their physiological force. They repeatedly engage with suffering and conflicted psyches, writing the experience of affect on the lived-body, often in extreme ways. And they engage too with the processes of thinking and feeling, demonstrating the crucial interplay of affective and cognitive elements in emotion. These elements animate medieval romance writing and assure its resonance for readers so many centuries later.

---

[1] This essay owes much to the 'Hearing the Voice' project (http://hearingthevoice.org), a collaborative interdisciplinary study of the phenomenon of hearing voices without external stimuli, based at Durham University and funded by a Wellcome Trust Strategic Award (WT098455MA); and to the 'Life of Breath' project, also funded by a Wellcome Trust Award (WT103340). I am grateful to the Trust for supporting my research, and to my colleagues for their insights.

Medieval Psychology: Thinking and Feeling

Medieval ideas of body and mind were much more integrated: to be embodied was to be human, and connection with the world was through the lived-body, fallen though this was. Hippocrates' theory of the humours, developed by Galen in the second century and central to medieval medical thought, necessitated the idea of a mind–body continuum. Both physical and mental health depended on the balance of the four humours, as did individual temperament and complexion, while each humour was also linked to the stars and planets.[2] The body was viewed as at once responsive to the forces of the cosmos and reflective of the inner self, the soul. The distinction between mind and body was complex and more fluid than in post-Cartesian thought, complicated by ideas of the soul, by different views on where in the body faculties were situated and by the integration of thought and affect. The term 'mind' originated with the concept of memory, but quickly came to overlap with notions of the soul, and took on at least some aspects of current definitions of mind: 'The seat of awareness, thought, volition, feeling, and memory; cognitive and emotional phenomena and powers considered as constituting a presiding influence; the mental faculty of a human being.'[3] Aristotle had situated the rational or intellective quality within the soul, and had located the heart as the centre of senses and cognitive faculties; Galen, by contrast, associated these with the brain, though popular notions persisted throughout the Middle Ages and beyond of the heart as site of understanding and feeling. Neo-Platonic theories situated the immortal and rational part of the soul in the head, the appetites and emotions (termed 'passions' or 'affections', because they were suffered involuntarily) in the trunk of the body. Augustine saw the will as a faculty of the 'superior part of the soul' and emotions as 'movements of the lower parts'. Yet he also saw emotions as having both cognitive and bodily aspects: they were 'special states of the soul involving evaluative judgements, behavioural suggestions, which are voluntarily complied with or repelled, and

---

[2] See Roy Porter's summary, *The Greatest Benefit to Mankind: A Medical History of Humanity from Antiquity to the Present* (London, 1997), p. 9, and his discussion of classical and medieval medicine, pp. 44–134; see further S. Kemp, *Medieval Psychology*, Contributions in Psychology 14 (New York, 1990). For general studies of medieval medicine, see M. L. Cameron, *Anglo-Saxon Medicine*, Cambridge Studies in Anglo-Saxon England 7 (Cambridge, 1993), F. Getz, *Medicine in the English Middle Ages* (Princeton, 1998), N. G. Siraisi, *Medieval and Early Renaissance Medicine: An Introduction to Knowledge and Practice* (Chicago, 1990), and C. H. Talbot, *Medicine in Medieval England* (London, 1967).

[3] *OED n*¹ IV.19a). Instances given include Chaucer's *Parson's Tale*, 'Thoghtes that ben enclosed in mannes mynde, whan he gooth to slepe' (914), and *Legend of Good Women*, 'Moche sorwe hadde he in his mynde' (946).

pleasant or unpleasant feelings'.⁴ Augustine's primary concern was the relation of emotions to the will, in the context of original sin.

By the end of the thirteenth century a new interest in psychology was developing. Qualities once attributed to the rational soul were now situated in the brain, probably as a result of medical observation of the effects of head injuries. Medical and philosophical views held broadly that cognition was two-part: processes mediated by the physiological mechanisms of the cerebral ventricles and processes within the rational soul/mind. They drew on the Arabic theory of three types of spirit: natural, vital and animal.⁵ The natural spirit was produced in the liver and sent through the veins: it enabled generation, nutrition and physical growth. The vital spirit was produced in the heart and moved through the arteries to give life to the body. In the brain, the vital spirit was transformed into the animal spirit, which controlled sensation and movement but also imagination, cogitation and memory. The senses, each connected with its own organ, were understood to be put together by the inner senses, situated in the ventricles of the brain, the centre of both sensory and cognitive faculties. Thoughts were dependent on 'forms', *imagines, simulacra* or *phantasmata* (Aristotle also uses *eikón*, copy), sense impressions involving perception and response, put together by the inner senses, and passing through imagination, cognition and memory. Avicenna's *De anima*, translated (into Latin) in the twelfth century, gives an account of the process, describing the five cells of the brain: at the front, the *sensus communis* (where information was processed, with impressions retained briefly) and *imaginatio* (a temporary memory retaining forms) – together comprising the *phantasia*; in the middle *imaginativa* ('a creative power, able to separate or combine the forms that it retrieves from *imaginatio*, thus providing man with the mental power to imagine things, even things that do not exist')⁶ and *estimativa* (the site of cognitive processes, where judgements were made, and which could draw on memory); and at the back *memorialis* (the storehouse of memory, where these 'phantasms' or memory-pictures were kept, imprinted, literally marked on the body through the physi-

---

⁴ See S. Knuuttila, *Emotions in Ancient and Medieval Philosophy* (Oxford and New York, 2004), pp. 168, 158. See, in particular, *The City of God* 14.6–7 and 14.19.

⁵ The theory of the three kinds of spirits is discussed in Johannitius' *Isagoge ad artem Galeni* (a brief translation of an Arabic treatise), translated by Constantine the African and circulated as part of the *Articella*, with a group of six medical texts translated in the twelfth century from Arabic into Latin: see Knuuttila, *Emotions*, pp. 212–13.

⁶ J. Tasioulas, '"Dying of Imagination" in the First Fragment of the *Canterbury Tales*', *Medium Ævum* 82 (2013), 212–35, at 216–17; the details given here of the five cells are indebted to Tasioulas' lucid summary. See Avicenna, *Liber de anima seu Sextus de naturalibus*, ed. S. E. van Riet (Leiden, 1968), and the detailed discussion in R. Harvey, *The Inward Wits: Psychological Theory in the Middle Ages and the Renaissance*, Warburg Institute Surveys 6 (London, 1975), pp. 43–64; and see further M. Karnes, *Imagination, Meditation and Cognition in the Middle Ages* (Chicago, 2011), in particular pp. 41–5.

ological process triggered by the senses).[7] *Phantasmata* are the products of 'the entire process of sense perception': quasi-pictures or representations, derived from sensory processes but with affective weight, 'emotionally charged'.[8] Roger Bacon used a similar paradigm in the thirteenth century. The middle cell, *imaginativa* or *phantasy*, had the dangerous potential to deceive reason, *estimativa*, as Albertus Magnus emphasised in his widely circulated *De apprehensione*.[9] Such ideas underpinned theories of mental illness: if the melancholy humour was dominant (an excess of black bile), then the cognitive processes at the central part of the brain were affected, potentially resulting in depressive illness, lethargy and withdrawal; if the choleric humour was dominant (an excess of yellow bile), then the imagination at the front of the brain was affected, bodying forth too many images, potentially resulting in mania.[10]

Emotions were understood as occurring through the movements of the vital spirit and natural heat, produced in the heart and travelling through the arteries. They might be triggered by sensory experience of different kinds or by the workings of imagination and memory, and they had both physiological and mental consequences. In excessive joy or anger, the vital spirit and accompanying heat moved out of the heart to other parts of the body – causing, for example, blushing for joy or shame. In excessive grief, distress or fear, by contrast, the vital spirit and heat withdrew from the arteries into the heart, with the possibility of causing unconsciousness or even death. Emotions, or 'accidents of the soul', were of medical interest because of their 'physiological consequences',[11] but they also raised complex psychological questions, explored and developed by a wide range of natural philosophers and theologians – Avicenna, John of La Rochelle, Hugh of St Victor, Roger Bacon, Albertus Magnus.

Thomas Aquinas' ideas of mind, body and affect were especially sophisticated, spanning the physiological and theological to develop a complex psychology. For Aquinas, the human was a compound of body and soul. The faculties of the soul – intellectual apprehension and intellectual appetite – were not themselves material, but their operations depended on brain and bodily processes:

---

[7] M. Carruthers, *The Book of Memory: A Study of Memory in Medieval Culture*, Cambridge Studies in Medieval Literature 10 (Cambridge, 1990), p. 17. See further *The Medieval Craft of Memory: An Anthology of Texts and Pictures*, ed. M. Carruthers and J. M. Ziolkowski, Material Texts (Philadelphia, 2002), and M. Carruthers, *The Craft of Thought: Meditation, Rhetoric and the Making of Images, 400–1200*, Cambridge Studies in Medieval Literature 34 (Cambridge, 1998).

[8] Carruthers, *The Book of Memory*, p. 59.

[9] See C. Collette, *Species, Phantasms, and Images: Vision and Medieval Psychology in the Canterbury Tales* (Ann Arbor, 2001), and Tasioulas, 'Dying', p. 216.

[10] See further my essay '"The thoghtful maladie": Madness and Vision in Medieval Writing', in *Madness and Creativity in Literature and Culture*, ed. C. Saunders and J. Macnaughton (Basingstoke, 2005), pp. 67–87, at pp. 70–71.

[11] Knuuttila, *Emotions*, p. 15.

It is clear that for the intellect to understand actually, not only when it acquires fresh knowledge, but also when it applies knowledge already acquired, there is need for the act of the imagination and of the other [interior sensory] powers. For when the act of the imagination is hindered by a lesion of the corporeal organ, for instance, in a case of frenzy; or when the act of the memory is hindered, as in the case of lethargy, we see that [a person] is hindered from actually understanding things of which he had a previous knowledge.[12]

Mind, body and affect are interconnected, and the emotions necessarily have a cognitive as well as an affective aspect: 'emotions are acts of the sensitive motive powers caused by external objects through the evaluations of the estimative power and necessarily accompanied by movements of the heart and the spirits' – the latter felt in the body.[13] They are not Cartesian private events, nor motions of a non-rational or animal part: they require the process of *phantasmata*, sensory images put together in the brain. They could be affective, focused on pleasurable or aversive objects (love and hatred, desire and aversion, pleasure and sadness), or spirited, involving striving for an outcome (hope and despair, fear and courage). Aquinas recognises that emotions are both cognitive and affective; he also recognises the influence of emotion on cognition.

Romance Minds and Bodies

Many of these ideas are clearly visible in the religious writing of the Middle Ages. Visionary and devotional literature relies on the notion that affective experience can open the way to the soul's deeper understanding of the self and the divine. Such understandings of human psychology also inform the 'psychomachia' tradition, in which personified aspects of the will, desires and forces beyond the self, both good and evil, figure as bodies battling over the soul: in Langland's *Piers Plowman*, for instance, Will debates with both affective and cognitive forces – Anima and Conscience.

How are such notions of mind, body and affect relevant to romance writing? Here too the body is both responsive to external forces and reflective of interior being. Affect is visibly written on the body, but also shapes and transforms the mind and creates individual identity. In particular, medieval understandings of mind, body and affect shape the most influential romance topos of all, that of love-sickness. Courtly romance is deeply engaged with inner psychology and its writing on the body,

---

[12] Aquinas, *Summa Theologiae*, ed. P. Caramello, 4 vols (Turin, 1952–6), I, 84.7; and see further A. Kenny, *Aquinas on Mind*, Topics in Medieval Philosophy (Oxford and New York, 1993), and D. F. Cates, *Aquinas on the Emotions: A Religious-Ethical Inquiry*, Moral Traditions (Washington, DC, 2009).
[13] Knuuttila, *Emotions*, p. 239.

especially in the context of love. Chaucer, with his interests in natural philosophy and medicine, treats notions of mind, body and affect with sophistication and originality – particularly in *Troilus and Criseyde*, where the physiological and psychological detail is quite remarkable.[14] But what of English Arthurian romances? It is a critical commonplace that in these narratives ideas of character are shaped not through the exploration of interior psychology but by the gradual accruing of action. Yet examination of individual works shows that action is accompanied by an emphasis, understated but essential, on both thought and feeling, that writers employ terms such as 'heart' and 'mind' in nuanced ways and that these are integrated with bodily responses, to suggest at the very least a broad cultural familiarity with ideas of mind, body and affect. We can therefore go beyond the notion of stylised gesture as accompanying emotion to see bodily attitudes in imaginative literature as indeed conventional but also as reflecting medieval understandings of emotion, comprised of affective and cognitive elements, written on the body and felt in the mind.

Arthurian romance is to some extent constructed upon the antithesis of reason and passion, often played out in the notions of love-sickness and love-madness. The works of Marie de France and Chrétien de Troyes repeatedly revisit this antithesis, famously stated in *Le Chevalier de la Charrete*, when Reason 'qui d'Amors se part' (who does not follow Love's command) advises Lancelot against climbing into the cart: 'N'est pas el cuer, mes an la boche, / Reisons qui ce dire li ose' (Reason, who dared tell him this, spoke from the lips, not from the heart).[15] The physically transformative power of profound emotion is memorably imaged in Lancelot's crossing of the sword bridge, so inspired by love that he feels no pain. Chrétien's *Le Chevalier au Lion* takes the exploration of passion further in its depiction of Yvain's madness on realising that he has betrayed his lady and lost her love. Grief and guilt overthrow his mind:

> Lors se li monte uns torbeillons
> el chief, si grant que il forsane;
> si se dessire et se depane
> et fuit par chans et pars arees,
> et lessa ses genz esgarees
> qui se mervoillent ou puet estre:
> ...
> por qant mes ne li sovenoit
> de rien que onques eüst feite.
> Les bestes par le bois agueite,

---

[14] See further my essays 'The thoghtful maladie', pp. 74–5, and 'The Affective Body: Love, Virtue and Vision in Medieval English Literature', in *The Body and the Arts*, ed. C. Saunders, U. Maude, and J. Macnaughton (Basingstoke, 2009), pp. 87–102, at pp. 89–90.

[15] Chrétien de Troyes, *Le Chevalier de la Charrete*, ed. M. Roques, *Les Romans de Chrétien de Troyes*, Les Classiques français du Moyen Age, 5 vols, vol. III (Paris, 1972), ll. 365, 370–71; *The Knight of the Cart (Lancelot)*, in *Arthurian Romances*, trans. W. W. Kibler and C. W. Carroll (Harmondsworth, 1991) pp. 207–94, at p. 212.

> si les ocit; et se manjue
> la venison trestote crue.
> Et tant conversa el boschage
> com hom forsenez et salvage.
>
> (Then such a great tempest arose in his head that he went mad; he ripped and tore at his clothing and fled across the fields and plains, leaving his people puzzled and with no idea of where he could be ... yet afterwards he did not remember anything he had done. He stalked wild animals in the forest and killed them and ate their raw flesh. He lived in the forest like a madman and a savage.).[16]

Intense emotion completely inhibits rational processes, and the trappings of civilisation are lost: Yvain returns to a bestial state. The scene is extreme yet can be seen as exemplifying the medieval physiology of acute melancholia or even love-madness, according to which frenzy could be caused by the obsessive bodying forth of images of the beloved occasioned by extreme emotion: the orderly processes of the brain were overthrown and the wits sent wandering.[17]

The English *Ywain and Gawain*, though it reduces and renders more colloquial Chrétien's work, retains the connection between mind, body and affect:

> In sorow than so was he stad
> That nere for murning wex he mad.
> It was no mirth that him myght mend;
> At worth to noght ful wele he wend,
> For was he es ful wil of wane.
> 'Allas, I am myne owin bane!
> ...
> An evyl toke him als he stode;
> For wa he wex al wilde and wode.[18]
>
> (He was beset by such sorrow then that he became nearly mad with grief. There was no pleasure that could restore him; he was convinced he was ruined, for he was wholly bewildered. 'Alas, I am my own murderer!' ... An illness seized him as he stood; he grew all wild and mad from grief.)

---

[16] See Chrétien de Troyes, *Le Chevalier au Lion (Yvain)*, ed. M. Roques, *Les Romans de Chrétien de Troyes*, Les Classiques français du Moyen Age, 5 vols, vol. IV (Paris, 1982), ll. 2806–2830; *The Knight with the Lion*, in *Arthurian Romances*, pp. 295–380, at p. 330. Subsequent references to *Yvain* are to this edition and translation, cited by line and page number respectively.

[17] See the accounts of this physiological process in S. Kemp, *Cognitive Psychology in the Middle Ages*, International Contributions in Psychology 33 (Westport, CT, 1996), p. 51, and Tasioulas, 'Dying', p. 218.

[18] *Ywain and Gawain*, in *Ywain and Gawain, Sir Percyvell of Gales, The Anturs of Arther*, ed. M. Mills (London, 1992), pp. 1–102, ll. 1639–50. References are to this edition, cited by line number. The work exists in a single fifteenth-century manuscript. On the work's adaptation of *Le Chevalier au Lion*, see D. Matthews, 'Translation and Ideology: The Case of *Ywain and Gawain*', *Neophilologus* 76 (1992), 452–63.

While Ywain appears to be seized by an external 'evyl', illness, the cause of his 'wa' is made explicit. Later, the maiden who recognises the sleeping Ywain – through a physical sign that, unlike the inner wits, is unchanging, a scar – diagnoses his state of mind in similar terms: 'Sorow will meng a mans blode / And make him forto wax wode' (Sorrow will disturb a man's blood / And make him grow mad, 1739–40), lines translating and elaborating Chrétien's comment, 'an puet bien de duel forsener' (one can certainly go mad with grief, 2924, p. 332). Here the affective phenomenon is made more explicit through the suggestion of the medieval physiology of furious grief. In such cases of extreme emotion, an excess of vital spirit travelled out through the blood via the arteries to the brain, and could lead to madness, frenzy of mind and body, disorder of the wits – the reverse effect of sadness, which caused the vital spirit to withdraw into the heart. Thomas Hoccleve in his autobiographical *Complaint* and *Dialogue with a Friend* describes his mental illness in terms that evoke a similar frenzy or 'wyldnesse': 'the wylde infirmitee / … which me out of myself / caste and threew' (the wild sickness which took and threw me out of myself); it occasions loss of memory, 'the substance / of my memorie / Wente to pleye / as for a certein space' (the substance of my memory went to play for a while), and Hoccleve repeatedly uses the image of his wits wandering and returning home.[19]

In the world of romance, the maiden's magical ointment has the power to draw the wits of the man who is 'braynwode', brain-mad (1756), back into order. In a medically detailed passage not included in *Ywain and Gawain*, Chrétien's narrator comments on the maiden's folly in using the entire box of magical ointment obtained from Morgan le Fay, rubbed on so vigorously by an attentive damsel 'que del cervel li trest si fors / la rage et la melencolie' (that she expelled the madness and melancholy from his brain, 3000–01, p. 332). Chrétien explains that it is only necessary to anoint the temples and forehead (2962–9), because Yvain only suffers in his brain, and he attributes Yvain's recovery to warmth and massage of the head, with the implication that the movement causes the excessive vital spirit to withdraw. The maiden's generous action in anointing the whole body can be seen as a natural response to Yvain's beautiful body, contravening medical logic – but could also be seen as medically appropriate in its recognition of the continuum between mind and body: bodily affect propels the vital spirit into the brain and dominates the inner senses, causing madness, and it is fitting to treat body and head together.

Ywain and Gawain indicates the typical balance of Middle English romance – normally avoiding medical detail, yet attuned to and playing on the interdependence of mind, body and affect. These qualities are

---

[19] *Thomas Hoccleve's Complaint and Dialogue*, ed. J. A. Burrow, EETS OS 313 (Oxford, 1999), ll. 107, 40–42, 50–51, and see also 2, 7, 9–10. Hoccleve's illness appears to have been suffered for some months in 1416.

exemplified in Thomas Chestre's *Sir Launfal*, which rewrites Marie's brief, allusive *lai* of *Lanval*. The material detail of *Sir Launfal* has frequently been seen as reductive, lessening the psychological impact of the narrative, yet emotion plays a key role, and the material aspects of the work often reflect its bodily, affective emphases. The focus is repeatedly on the heart as the site of the emotions, as for instance in the extended scene at the Mayor's house added by Thomas. Launfal responds affectively to the Mayor's daughter's invitation to dine with her:

> 'Damesele,' he sayde, 'nay!
> To dyne have I no herte.
> Thre dayes ther ben agon
> Mete ne drynke eet y noon,
> And all was for povert.
> ...
> No wonther dough me smerte![20]
>
> ('Damsel,' he said, 'no! I have no heart to dine. Three days have gone by in which I have had neither meat nor drink, and all because of poverty. ... No wonder that I am in pain!')

The passage is simple and colloquial, but clearly employs a physiological model of affect: Launfal's rejection of the invitation despite his physical hunger, the use of the term 'heart' and its rhyme with 'smerte' emphasise that distress motivates Launfal's response. When Launfal encounters the faery Tryamour, Thomas, like Marie, uses the neo-Platonic convention of love occurring through the eyes, though without elaboration: 'Launfal beheld that swete wyghth – / All hys love yn her was lyghth' (Launfal beheld that sweet creature / All his love settled on her, 307–8). Later, the material loss of worldly goods which 'malt as snow ayens the sunne' (melted like snow in the sun, 740) is followed by a more extended depiction of the physical affect of sorrow on Launfal:

> He bet hys body and hys hedde ek,
> And cursede the mouth that he wyth spek,
> Wyth care and greet dolour.
> And for sorow, yn that stounde,
> Anoon he fell aswowe to grounde. (751–5)
>
> (He beat both his body and his head, and in distress and deep misery cursed the mouth with which he had spoken. And for sorrow, in that moment, he straight away fell swooning to the ground.)

These are the conventional gestures of grief, and its affective vocabulary – dolour, care, sorrow. Yet there is also physical realism according to medi-

---

[20] *Sir Launfal*, in *Of Love and Chivalry: An Anthology of Middle English Romance*, ed. J. Fellows (London and Rutland, VT, 1993), pp. 199–229, ll. 194–204. Subsequent references are to this edition, cited by line number. The poem dates to the end of the fourteenth century, and exists in a single manuscript.

eval physiology: the flight of the vital spirit into the heart occasioned by grief causes Launfal to swoon and fall. It is fitting that Tryamour's final gesture is also explicitly bodily, the inverse of the love her look inspires in Launfal: her breath, blown on the treacherous queen, punishes her by blinding – a literally striking expression of affect. The image takes up and reshapes the idea of the supernatural, invasive force, its affect rendering physical the queen's metaphorical blindness rather than causing love-sickness. Like the author of *Ywain and Gawain*, Thomas Chestre uses affect quite simply, yet powerfully, in ways that are not empty literary conventions but which exploit the connection between mind, body and affect.

What of a poem that at so many points seems to contravene expectation and convention, *Sir Gawain and the Green Knight*? Here not lovesickness but more existential concerns are the focus, interwoven with chivalric challenges. The poet conveys much through action and dialogue, combined with third-person description, but is also evidently interested in psychology and in affective and cognitive processes. Both bodily affect and mental processes are described in nuanced ways from the start, as in the description of Arthur's 'ʒonge blod and his brayn wylde' (young blood and wild brain).[21] The term 'wylde' (glossed by Andrew and Waldron as 'restless') implies disorder, an excess of vital spirit as a result of youth. The affect of angry shame is evident in Arthur's blush, 'Þe blod schot for scham into his schyre face' (for shame the blood rushed into his fair face, 317), at the Green Knight's derision, as well as in his verbal retort. Across the poem, Gawain's character is portrayed in terms of the complex intersections of mind, body and affect. The Pentangle makes clear that mental, spiritual and physical virtues are all interwoven. The 'fyue wyttez' (640), typically glossed as the five senses, signify the inner senses found within the brain, which put together and interpret sensory perceptions, and which form one point of the endless knot. Direction of mind as well as action is crucial, and the wits must be fittingly used: Gawain's 'þro þoȝt' (eager thought, 645) is focused on the five joys of Mary. His thoughts are repeatedly emphasised, 'Now þenk wel, Sir Gawan' (Now think well, Sir Gawain, 487); 'Þen þenkkez Gawan ful sone / Of his anious uyage' (Then Gawain suddenly thought of his difficult journey, 534–5). The 'care at ... hert' and 'derue doel' (distress at heart; great misery, 557–8) of the court, like Arthur's 'brayn wylde' earlier, are set against Gawain's more intellectual response, 'What may mon do bot fonde' (What can man do but try, 565)?

Fittingly for a poem that privileges thought, Gawain's quest begins with a parodic account of romance action, as he is challenged in the space

---

[21] *Sir Gawain and the Green Knight*, in *The Poems of the Pearl Manuscript: 'Pearl', 'Cleanness', 'Patience', 'Sir Gawain and the Green Knight'*, ed. M. Andrew and R. Waldron, 5th edn (Exeter, 2007), pp. 207–300, l. 89. References are to this edition, cited by line number.

of one stanza by enemies at every ford, by dragons, wolves, wild men, bulls, bears, boars and giants. By contrast, the poet evocatively conveys Gawain's mental and physical suffering in the wintry weather: the realities of travel in midwinter afflict both body and mind. The poet recounts his inner dialogue: the prayers that precede his arrival at Hautdesert and his thoughts once he enters the place where both mind and body will be tested through the affective lures of sexual desire and love of life. Gawain's thoughts process sensory perceptions and affective responses: he thinks that the castle he sees is 'fayr innoghe' (very fair, 803) and that the lady he sees is fairer than Guinevere. They are contrasted by the affect of laughter that characterises Hautdesert and its larger-than-life host ('Þe lorde ful lowde with lote and laȝter myry' [the lord, with very loud words and merry laughter, 1623]; 'With merþe and mynstralsye ... / Þay maden as mery as any men moȝten, / With laȝyng of ladies, with lotez of bordes' [with mirth and minstrelsy they made as merry as any men might, with the laughter of ladies and with jesting words, 1952–4]). For the attentive reader, this emphasis may recall the affect of 'gomen' (game, 273, 283) associated with the Green Knight, who 'laȝes so loude' (laughs so loudly, 316) at the fear his request inspires. Especially complex and revealing are Gawain's responses to the lady, which conceal affect in highly unnatural, self-conscious ways that separate mind and body. Thus he 'schamed' (was embarrassed, 1189) on seeing the lady enter slyly; as he pretends sleep, the audience is offered an account of his cognitive processes: he 'Compast in his concience to quat þat cace myȝt / Meue oþer amount. To mervayle hym þoȝt' (considered in his conscience what the situation might portend or amount to. He thought it a marvel, 1196–7). He is 'al forwondered' and 'wroth with hymseluen' at her flirtatious behaviour at dinner (completely bewildered, angry with himself, 1660) – and his suave exterior is countered by the more revealing affect of sleep, as 'drowping depe' (in a deep and troubled sleep, 1748), he dreams and mutters, reflecting the 'mornyng of many þro þoȝtes' (the grief of many pressing thoughts, 1751). The narrator's statement that 'Gret perile bitwene hem stod' (There was great danger between them, 1768) signals the severe strain of the affective experience on the mind – strain countered by Mary's memory of the knight, keeping him in mind: 'mynne' (1769). When Gawain comes to accept the girdle, however, it is feeling rather than thought that is emphasised through the mention of the heart, 'Þen kest þe knyȝt, and hit come to his hert' (then the knight considered, and it came into his heart, 1855) – and by the time Gawain goes to make his confession, we no longer hear his thoughts clearly.

Bodily affect is foregrounded in the account of Gawain's last night at Hautdesert: he sleeps little, listening to the sounds of the weather. Sensory perceptions – the sight of the barrow and boiling stream, the sound of the axe being sharpened – colour the depiction of the Green Chapel and Gawain's interpretation of it as a demonic place. Fear is written on his body as he shrinks slightly from the axe. Gawain's response to Bertilak's revelation of his failure recalls and heightens the affective emphases of the opening of the poem – the shame of Arthur and the court at the Green Knight's challenge. Gawain stands 'in study' (2369):

> So agreued for greme he gryed withinne.
> Alle þe blode of his brest blende in his face,
> Þat al he schrank for schome þat þe schalk talked. (2370–72)
>
> (So aggrieved for his shame that he suffered within. All the blood within his breast rose to his face, so that he shrank for shame at what the man had said.)

The term 'study' emphasises the cognitive element of shame, while its emotive force is reflected in the physical blush that marks Gawain's response. Mind, body and affect align once again in Gawain, as he realises that human desire to preserve his life has led him to misbelieve, misinterpret, mislead by taking the green girdle. He has privileged affect, rather than harnessing it to thought and will, placing individual desires above trust in God and loyalty to the chivalric code. On the one hand, his instincts and desires have been unruly; on the other, they have been comprehensible, reflecting the love of life that is a natural human response. Gawain learns humility: learns, that is, the continual need to bring thought and judgement to bear on sensory responses and feelings, to refine emotion with cognition and to order the mind – the impulses of perceptions, desires and affects, the forces of imagination, the multivalent *phantasmata* with such sensory and cognitive power. He also, however, learns the impossibility of absolute control over such impulses, forces and images, and hence the crucial need for affect to play a positive role in cognitive processes – to evoke shame, pity and humility, to fuel imagination and thought, and ultimately to seek grace.

Writing from the Heart: Malory's 'Morte Darthur'

Malory's *Morte Darthur*, despite its very different prose style, is not as dissimilar as we might expect. Malory, like the romance writers who precede him, makes natural the conventions of behaviour associated with love-sickness and grief, in particular, which play such essential roles in Arthurian history. These emotions, above all, underpin the key moments in the narrative: Uther's love-sickness for Ygrainne, the loves of Launcelot and Tristram, both manifest in madness, the grief and penance of Launcelot in the Grail Quest, and the great laments and losses of the last books. Thought and feeling are most often conveyed through dialogue – and sometimes through inner speech. But Malory also creates his emotional tapestry through the use of repeated affective terms – 'dole', 'abase', 'marvel', 'mourn' – to which layers of meaning and dramatic association attach themselves in the course of the narrative.[22] These emotive terms are frequently accompanied with concisely stated but telling physical affects – tears, swoons, sickness, madness, changes in colour, laughter.[23] Cognition and affect merge: Arthur is 'passynge hevy', 'in grete thought' and 'in a study', 'pensyff' after his dream of griffins and serpents and sight of the questing beast that precede Merlin's prophecy of his fall (I.19, 34–35); Palomides gains 'suche a rejoysynge' by looking at Isode that he strikes down all he encounters (X.70, 580); Gareth's heart is 'lyght and joly' when he looks on his lady in battle (VII.17, 252), he 'walowed and wrythed' burning for love of her but is also 'mervaylously wytted' (VII.19, 255; VII.26, 267). By contrast, Tristram is 'oute of hys mynde' on account of his love for La Beale Isode (IX.19, 391); Guinevere swoons, 'sore abaysshed' at the accusations made against her (XVIII.3, 794). Morgan's treachery is reflected in the fact that she 'kepte hir countenaunce and made no sembelaunte of dole' on Accolon's death (IV.14, 118): she is able, unnaturally, to subdue the affective with the cognitive even while the narratorial comment makes clear the presence of grief. For Malory such containment of emotion is negative, indicating lack of true feeling, unnatural assertion of mind over body and conscious deviance from the affect that should underpin virtue.

Malory's depictions of conflicted psyches are especially revealing, as for example his probing of Balin's repeated series of wrong but somehow inevitable choices. The promise of adventure 'reysed his herte' (II.2, 49) – a physical reference to the movement of the vital spirit outwards. The convention of thought as situated in the heart allows Malory naturally to combine affective and cognitive elements. Despite Balin's poverty, 'in hys herte he was fully assured to do as well', a sentiment he repeats to the damsel bringing the sword that she prophesies will destroy him (II.2, 49). Balin repeatedly 'takes the adventure' (II.2, 50) despite grievous outcomes and ill omens, privileging interior judgement over external signs. Malory subtly conveys the peculiar mixture of regret, resignation and tenacity, emotion and intellect, that characterises Balin's responses just before his death. He hears the horn blown and draws the conclusion, 'That blast ... is blowen for me, for I am the pryse; and yet am I not dede' (II.17, 70). He hears of the tradition of jousting and responds in terms of the heart, 'though my hors be wery my hert is not wery. I wold be fayne ther my deth should be' – feeling and thinking; and after being warned about accepting a strange shield, concludes 'Me repenteth ... that ever I cam within this countrey; but I maye not torne now ageyne for shame' (II.17, 71). The heart is both willing and regretful, its complex mix of affective and cognitive reflected in Balin's conflicted response as he articulates his

---

[22] See further Andrew Lynch's discussion of 'cheer' in this volume.
[23] References are to Sir Thomas Malory, *Le Morte Darthur*, ed. P. J. C. Field, Arthurian Studies LXXX, 2 vols (Cambridge, 2013), vol. 1, cited by book, section, and page number.

wish to turn from the adventure yet chooses to pursue what he views as the path of honour.

The story of Balin probes the psychology of the quest, a recurrent theme in the earlier parts of the book. From the Grail Quest onwards, the emphasis begins to shift further towards the psychology of love, from both secular and religious perspectives. The portrayal of Elaine of Astolat is particularly detailed in its reference to mind, body and affect. Elaine responds with extreme physical affect to the changes effected in Launcelot by his illness: seeing him 'syke and pale', she swoons and shrieks; finding him wounded again, she 'cryed and wepte as she had bene wood' (XVIII.15, 819; XVIII.17, 823); Bors too, on seeing Launcelot 'dede pale and discoloured', 'loste his countenaunce' (XVIII.16, 820). Elaine's response to Launcelot's rejection of her love is again characterised by high affect: grief, manifest in shrill shrieks and swoons, not eating for ten days and, finally, death. But this is wonderfully accompanied by an emphasis on the cognitive aspects of emotion, articulated in Elaine's speech:

> 'Why sholde I leve such thoughtes? Am I nat an erthely woman? And all the whyle the brethe ys in my body I may complayne me, for my belyve ys that I do no offence, though I love an erthely man, unto God, for He fourmed me thereto, and all maner of good love commyth of God. And othir than good love loved I never Sir Launcelot du Lake.' (XVIII.19, 827)

Breath in the body signifies life and feeling, but also the ability to speak, to interpret and to combine affect and intellect in order to produce complex emotion. The notion of love that is natural, arising from the 'harte selff' (XVIII.20, 830), is one of Malory's great subjects, and it is the ways such affect plays out cognitively and physically, how mind and body respond to it, that shape the pattern of the narrative.

Conflict between mind and body, and the crucial role of affect, are nowhere more apparent than in Malory's treatment of Launcelot's psychology. Earlier, his rejection by Guinevere, like Tristram's by Isode, results in madness: like Chrétien's Lancelot and Yvain, the noblest of Malory's knights experience extremes of emotion with the power to overthrow the mind – in contrast to the enchantresses, who are able to manipulate feeling to their own ends. In the Grail Quest, however, Launcelot's love 'oute of mesure' (XIII.20, 696) for Guinevere is manifest not in the affects of love, but in physical paralysis. Unable to enter the chapel he finds, he is 'hevy and dysmayed' (XIII.17, 693), lying half-waking as the Grail passes – affects that he himself interprets: 'myne olde synne hyndryth me and shamyth me, that I had no power to stirre nother speke whan the Holy Bloode appered before me' (XIII.19, 695). The teachings of the Quest urge him through affect to action: 'tho wordis wente to hys herte' (XIII.19, 695). They are enacted in Launcelot's adoption of a life of affective piety – his abstinence, penance and wearing of a hair shirt. Gawain fails in the Quest because he refuses this mode, placing his trust only in deeds of arms; his quest, like his spirit, is barren. Affective piety brings together physical and mental practices, fuses affect and intellect, to produce the most profound spiritual response. It is fitting that only within a state of bodily unconsciousness – the most heightened of affects, in which the spirit withdraws into the heart – does Launcelot achieve the vision of the Grail. His earlier inability to enter the chapel echoes his inability to enter the Grail chamber, but the resulting swoon is a positive rewriting of the earlier sinful sleep, an affective response that leads to spiritual revelation.

The hermit who counsels Launcelot in the Quest warns, 'loke that your harte and youre mowth accorde' (XIII.20, 696), but the last books focus on heightened division within Launcelot, set 'in hys prevy thoughtes and in hys myndis' on the Queen, while his outward self seems turned towards God (XVIII.1, 790). Awareness of this division is memorably depicted by Malory in Launcelot's searching of Urry's wounds, which goes 'sore ayeynste [his] harte', causing him to weep 'as he had bene a chylde that had bene beatyn' (XIX.12, 867–8). Lament again and again characterises Launcelot in the course of the downward spiral of the work, as the conflict of love and loyalty works to effect the deaths of Gareth and Gaheris, the vengeance of Gawain, the treachery of Mordred and the fall of the kingdom. With each successive event, it is grief, expressed through laments that recognise and articulate loss, that most characterises Launcelot, rather than any positive affect of love or chivalry. His sentiments contrast with Gawain's insistence on vengeance, an attribute fleshed out by Malory through the accruing actions of Gawain and his brothers from early on in the narrative. Ultimately Gawain too experiences an affective turn, recognising, as he lies dying, the effects of his vengeance, forgiving and sending for Launcelot. His redemption is marked through his visitation of Arthur in dream.

At the end of the work, heart and mouth – mind, body and affect – accord as Launcelot mourns the death of Guinevere:

> 'Truly ... I trust I do not dysplese God, for He knoweth myn entente, for my sorow was not, nor is not, for ony rejoysyng of synne. But my sorow may never have ende ... truly myn herte wold not serve to susteyne my careful body.' (XXI.11, 936)

The recollection of his role in their fall causes the vital spirit to withdraw: 'this remembred, of their kyndenes and myn unkyndenes, sanke so to myn herte that I myght not susteyne myself' (XXI.11, 937). The affective power of thoughts, phantasms stored in the memory, effects a strong physiological response. As in the Grail Quest, the affects of grief are also manifest in penance and abstinence, conscious actions that bring together mind and body so that Launcelot 'waxed ful lene': after the death of Guinevere, he 'never after ete but lytel mete, nor dranke, tyl he was dede; for than he seekened more and more, and dryed and dwyned awaye' (XXI.10, 935; XXI.12, 937). Lament and the withholding of sustenance are countered in death, however, by the bishop's laughter and vision of Launcelot with the angels in heaven, and by the affects of holiness: 'he laye as he had smyled and the swettest savour aboute hym that ever they felte' (XXI.12, 938). In death, the vital spirit has moved once more out of the heart, to be positively marked through joyfulness of expression and sweetness of smell. The book ends with 'wepynge and wryngyng of handes, and the grettest dole … that ever made men' (XXI.12, 938), but also with profoundly positive spiritual affect, the wonder of sanctity and redemption, as the perspective shifts from the earthly to the celestial.

Conclusion

Ywain and Gawain, Sir Launfal, Sir Gawain and the Green Knight, Le Morte Darthur: though all treat Arthurian subjects, they remain very different works. Yet all also share an engagement with emotion that reflects and reflects on the deep connections between mind, body and affect. None of these writers enjoys Chaucer's precise medical knowledge, but all draw on the notion of a mind–body continuum that is so central to medieval being in the world. *Ywain and Gawain* takes up and adapts the motif of frenzy effected through grief in love; the ways that extreme affect can overthrow the mind, and the possibility of a marvellous cure. *Sir Launfal* explores the marvellous from a different perspective, depicting first the affect of love for the wondrous faery lady, and then the affects of loss on body and mind, finally and dramatically reversed. *Sir Gawain* probes deeply the complex relations of thinking and feeling, conscious and unconscious being, to illuminate the pursuit of virtue in a fallen, treacherous world where human and supernatural meet. Malory's tragic tapestry is coloured by the accruing affects of love and loss, written on the bodies, minds and hearts of his characters, to illuminate the complex workings of destiny and free will that lead inexorably to the fall of the Arthurian world but also lead to redemption. Naturally and easily, yet with profound affective power, these romance works draw on, are inspired by and engage with the complexities and tensions of the mind–body–affect nexus that has so challenged thinkers from the early modern period to the present.

3

'What cheer?' Emotion and Action in the Arthurian World

ANDREW LYNCH

I

Although the history of emotions is at present a boom area in humanities research, not least in medieval and early modern studies, the current widespread interest in emotions has not been led by the humanities.[1] In the field of psychology, for instance, emotions, once regarded as a distraction from sound rational function, have been seen as vital to mental wellbeing for a good while now.[2] Outside academia, from primary education to the commercial workplace, the terms 'emotional intelligence' and 'emotional literacy' are commonly used. In that context, the emphasis is primarily instrumental and goal-oriented. To quote a popular source, emotional literacy is

> the ability to express emotions productively. To be emotionally literate is to be able to handle emotions in a way that improves your personal power and improves the quality of life around you. Emotional literacy improves relationships, creates loving possibilities between people, *makes co-operative work possible, and facilitates the feeling of community*.[3]

To me, this formulation of the role of the emotions in life is problematic. It seems full of kind assumptions about the benign social tendencies of empowered individuals. It champions the 'quality of life' yet is apparently mainly driven by an unexamined desire for productive labour in whose service both individual 'emotional expression' and 'the feeling of community' are enlisted. It does not favour a potentially dissenting or adversarial emotional reading, one which might question its implied

---

[1] I acknowledge the support of the Australian Research Council Centre of Excellence for the History of Emotions, Europe 1100–1800 (CE110001011) in the preparation of this essay.
[2] C. E. Izzard, *The Psychology of Emotions* (New York, 1991), p. 1, writes that '[t]he significance of emotions for self-confidence, social commitment, creative endeavors and courageous actions' was long obvious, 'but until the 1980s most of psychology ignored them'.
[3] C. Steiner, with P. Perry, *Achieving Emotional Literacy* (London, 1997), p. 11, my emphasis.

construction of the common good or the reality of the community it wants people to internalise as their own. It does not ask in whose interests all this labour might be required. But if one considers the firm relation of individual emotions to a collective aim, the cultivation of a feeling of community, the linking of collectivity with a higher quality of life, the enabling of love and, especially, the relation of emotion to productive action, one answer to that question within medieval literary culture could be 'in King Arthur's interests'. Arthur's reign, Camelot and the fellowship of the Round Table might be read retrospectively (if rather reductively) in these popular contemporary terms as a project to mobilise workplace emotions in the interests of the company owner. In this essay I examine how the Arthurian emotional project looks in three English examples stretching over three centuries: the early thirteenth-century *Brut*, by Laʒamon; Thomas Chestre's late fourteenth-century tail-rhyme romance, *Sir Launfal*; and Thomas Malory's *Le Morte Darthur* (1469).

Of course, it is not adequate to apply contemporary terminology directly and without discrimination to a medieval Arthurian literature which is of such varied nature, provenance and intellectual formation. Especially, it is problematical to write about medieval 'emotions', given that the word is not found in its modern sense until much later. Nevertheless, many modern names for 'emotions' – love, hatred, fear, pity, anger, envy, joy – are found in medieval texts, and seem to have been considered operative in daily life, though they may well have meant something different in the very different material and conceptual realms medieval people inhabited. Generally the abstract words vaguely comparable to modern 'emotion' used in medieval English occur principally in different senses from the modern: such as 'passions', often found in the sense of 'sufferings', 'afflictions' or the senses as a whole, as acted upon by external force; 'affect', the 'capacity for being affected emotionally', 'emotional bent or disposition'; or 'feeling', which in its non-literal uses seems closest to 'emotional sensibility' in general.[4] None of these terms covers quite the same ground as 'emotions' in the modern sense. They are either too much about responses to external forces, or about something too stable, general and unimmediate.

Individual emotion terms, as distinct from more tangible bodily 'feelings', are always culturally loaded and semantically slippery: in short, historical, that is, 'located in time'.[5] Also historical is 'emotionology', 'the attitudes or standards that a society, or a definable group within a society, maintains toward basic emotions and their appropriate expression',

---

[4] *Middle English Dictionary*, 'passioun' (n.); 'affect' (n.); 'felinge' (ger.(1)), 5.(a), (b).
[5] See A. Wierzbicka, 'The "History of Emotions" and the Future of Emotion Research', *Emotion Review* 2.3 (2010), 269–73, at p. 270. See also p. 272: 'There are no emotion terms which recur with the same meaning, across languages, cultures, and epochs. There are, on the other hand, certain recurrent themes, associated, for the most part, with good or bad feelings.'

requiring readers of the past to keep in mind the 'dynamic relationship between emotionology and emotional experience'.[6] No single or separate discourse controls either term in that relationship; emotions are an area of medieval life and thought where many discourses overlap, including the traditions of virtue and vice, of sin, of physiological, psychological and medical studies, and class- and gender-based ideologies also, such as the written traditions of war, courtliness and love.

Nevertheless, something relevant to the medieval in the word 'emotion' is its underlying sense of 'motion', of 'movement' (originally applied to political disturbances),[7] movement whether intransitive, transitive or reflexive, potentially both being moved or displaced by something and also actively moving oneself or others towards somewhere.[8] To 'move' in medieval English (as in Latin 'movere') is metaphorically 'to excite, arouse, stir up', and 'stirring' is a medieval English word also used for emotional excitation in much the same way. To move, or stir, oneself is to become excited or angry; to be perturbed, to stir or arouse oneself to action, and frequently in the passive, to be 'stirred'.[9] Both moving and stirring in their metaphorical senses closely associate emotional activity with literal physical activity, and that fits well with the medieval Galenic physiology of emotion, in which blood carrying the 'vital spirits' surged from the heart or towards it, according to a person's emotional state, empowering or disabling physical activity. Simo Knuuttila provides this diagram to illustrate 'a commonly known [medical] model' in the early thirteenth century.[10]

	Centrifugal	Centripetal
Slow	Joy	Distress
Quick	Anger	Fear

The process illustrated is not solely a physical one, but 'psychosomatic', relating mind and body, and treating human emotions as 'subject to the rational power'.[11] Still, emotions can lead the way: for instance, cures for problems arising from excessive coldness, such as timidity, could be effected by deliberate excitation of joy, gladness or anger, which would

---

[6] P. N. Stearns with C. Z. Stearns, 'Emotionology: Clarifying the History of Emotions and Emotional Standards', *American Historical Review* 90.4 (1985), 813–36, at p. 813. J. Corrigan, *Business of the Heart: Religion and Emotion in the Nineteenth Century* (Berkeley, 2002), p. 274.
[7] *Oxford English Dictionary*, 'emotion', *n.* 1.a.
[8] For a discussion of 'motive' in medieval literature see R. Morse, 'Temperamental Texts: Medieval Discussions of Character, Emotion, and Motivation', in *Chaucer to Shakespeare: Essays in Honour of Shinsuke Ando* (Cambridge, 1992), pp. 9–24, especially pp. 11–14.
[9] See *Middle English Dictionary*, 'meven' (v.), and 'stiren' (v.); *Oxford English Dictionary*, 'stir, v.' and 'move, v.'.
[10] S. Knuuttila, *Emotions in Ancient and Medieval Philosophy* (Oxford and New York, 2004; repr. 2006), p. 216.
[11] Knuuttila, *Emotions*, p. 214

awaken the 'vital spirit and natural heat' and change the humoral imbalance.[12]

In considering the medieval idea of emotions we are therefore dealing with active movements and stirrings, not simply 'states' of emotion, and with movements that occur within ever-changing situations. So a concern with medieval emotions is not only with the definition of individual emotion names or categories of emotion, as some historians look for, but with tracing the mobilisation of emotions in a story of active and never-ending processes. This is roughly in line with the school of modern psychology which distinguishes 'emotions' from 'feelings' by stressing their involvement in the 'management' of daily life concerns and 'goals'. Keith Oatley, referencing what he calls Aristotelian 'functionalism' about emotions, describes them as 'biological solutions to just those problems in the management of human actions that cannot be tackled in technical plans'[13] and says they 'depend on evaluations of what has happened in relation to the person's goals and beliefs'.[14] Building on the work of Nico Frijda, he argues that 'the core of an emotion ... is a mental state of readiness for action, or a change of readiness'.[15] The underlying mental state of an emotion, according to Oatley, will include 'accompaniments of conscious preoccupation, bodily disturbance, and expression. It will also issue in some course of action prompted by the emotion.'[16] Emotions are 'communicative', he adds, both within the different parts of an individual's cognitive system, and in a social context amongst individual people.[17]

Carolyne Larrington has remarked that Frijda's theory is helpful for reading situated emotions in medieval texts: 'Emotion does not occur without a proximate cause, and it results in some action; it often appears in the text to explain motivation: "emotions arise out from the interaction of situational meanings and concerns".'[18] One might say that in this view emotions become inseparable from the narratives in which they occur. As readers of medieval narrative we deal with literary performances and articulations of emotion, not with the natural outcropping in literature of social or biological realities in an unmediated form. Different literary achievements in these performances and articulations, insofar as we are able to perceive them, can make similar-looking emotions – pity, anger, joy, sorrow – mean different things and relate to action in different ways.

---

[12] Knuuttila, *Emotions*, p. 214.
[13] K. Oatley, *Best Laid Schemes: The Psychology of the Emotions* (Cambridge, 1992), p. 4.
[14] Oatley, *Best Laid Schemes*, p. 19.
[15] Oatley, *Best Laid Schemes*, pp. 19–20, citing the work of N. Frijda, *The Emotions* (Cambridge, 1986), See especially Chapter 2, 'Emotional behaviour'.
[16] Oatley, *Best Laid Schemes*, p. 21.
[17] Oatley, *Best Laid Schemes*, p. 44.
[18] C. Larrington, 'The Psychology of Emotion and Study of the Medieval Period', *Early Medieval Europe* 10.2 (2001), 251–6, citing N. H. Frijda, 'The Laws of Emotion', *American Psychologist* 43 (1988), 349–58, reprinted in *Human Emotions*, ed. J. Jenkins, K. Oatley and N. Stein (Oxford, 1998), pp. 270–87, at p. 274.

As in the self-narrative of confession the medieval penitent had to name 'those circumstances and details that identify a sin for what it is', in Valerie Allen's phrase, so the emotions in medieval narratives are inherently circumstantial and situational, not represented in the abstract.[19] Accordingly, if it is true that 'evaluation of an emotion seems context dependent in a way that the type of emotion is not', as Robert C. Roberts has suggested, we will understand Arthurian emotions better as attentive readers of narrative than as quasi-scientific taxonomists looking for evidence leading us to facts and systems of thought beyond the text.[20]

II

Arthurian narratives are also always political documents. The emotions within them rarely occur in a value-free zone, as a matter of free choice or ethical neutrality. There is a medieval, and perhaps especially an Arthurian, authority politics of emotion, rather as in the texts of medieval Christian affective piety, where readers are emotionally bound to acknowledge both their debt of gratitude to Christ and their sinful ingratitude. At the political bottom line, Arthurian emotions, especially in the chronicle tradition stemming from Geoffrey of Monmouth, are similarly enjoined on the king's subjects; the extent to which others share them with him is a sign of his strength, the 'love' which his subjects bear: if Arthur is your lord, or has made himself so, then you should have the same grounds as him for joy or sorrow, fear what he fears and hope as he hopes, unless you are a traitor who has something radically wrong with you. Emotion therefore has an ethical bent, and people are more morally responsible for their 'feelings' than we are used to thinking, much as Richard Abels has observed of Anglo-Saxon texts, where cowardice, for instance, which Aristotle considers an an excess of the emotion of fear, is seen instead as a 'wilful choice, ... not a specific moral failing concerned with fearfulness in war. ... actions that one might term "cowardly" were presented as failures to perform military duties owed a lord due to insufficient love and loyalty'.[21] In this cultural milieu, '[p]assion and desire are seen as conscious choices of the rational soul'.[22]

---

[19] V. Allen, 'Waxing Red: Shame and the Body, Shame and the Soul', in *The Representation of Women's Emotions in Medieval and Early Modern Culture*, ed. L. J. Perfetti (Gainesville, FL, 2005), pp. 191–210, at p. 193.

[20] R. C. Roberts, *Emotions: An Essay in Aid of Moral Psychology* (New York, 2003), p. 198.

[21] R. Abels, '"Cowardice" and Duty in Anglo-Saxon England', *Journal of Medieval Military History* 4 (2006), 29–49, at p. 31.

[22] See M. R. Godden, 'Anglo-Saxons on the Mind', in *Learning and Literature in Anglo-Saxon England: Studies Presented to Peter Clemoes*, ed. P. Clemoes, M. Lapidge and H. Gneuss (Cambridge, 1985), pp. 271–88, at p. 286. Godden is cited by R. Morse in 'Temperamental Texts'.

The military leader, for his part, has to act reciprocally, both nurturing and returning the love and loyalty of his men. Although it is correct to say, as Barron and Weinburg do, that the Arthur of Laȝamon's *Brut*, as a 'public figure', has no 'inner life', and so, for instance, does not express a 'personal' religious consciousness, even 'in moments of greatest anguish', the public nature of his emotional life can be seen as a sign of his political success, not as a detraction from the strength of his personal feelings.[23] Erin Mullally has pointed out that 'friendship' in Laȝamon very often refers to military and political alliance.[24] Your true 'friends' are people who act in your interests and make common cause. Arthur prides himself on his lack of singularity: 'Ne biwan hit ich noht ane ah dude we alle clæne' (I did not triumph on my own, for we did it all together).[25] He is a king who not only knows how to feel appropriately in the public sphere but can also rely on others to act on the same feelings.

So, the emotions that Laȝamon's Arthur displays, following on from Geoffrey of Monmouth and Wace, are what can be called 'functional' emotions, operating in tandem with the action. Behind this partnership lies the necessary heroic connection between words and deeds, based on courage: '"Nis noht wurð þrætte buten þere beo dede eac"' ('Threats are worth nothing unless there are deeds as well') (l. 13254). Arthur, the 'most courageous of all kings' ('baldest alre kingen') (ll. 13066, 21680, 26178), is often emotionally stirred by shameful events; the shame is always political or military, to the land at large. On hearing of the death of Uther, by Saxon treachery, and of his own succession, Arthur literally embodies a change from grief to pity to regal and military purpose:

> þus heo gunnen tellen   and Arður sæt full stille
> ænne stunde he wes blac   and on heuwe swiðe wak,
> ane while he wes reod   and reousede on heorte.
> þa hit alles up brac   hit was god þat he spac. (ll. 9923–6)

> (Thus they spoke and Arthur sat quite still; one moment he was pale and quite lacking in colour; next instant he was red with heartfelt grief. When it all burst out, what he said was fitting.)

He first sits still as the blood rushes the vital spirits to his stricken heart, making him pale and weak; then the blood is expelled from his heart in generous pity, making him red again. Emotion bursts out in a fervent prayer for divine help as he sets out immediately to cross to Britain with his forces.

---

[23] *Layamon's Arthur: The Arthurian Section of Layamon's 'Brut'*, ed. W. R. J. Barron and S. C. Weinburg, (Exeter, 1991), p. lxiv.

[24] E. Mullally, 'Registers of Friendship in Layamon's *Brut*', *Modern Philology* 108.4, (2011), 469–87.

[25] *Layamon's Arthur*, ed. Barron and Weinburg, l. 12470. Subsequent in-text references to Layamon's *Brut* are to this edition.

La3amon's Arthur is also highly successful in controlling the communication of emotion to his men. So when the Roman ambassadors' letter is read, demanding tribute, Arthur, like a 'lion', forbids casual violence to them from his knights and calls a council (l. 12400). Then in the formal war council he expresses a deep sense of anger and shame (l. 12487) with many reasons that leave his followers 'so incensed that they all shook with rage' (ll. 12596–2597), but again he stills them, even though he is *abol3en* (swollen) with anger, and explains what he will 'do':

> þe king wes abol3en.
> 'Sitteð adun stille,   cnihtes inne halle,
> and ich eou wolle telle   what ich don wulle.' (ll. 12599–600)
>
> (the king was furious. 'Sit down quietly, knights in hall, and I will tell you what I intend to do.')

What Arthur does is to send writs to the Emperor with a declaration of war, after which he gathers his forces and sets out as soon as possible. Arthur has felt an equal anger with his men, or a greater, but his anger has managed the occasion, directing it so as to give the utmost active political consequences. It is a more drawn-out, communal version of the frequent La3amon formula 'Arður hine biðohte whæt he don mahte' (Arthur considered what he could do) (10022), and, more specifically, a communal version of a sequence in which Arthur observes harm come to his land or men, then, as if consciously, has 'angered *himself* extremely' (wraðde hine sulfne wonderliche swiðe) before making a call to arms or a battle move (10151, 20345). His anger is spontaneous, 'sincere', we would say, and of the moment, but also future-oriented, something between an unpremeditated event and a studied control of himself and others. He 'feels' furiously angry – this is no mere matter of 'countenance'[26] – but it does not seem only a personal indulgence, a *furor*, because it is successfully communicated to a whole group. As long as the emotional communication between Arthur and his people is maintained – the feeling of *we alle* that La3amon emphasises – envoys or courtiers or whole armies 'work for the king emotionally', as if under licence.[27] Unity of feeling, rather than sheer possession of land, is what keeps a monarchy operative in La3amon.[28] As the most effective monarch, Arthur enjoys that unity more than any other. Objections that Arthur's anger is the sign of an 'alienation' that prevents him 'from sustaining his human relationships

---

[26] S. A. Throop, 'Zeal, Anger and Vengeance: The Emotional Rhetoric of Crusading', in *Vengeance in the Middle Ages: Emotion, Religion and Feud*, ed. S. A. Throop and P. R. Hyams (Aldershot, 2010), pp. 177–202, at p. 193.

[27] L. Diggelmann, 'Emotional Excess in Two Twelfth-Century Histories: Wace's *Roman de Brut* and *Roman de Rou*', unpublished paper, 'Emotions in the Medieval and Early Modern World' conference, University of Western Australia, 9–11 June 2011.

[28] See A. Sheppard, 'Of This Is a King's Body Made: Lordship and Succession in Lawman's Arthur and Leir', *Arthuriana* 10.2 (2000), 50–65.

and protecting his people' underrate the emotionally communicative aspect of successful rule in Laȝamon, despite one reference to Arthur's fierce personality making his counsellors reluctant to contradict him (ll. 10428–30).[29] In its purposefulness, Arthur's controlled emotion parallels the 'cogitative' nature of correct medieval imagination, the 'deliberative' use of the *vis imaginativa*, with its judgemental quality.[30]

Françoise Le Saux notes a special quality of emotional restraint in Wace's Arthur: 'Arthur's defense of the envoys against the wrath of his men ... illustrates his self-restraint and respect of higher principles – in this case the immunity of messengers – even in so extreme a situation.'[31] By contrast, there is no sense that Laȝamon's Arthur needs to restrain emotion in order to act rightly, only to channel it in the right direction. His 'heart', often described as 'swollen' (*abolȝen*) with anger, leads him correctly. There is no suggestion of the ascetic or Stoic attitudes to emotion often found in Old English poetry. Perhaps because Laȝamon's Arthur is a man called on to take worldly action, not to despise the world, the narrative takes a secular view of his emotions as reliable indicators, something also found in the later romance tradition. In Thomas Malory's *Le Morte Darthur*, Arthur knows his disguised nephew Gareth emotionally – 'myne herte gyvyth me to the gretly that thou arte com of men of worshyp' – in a manner perfectly in line with his separate mental estimation – his 'conceyte' – that the unknown youth will 'preve a man of ryght grete worshyp'.[32] Gawain's brotherly 'bloode' and Lancelot's 'jantylnesse and curtesy' have the same informative functions (1. 295), through the mystical cognition of noble kinship or affinity that sets up an emotion-action cycle. How you feel in such cases makes you act in a way that reflects and shows who you are.

Joy, the other principal emotion of the Arthurian chronicle tradition, is, like royal anger, public and political in its operations. But whereas anger comes before action, joy comes after action, as if it has to be earned. And since, in the Arthurian chronicle tradition, joy is most frequently associated with military success, anger can be regarded as the necessary prelude to joy, as victorious war is to peace. The opposite of joy is 'sorrow', as is felt after military losses. Sorrow is at its height when events are perceived to have reached a stage which no subsequent military action can be imag-

---

[29] D. P. Donahue, 'The Darkly Chronicled King: An Interpretation of the Negative Side of Arthur in Lawman's *Brut* and Geoffrey's *Historia*', *Arthuriana* 8.4 (1998), 135–147, at pp. 135–6.

[30] M. Carruthers, *The Book of Memory: A Study of Memory in Medieval Culture*, Cambridge Studies in Medieval Literature 10 (Cambridge, 1990; 2nd edn 2008), p. 244.

[31] F. H. M. Le Saux, *A Companion to Wace* (Cambridge, 2005), p. 135.

[32] *The Works of Sir Thomas Malory*, ed. E. Vinaver, rev. P. J. C. Field, 3 vols (Oxford, 1991), I: 294. Subsequent in-text references to *Le Morte Darthur* are to volume and page numbers in this edition.

ined to redeem. Waking from a dream obscurely warning of Mordred's and Guenevere's treachery, Laȝamon's Arthur says:

> 'for ich what to iwisse igon is al mi blisse:
> for a to mine liue sorȝen ich mote driȝe.
> Wale that ich nabbe here Wenhauer mine quene!' (ll. 14019–21)

> ('for I know with certainty that all my happiness is ended; for as long as I live I must endure sorrow. Alas that Guenevere my queen is not here with me.')

The necessary conversion of emotion to action is deeply challenged here. The narrative register of emotions tells us that everything is over before the actual events do. Arthur's premonitory dream anticipates the emotional effect of Wenhauer's defection. His longing for her at the very moment when her disloyalty has been obscurely sensed shows how uncertainly emotion relates to cognitive appraisal of 'goals' in this case, and explains his refusal to believe the messenger when the idea of her treachery is first raised: 'Longe bið æuere þat no wene ich næuere' (As long as time shall last I will never believe that, 1.14036). He knows emotionally the impossibility of admitting so horrible a fact to consciousness and remaining the same person that he was before; the 'I' that believes it will be irrevocably changed. When he accepts the news as true, Arthur tries to maintain his policy of emotional control by personally regulating the general reaction to the news of rebellion, using the same words he has used to control anger at the Romans:

> 'Sitteð adun stille, cnihtes inne halle,
> and ic eou telle wulle speles vncuðe.' (ll. 14061–2)

> ('Sit down quietly, knights in the hall, and I will tell you matters strange to hear.')

Nevertheless, in this case, he must suffer (*driȝe*) sorrow ineluctably, whatever he does. He can punish the traitors and revenge himself by force of arms – the messenger suggests this as a consolation – but he cannot have their loyalty again. The collective context in which 'joy' is possible has been destroyed by the defection of these intimates, so the emotional situation cannot be managed by force as external attacks have been. In the logic of Arthur's dream it is after the killing of Modred and Wenhauer, and the thrusting of her dismembered body into a black pit, that Arthur finds all his people desert him as he stands alone (just *miseolf*) upon a hill, deprived of the communal resources for happiness, politically or personally. Arthur's dream of lonely and helpless sorrow is a completely original insertion by Laȝamon in Geoffrey's and Wace's accounts. It expresses in its extension of the story's generic range an emotional condition that can neither manage nor be managed by future actions. Although 'me imette a sweuen' is 'I dreamed a dream' in modern English, in Laȝamon's idiom it is the dream that impersonally acts on Arthur ('a dream dreamed to me'), in a great difference from the confident reflexives we have seen when he acts emotionally on himself, and from the imperatives by which he has controlled others' emotion. The grammar of the dream expresses the unthinkable scandal of the emotions of intimates (wife and sister's son) not 'working for the king' but working for themselves, just as in its inception the dream suggests that Arthur has not himself really been in control of his previous life: 'Me imette þat mon me hof uppen are halle' (I dreamed that I had been reared high upon a hall, l. 13984). It dreams to him that somehow, by an impersonal and unspecified force, he has been raised up onto the roof of a hall which Modred and Wenhauer tear down.

Arthur says later that the dream showed that sorrows, including the later death of Gawain, were 'ordained' (ʒeueðe) for him (l. 14145). From that point, his anger and ruthless punishment of opposition are factors that cannot restore 'joy' (*blisse, wunne*), no matter how actively they proceed, just as in the dream he has concluded 'al wet and weri of sorʒen and seoc' (all wet and weary then, sick with sorrow) *after* killing Mordred and Guenevere (l. 14014). The anger continues – including a massacre of the whole city of Winchester – and one cannot see that Laʒamon thinks it is excessive, but the ameliorative emotional effect is notably missing. Arthur's last speech is spoken 'mid sorhful heorte' (l. 14271), and his departure communicates a general 'sadness beyond measure' – *vnimete care* – (l. 14289) to the nation. 'Joy' (*wunne*) is only to be expected on his return. The *Brut* is a compelling narrative of the power of emotions to exceed and critique the 'life goals' that they are supposed to facilitate.

III

Arthurian masculine 'emotional' regimes are normally distinguished by their collectivity: 'manhood is a collective enterprise.'[33] So Arthurian narratives tend to desire the joy of a whole people (as in Laʒamon), or of a court (as in Chrétien's *Erec*), or of a chivalric fellowship (as in Malory), under the king's rule. Where the story develops in a way that legitimately privileges an individual's interest over that of the king's group, as in Thomas Chestre's *Sir Launfal*, a version of Marie de France's *Lanval*, the quality of the emotional narrative is altered – not semantically, the same limited vocabulary is used throughout – but by the force of its circumstantial re-applications.[34] Over the course of the story, Launfal's stolid nature and knightly instincts never change, and the narrative repertoire

---

[33] A. Baden-Daintree, 'Blood, Tears, and Masculine Identity in the Alliterative *Morte Arthure*', unpublished paper, XXIIIrd Triennial Congress of the International Arthurian Society, University of Bristol, 25–30 July 2011 (see also this volume).

[34] Two earlier analyses informing the following discussion are: A. C. Spearing, *The Medieval Poet as Voyeur: Looking and Listening in Medieval Love Narratives* (Cambridge, 1993), pp.

of his emotions is typically underdeveloped – happy when things are going well, sad when they are not, not even showing surprise, as Marie's Lanval does, at his new-found love and fortune. But the idea of his happiness becomes increasingly detachable from his place in Arthur's court. The normally all-embracing justice, *joye* and *solas* of the Arthurian reign, celebrated at the poem's beginning, are later compromised by its concentration on an individual's material and personal sources of happiness, especially wealth and love.[35]

In Chestre's poem, Launfal's dislike of Guenevere's promiscuity and her failure to reward him with a gift drive him from the court and he falls into poverty. Excluded from good society, he is rescued from humiliation and sorrow by a billionaire fairy lover, Triamour, and restored to wealth, joy and a prominent place at court. Her warning not to tell others about their love, explicable as a magic demand and a *fin' amour* requirement, makes the sexual aspect of their happiness a private matter, and Launfal is not bothered:

> Tho was Launfal glad and blythe,
> He cowde no man hys joye kythe   [make known]
> And keste her well good won   [many times]   (ll. 358–60)

But sexual solace is not all he has; for seven years after his return to prosperity, Launfal sustains both public honour and private happiness. No one at court knows his real emotional state. Triamour's money and backing allow him success as an active knight in two military adventures, not found in Marie. When unwanted advances and taunts from Guenevere lead him to reveal his lover's existence, the poem remarks that along with her he loses his wealth, his horse and the magic servant who has helped him in tournaments, and that his armour becomes tarnished (ll. 728–44). Triamour is the greatest of his losses, but not the only one: 'All my joye I have forelore, / And the - that me ys worst fore' (ll. 748–9). Finally, in order to clear Launfal from treason, Triamour appears before the court, verifies the humiliating truth to Arthur, punishes Guenevere, and they leave together for a magic island realm.

The English poem differs from Marie's *Lanval* in some respects that alter the emotional force of its ending. Launfal has begun the story 'working emotionally', in Diggelmann's terms, for Arthur through his limitless largesse as steward at court and by his loyal dislike of Guenevere's infidelity, which is said to be shared by other 'courteous' ('hende') knights (l. 45). In Marie it is stressed that, despite his great service, Lanval is forgotten by Arthur, but in *Launfal* only Guenevere is at fault. Arthur

---

97–119; and M. Stokes, 'Lanval to Sir Launfal: A Story Becomes Popular', in *The Spirit of Medieval English Popular Romance*, ed. A. Putter and J. Gilbert (Harlow, 2000), pp. 56–77.

[35] *Sir Launfal*, in *The Middle English Breton Lays*, ed. A. Laskaya and E. Salisbury (Kalamazoo, 1995), ll. 1–12. Subsequent in-text references to *Sir Launfal* are to this edition.

shows great generosity and support to Launfal when he leaves court, and never learns of his poverty because his two nephews go along with Launfal's wish to disguise it. So Chestre preserves Arthur's credit as a 'good king' more carefully than Marie had, and is also more consistent in his representation of the court in general, Guenevere excepted, as an emotionally supportive place for Launfal as long as he can remain in it.[36] In Marie, Lanval's superior qualities make him envied by most of the court, so that he begins the story not as part of a 'community' in the same way as Launfal does, but as a typical example of an outsider who does not know how to work the system: 'hume estrange descunseillez ... en autre tere' ('a stranger bereft of advice ... in another land').[37] He later gains support from the other knights, but only following his generosity and prominence at court after he receives the fairy gold.

In Marie, the fairy lover's sexual bounty brings Lanval into a happiness that he apparently does not know at court or as a knight, even when restored to wealth and honour, a joy which he can only find in her and when alone:[38]

> mut ot Lanval joie e deduit:
> u seit par jur u seit par nuit,
> s'amie peot veer sovent (ll. 215–18)

(Lanval experienced great joy and pleasure, for day and night he could see his beloved often.) (p. 75)

> Lanval s'en vait a une part,
> mut luin des autres; ceo l'est tart
> que s'amie puïst tenir,
> baiser, acoler e sentir;
> l'autrui joie prise petit,
> si il nen ad le suen delit. (ll. 253–8)

(Lanval withdrew to one side, far from the others, for he was impatient to hold his beloved, to kiss, embrace and touch her. He cared little for other people's joy when he could not have his own pleasure.) (p. 76)

When his lover seems gone for ever, Lanval laments only the loss of her, and realises it emotionally before any other effects of her absence. His friends deride his emotional life:

---

[36] See Spearing, *The Medieval Poet as Voyeur*, p. 108.

[37] *Lanval*, in *Marie de France, Lais*, ed. A. Ewert (Oxford, 1969), ll. 36–7. *The Lais of Marie de France*, ed. and trans. K. Busby and G. Burgess (Harmondsworth, 1986), p. 73. Subsequent in-text references to the poem are to this edition and translation.

[38] See Spearing, *The Medieval Poet as Voyeur*, p. 99; Stokes, 'Lanval to Sir Launfal', pp. 67–9.

> mut l'unt blasmé e chastïé
> k'il ne face si grant dolur,
> e maudïent si fol'amur. (ll. 408–10)
>
> (They chastised him and urged him strongly not to be so sorrowful and cursed such foolish love.) (p. 78)

Marie's story consistently sets Lanval's love and the joy of sexual union against the apparently superficial emotional life of a knight at Arthur's court until finally he is 'borne' away by his lover to Avalon – 'la fu ravi li dameiseaus' (l. 644) (thither the young man was borne; p. 81) – on the back of her palfrey, and never heard of again. Loving her constitutes an emotional regime in opposition to Arthur's, signalling 'a dissent from the fundamental premises of the patriarchy'.[39] In *Sir Launfal* the hero chooses to ride his war-horse Blanchard to Triamour's country, and although he leaves the Arthurian world he remains an active knight, re-appearing once a year to joust with all takers (ll. 1024–32). Without Launfal's changing his ordinariness in any way, or even being moved to do anything special to advance his own cause, his career redefines the nature of his 'joy' as a set of individual material requirements, which remain those of a supreme Arthurian knight, but which in this case can finally be better satisfied outside the Arthurian environment. Triamour offers Launfal the added joy of love as a complement to knightly life, not an alternative; she is herself a better source of knightly patronage than Arthur. So Launfal's emotions remain 'Arthurian', as part of an 'emotional community' in Barbara Rosenwein's limited sense of a 'group … in which people adhere to the same norms of emotional expression[,] and value – or devalue – the same or related emotions', but he is no longer emotionally working for Arthur.[40] In this largely apolitical context, lacking even Marie's sketchy placement of the story in Geoffrey of Monmouth's time-line, the king has not been opposed or betrayed – he will go on being 'good King Arthur' – but he has become emotionally redundant to his former vassal.

IV

Sir Launfal shows how the Arthurian imaginary has political trouble in accommodating the variety of 'emotional communities' that Barbara Rosenwein envisages as existing in any one historical period.[41] Differing legitimate emotional evaluations, like those imported by the Quest of the Holy Grail, cause serious political problems in Arthur's world, as do rival centres of emotional attention such as Mordred – 'dearest of all

---

[39] S. Kinoshita, 'Cherchez la femme: Feminist Criticism and Marie de France's *Lai de Lanval*', *Romance Notes* 34 (1993–4), 262–73, at p. 272.

[40] B. Rosenwein, *Emotional Communities in the Early Middle Ages* (Ithaca, NY, 2006), p. 2.

[41] Rosenwein, *Emotional Communities*, p. 2.

men' to Guenevere in Laȝamon's *Brut* (l. 14101) – and Lancelot. Nevertheless, it is possible to note a wider role for emotions in romance scenarios, where they may become involved in the action as 'characters' that seem to dictate the political development of a story, or even to go beyond it, rather than merely serving it as 'actants'. These are not necessarily Arthurian romance features, of course. In the quasi-Arthurian English *Ipomadon*, for instance, the proud heroine has sworn to love only a knight of proven highest prowess, as in Geoffrey of Monmouth's tournament scenario (where the pairing up of the bravest and the most beautiful can only improve the aristocracy's genetic stock), but she falls in love with a young man when she sees him cutting up a deer, a man reputed not to be of prowess. She cannot correct her love of him by reason or by reference to her normal standards, though she tries:

> She thynkys to haue Ipomadon
> And thought agayne, 'Thynke not thereon',
> Thus turnys she tow and fro. (ll. 699–701)

> (She thinks she will have Ipomadon and thought again, 'Don't think of it', thus she turns to and fro.)

She knows she cannot love a coward and yet she loves a coward. Love conquers:

> Att the laste, of love drewry
> Dystrwes defaute of chevellrye. (ll. 702–3)

> (In the end, the power of [her] love overides [his] lack of chivalry.)[42]

Even though the audience knows who the young man really is, emotion seems to lead the way here, waiting for the plot to catch up. We see many similar romance situations, Arthurian and otherwise, where emotion itself seems the narrative priority, and these often seem to be constructed around a negative or insufficient or unwanted relation of emotion to action. In Malory, when Arthur weeps helplessly at the course of his unwanted war with Lancelot – '"Alas, alas, that ever yet thys warre began"' (3.1193) – it is a sign of lessened political power, which has rendered his emotion private (i.e., politically deprived), divorced from effective regal action. Yet this emotion still matters – Arthur remains a highly privileged character in that the narrative cares so much about his conflicted emotional life – and Arthur's manifest emotions become actions in themselves in the private sphere. That can be seen as a major difference in Malory from *La Mort le roi Artu*, which, as Norris Lacy says, routinely 'remove[s] the emotional center of the story'[43] from the king, and which lacks the king's tears and the

---

[42] *Ipomadon*, ed. R. Purdie, EETS, OS 316 (Oxford, 2001), ll. 698–701.
[43] N. J. Lacy, 'The Ambiguous Fortunes of Arthur: The Lancelot-Grail and Beyond', in *The Fortunes of King Arthur*, ed. N. J. Lacy (Cambridge, 2005), pp. 92–103, at p. 100.

sad privacy of this speech in Malory; in the French it is made 'in front of all those who were with him'.[44] Malory's Arthur's problem here is the lack of possible action that could answer to his emotional state. When Arthur has recovered something significant to do, the disposal of Excalibur, and has caught up with the action again, non-functional emotion is put in its normal place: '"Now leve thys mournynge and wepyng, jantyll knyght, ... for all thys woll nat avayle me"' (3.1238). When situations are normal, tears in romance must typically be 'left', so that something more useful can be done. Bors says in exasperation to Guenevere, who has driven Lancelot away in madness, '"Now, fye on youre wepynge! ... For ye wepe never but whan there is no boote"' (2.808); that is, 'no remedy' / 'nothing that can be done to help'. Tears should predicate remedial action. Action should do away with tears.

And yet Malory's narrative reveals an over-simplicity in this normative relation of emotion to action. Like Laʒamon's Arthur on hearing the news of Mordred and Guenevere, Malory's Gawain, hearing that Lancelot has killed Gareth, both '"may ... nat beleve"' (3.1184) that the news is true, yet knows that '"now ys my joy gone"' (3.1185), not principally because of his personal anger at the death of his brother, but because the unthinkable has happened between two other people. In Gawain's eyes, Lancelot's killing of Gareth, who '"loved hym bettir than me and all hys brethirn and the kynge bothe"' (3.1185) has destroyed the public conditions, the emotional atmosphere, in which joy could be a possibility. Now, as we saw in Laʒamon, only revenge and death are possible. Emotion still drives to action – '"I shall sle hym, othir ellis he shall sle me"' (3.1186) – but deprived of its wider communal potential, it shrinks within a purely personal scenario, in which Gawain reductively casts himself as the punisher of a '"false knight"' who has killed Gareth and Gaheris '"in the despite of me"' (3.1189). The political damage sustained by the Arthurian regime is reflected in its stark emotional division between Arthur's tears of regret and Gawain's implacable hatred, both equally inefficacious. While nothing else than a war with Lancelot could be expected politically, given what has happened, the narrative course of emotional life still shows the insufficiency of the normal active response to emotional events.

Conversely, spontaneous emotional expression, what Malory often calls 'cheer', can run counter to expected action, as Launcelot finds when Gawain refuses to make peace, yet he remains reluctant to lead his forces against Arthur:

> and when sir Launcelot had harde hir answere, than the tearys ran downe by hys chekys. And than hys noble knyghtes strode aboute hym and seyde,
> 'Sir Launcelot, wherefore make ye suche chere? Now thynke what ye ar and what men we ar, and lat us noble knyghtis macche hem in myddis of the fylde.'

---

[44] *The Death of King Arthur*, trans. J. Cable (Harmondsworth, 1971), p. 145.

> 'That may be lyghtly done,' seyde sir Launcelot, 'but I was never so lothe to do batayle. And therefore I praye you, sirres, as ye love me, be ruled at thys tyme as I woll have you.' (3.1113–4)

'Cheer' is one of Malory's main emotion words, surprisingly various and flexible in its usages, ranging from ordinary 'entertainment' at social gatherings, having or making someone else have 'good cheer' or 'merry cheer', with a possible sexual element – '"lye downe by his syde and make hym no strange chere but good chere"' (1.314) – to expressions of deep emotion: 'Lorde, the grete chere that sir Launcelot made of sir Gareth and he of hym! For there was no knyght that sir Gareth loved so well as he dud sir Launcelot' (1.360). Sometimes it relates to how a person 'looks' or 'seems to be feeling': 'with hevy chere' (1.329); '"me semeth by your chere ye haue ben diseased but late"' (1.443), and it extends to understanding of a person's feelings based on assessment of their actions: '"thou madist no chere to rescow me ... But untyll that tyme I wente ye had loved me"' (1.402); '"they woll nat oute of the fylde, I se by their chere and countenaunce"' (2.526). As a 'feeling' and yet a sign to others and an action towards others, 'cheer' is both personal and emotionally communicative, though it can be simulated, 'god chere shewynge outeward' (2.547), '"youre semble chere that ye made us"' (2.549), or used to hide anxiety, 'he was in grete feare to dye, but allwayes ... he batyd no chere' (1.143), or changed by effort: 'there was nother man nother woman that coude chere hym with onythynge that they coude make to hym' (2.783). 'What cheer?' means 'how do you feel?' or 'how do you do?',[45] and the answer sometimes reveals a cognitive element: to the question '"What chere?"' a knight can reply '"Well"' (1.451) or '"Nat good"' (1.108), or '"Truly, damesel ... never so ylle"' (1.258), but also 'I can not sey, fayre damesel ... for I wote not how I com into this castell' (1.257). 'Cheer' is one's own, yet, as in the view of Lancelot's kinfolk (3.1113–4), quoted above, the 'cheer' you 'make' in a particular situation will also be closely linked to a public idea of who you 'are' and what you should 'do'.

'Cheer', then, is inextricably linked to an emotional evaluation of the preceding action and to the potential within emotion for further action, but it also retains a spontaneity that can exceed both the prescriptions of emotionology and of political utility or any situated 'goal-oriented' behaviour. Through the 'cheer' that Launcelot and Arthur make, we understand that emotion has developed in them its own separate, and more satisfying, narrative trajectory. They find themselves invested in more than one 'emotional community', but only they are members of the second community that puts sorrow for lost love and fellowship above the demands of war. Lancelot 'makes cheer' that cannot be communicated

---

[45] It survives as 'wotcher'. See *Oxford English Dictionary*, 'cheer', n^1 3b, 'a familiar greeting'; 'wotcher, *int.*'.

spontaneously to others within his close group. It is not the manner of Launcelot's emotional display in itself that annoys them, or its breaking of any taboo against expressing feelings. At many other moments, such as the parting of Launcelot and Guenevere, where we are told anyone observing would be similarly affected (3.1253), open weeping is a proper behaviour. The problem is its situation in this particular course of events, where, counter-intuitively to Lancelot's kin, a knight's emotion is destroying motivation and inhibiting right action.

In conclusion, it can be seen that counter-active and counter-communal emotion in the Arthurian world accompanies and registers an extraordinary personal and political strain, a threat to normal functions of identity and a breaking of fellowship. But also, it seems to attract a narrative privilege; it is only Malory's emotional elite, Arthur and Lancelot, who realise the fullness of the unfolding situation and cannot therefore readily transform emotion into actions that others, less perceptive, would wish. Feeling more than one thing at a time is perhaps not a useful trait in times of crisis (and that may suggest that refined emotions are not necessarily an evolutionary advantage), but the greatest personages of *Le Morte Darthur* model it as a right reading of events. From their apparently reliable role in the 'management' of actions, Arthurian emotions seem to have become powerful entities to which no one course of action is a satisfactory response, just as in Laȝamon's *Brut* the emotions once harnessed to drive political goals eventually overwhelm the normal active measures taken in response to their demands. If the Arthurian world provides some perfect examples of the productive emotional mobilisation of a workforce, it also gives us a compelling narrative of the problems that arise when a more developed and intense 'emotional literacy' supplants a narrowly instrumental and goal-oriented reading of events.

PART II

BODIES, MINDS AND VOICES: INVESTIGATING EMOTION IN ARTHURIAN TEXTS

4

Ire, Peor *and their Somatic Correlates in Chrétien's* Chevalier de la Charrette

ANATOLE PIERRE FUKSAS

Emotions and the Medieval Romance

All readers know that the act of reading a novel triggers emotional responses. Literary texts written a thousand years ago, such as Chrétien's *Chevalier de la Charrette* and medieval verse romances more generally, can still produce emotional responses in modern readers because they describe emotion-related aspects of the human condition that are still part of our experiences of life. There is no doubt that literary descriptions embed emotions, even difficult emotions. And, surprisingly enough, the words or locutions for these are likely to trigger affective reactions in readers and/or audiences in ways that have yet to be clarified.

Recent advances in neuroscience may play a significant role in the understanding of such a crucial issue. David Havas, Arthur Glenberg and Mike Rinck introduce their article on emotion simulation by affirming that 'reading a passage from a favourite novel makes it clear that language evokes emotion'.[1] Again, assuming that 'there is no question that language and emotion affect one another', Glenberg and his collaborators observed that 'when we read a novel, the words may thrill, petrify, or titillate'.[2]

According to some experimental findings, the understanding of emotion-related descriptions may be based on an embodied knowledge that makes recognition possible.[3] Essentially, the understanding of emotion-related situations is likely to activate the neural representation

---

[1] D. A. Havas, A. M. Glenberg and M. Rinck, 'Emotion Simulation during Language Comprehension', *Psychonomic Bulletin & Review* 14.3 (2007), 436–41, at p. 436.
[2] A. M. Glenberg, B. J. Webster, E. Mouilso, D. Havas and L. M. Lindeman, 'Gender, Emotion, and the Embodiment of Language Comprehension', *Emotion Review* 1.2 (2009), 151–61, at p. 151.
[3] For a brief review of recent studies supporting this view see A. P. Fuksas, 'Embodied Abstraction and Emotional Resonance in Chrétien's *Chevalier de la Charrette*', *Cognitive Philology* 4 (2011), 1–14.

of the corresponding emotions in readers or listeners. This hypothesis is congruent with the idea that 'the body-sensing areas constitute a sort of theatre where not only the "actual" body states can be "performed", but varied assortments of "false" body states can be enacted as well, for example, as-if body states, filtered body states, and so on'.[4]

Antonio Damasio, one of the most prominent neuroscientists to have studied emotions, remarks that 'the commands for producing as-if body states are likely to come from a variety of prefrontal cortices as suggested by recent work on mirror-neurons in both animals and humans'.[5] A mirror-matching mechanism may be responsible for the understanding of emotions felt and expressed by others both in somatic and linguistic terms. Evidence provided by Arthur M. Glenberg and his colleagues supports this hypothesis, by showing that the full understanding of emotion-related language requires corresponding emotions to be simulated, or partially induced, using the same neural and bodily mechanisms as when experiencing analogous affective states.[6]

According to other studies, similar brain systems reflect the decoding of both biological and symbolic emotional signals of positive valence, differing mainly in the speed of meaning-access, which is faster and more direct for facial expressions than for words.[7] On the other hand, investigations based on the processing of single words presumed to vary in emotional valence show that the emotional arousal attributed to words does not cause a compulsory activation of the autonomic nervous system, but rather works on a cognitive level, facilitating word-processing.[8] Other studies of the influence of lexical relevance on the syntactic and semantic processes that occur during sentence comprehension showed that emotional valence in a word impacts on the syntactic and semantic processing of sentences.[9]

---

[4] A. Damasio, *Looking for Spinoza: Joy, Sorrow, and the Feeling Brain* (Orlando, 2003), pp. 117–18.

[5] Damasio, *Looking*, p. 118. On the literary and philological implications of theoretical studies and experiments concerning mirror neurons and embodied semantics cf.: A. P. Fuksas, 'The Ecology of the Sword Bridge through the Manuscript Textual Tradition of the *Chevalier de la Charrette* by Chrétien de Troyes', *Compar(a)isons* 26.2 (2007), 155–80; A. P. Fuksas, 'The Embodied Novel: An Ecological Theory of Narrative Reference', *Cognitive Philology* 1 (2008), 1–14; M. Salgaro, 'Stories without Words: Narratives of the Brain', *Cognitive Philology* 2 (2009), 1–8; and M. Salgaro, 'The Text as a Manual: Some Reflections on the Concept of Language from a Neuroaesthetic Perspective', *Journal of Literary Theory* 3.1 (2009), 155–66.

[6] A. M. Glenberg, D. A. Havas, R. Becker and M. Rinck, 'Grounding Language in Bodily States: The Case for Emotion', *The Grounding of Cognition: The Role of Perception and Action in Memory, Language, and Thinking*, ed. R. Zwaan and D. Pecher (Cambridge, 2005), pp. 115–28.

[7] A. Schacht and W. Sommer, 'Emotions in Word and Face Processing: Early and Late Cortical Responses', *Brain and Cognition* 69 (2009), 538–50.

[8] M. Bayer, W. Sommer and A. Schacht, 'Emotional Words Impact the Mind but not the Body: Evidence from Pupillary Responses', *Psychophysiology* 48.11 (2011), 1554–62.

[9] M. Martín-Loeches, A. Fernández, A. Schacht, W. Sommer, P. Casado, L. Jiménez-Ortega

This array of evidence does not prove beyond doubt that the processing of emotion-related descriptions is grounded in corresponding affective states, targeting both brain and body of the subject. It seems likely, however, that the full understanding of emotion-related language must be based on the idea of processing strategies similar to those responsible for processing corresponding emotional states triggered by other environmental interactions. This assumption throws the door wide open to the idea that readers or listeners understand emotion-related descriptions according to their own embodied experience of similar affective states.

It is therefore likely that responses to emotion-related descriptions vary according to individual and social experiences of corresponding emotional states, depending on the historical and/or cultural frame of reference.[10] In a seminal work specifically concerned with the study of emotions in medieval literature, Carolyne Larrington hypothesises that 'reference to somatic indices in historical or imaginative texts encourages readers to infer the presence of an emotion on the basis of their own experience of similar bodily changes'.[11] Courtly romances feature character-specific emotional responses to environmental and social circumstances that often entail the description of somatic correlates, such as trembling or blushing, in order to explain how selected characters feel such emotions.

Thus, descriptions of emotional responses to specific environmental and/or social circumstances affecting romance protagonists and minor characters are likely to modulate the emotional appraisal of the events described in readers and/or the audience. Larrington also suggests that 'the concepts of appraisal and action readiness help to explain the ways in which emotion is embedded within the texts we scrutinise'. Indeed, in accordance with the proposition that 'emotion often appears in the text to explain motivation', the emotional states that affect characters do not emerge without a proximate cause that results in some action.[12]

This assumption is consistent with an ecology of emotions rooted in the understanding of human affective states as adaptive, perpetually adjusting to environmental and/or social interaction. Accordingly, emotional responses modulated by perceptual events and/or emotion-related memories underlie decision-making processes and consequent intentional actions. Hence, it is impossible fully to understand the description of an action without being aware of its emotional back-

and S. Fondevila, 'The Influence of Emotional Words on Sentence Processing: Electrophysiological and Behavioral Evidence', *Neuropsychologia* 50 (2012), 3262–72.

[10] B. H. Rosenwein, 'Worrying about Emotions in History', *American Historical Review* 107.3 (2001), 821–45; B. H. Rosenwein, 'Problems and Methods in the History of Emotions', *Passions in Context* 1 (2010), 1–32; and S. Knuuttila, *Emotions in Ancient and Medieval Philosophy* (Oxford and New York, 2004; repr. 2006).

[11] C. Larrington, 'The Psychology of Emotion and Study of the Medieval Period', *Early Medieval Europe* 10.2 (2001), 251–6, at p. 254.

[12] Larrington, 'Psychology', p. 254.

ground, because the meaning of that very action depends on its affective implications.

A number of studies have elaborated and extended these arguments. For instance, Frank Brandsma posits a 'deliberate narrative strategy, intended to make the audience react to the described situations in the same way as the characters do; the characters mirror the reaction the author hopes to invoke in his audience'.[13] Providing evidence from medieval verse and prose romances, Brandsma has introduced the idea of 'mirror characters', who react to specific environmental circumstances in a way that aims to influence the audience's responses.

I have observed elsewhere that Chrétien de Troyes' emotion-related descriptions in the *Chevalier de la Charrette* typically present character-specific responses to perceptual events and/or underlie decision-making processes that lead to purposeful intentional actions.[14] Accordingly, I have postulated (and demonstrated) that descriptions of affective states are crucial to the 'realism' of medieval romances, because the emotions are perceived as 'real' and 'true', that is, appropriate to the environmental conditions the characters are facing, as marvellous and extravagant as they can be.[15]

The discussion below of other cases from the same romance, one of the most famous and a somewhat prototypical instance of the genre, offers additional evidence concerning the association between affective states and somatic correlates in descriptions of emotion-related circumstances. The investigation will focus on specific emotion words, but, in accordance with previous observations, these are not to be interpreted as triggering corresponding affective states in the reader and the audience *per se*. Rather the words directly refer to contexts, namely environmental descriptions, explaining what emotional state an individual person is likely to experience in such specific conditions, and to the ensuing actions, explaining why a given character acts the way he or she does.

The investigation specifically focuses on the nouns *ire* and *peor*, which co-occur with a third, the verb *trambler*, which clearly describes a somatic correlate of the affective states they indicate. Interestingly, the same bodily state affects different characters with respect to emotional states that are described as being different. The first case is the episode following the revolt by the people of Logres, in which Lancelot fights an arrogant

---

[13] F. Brandsma, 'Mirror Characters', in *Courtly Arts and the Art of Courtliness*, ed. K. Busby and C. Kleinhenz (Cambridge, 2006), pp. 275–84, p. 284, in particular, and cf. F. Brandsma, 'Arthurian Emotions', *Actes du 22ᵉ Congrès de la Société Internationale Arthurienne* (Rennes, 2008) [http://www.uhb.fr/alc/ias/actes/index.htm, 15 July, session 2 L2: Conte du Graal et emotions].

[14] Fuksas, 'Embodied Abstraction'.

[15] See also A. P. Fuksas, 'Characters, Society and Nature in the *Chevalier de la Charrette* (vv. 247–398)', *Critica del Testo* 12.2–3 (2009), 49–77.

knight who has treated him with contempt because he has ridden in the infamous cart (ll. 2732–9):

> Li chevaliers de la charrete
> De malvestié se blasme et rete
> Quant son oste voit qui l'esgarde;
> Et des autres se reprant garde
> Qui l'esgardoient tuit ansanble.
> D'ire trestoz li cors li tranble,
> Qu'il deüst, ce li est avis,
> Avoir molt grant pieç'a conquis
> Celui qui a lui se combat.[16]

(The knight of the cart curses himself while seeing his host and all the attending crowd who all together are watching him. Suddenly his body begins to shake with anger, for as far as he was concerned, he should have defeated his opponent long ago.)

Lancelot notices that the crowd is staring at him and realises that he has already fought too long before defeating his opponent; this awareness causes him to experience an emotional upheaval that triggers his final assault. Anger (*ire*) is the emotion that shakes (*tranble*) the protagonist's body (*cors*): the description of this affective state clearly entails a somatic correlate. Chrétien states that it is the visual appraisal of the situation that makes the hero's body tremble with anger, before relating how Lancelot fights even harder in order to win the battle (ll. 2740 ff.).

A philological investigation focusing on emotion words in a medieval literary text must necessarily take into account the variation inherent in manuscript tradition: the emotional system of a romance varies according to redactors' understandings of specific episodes and their emotional meaning. In this case the various readings create remarkable differences in the affective tone, and in the depiction of the association between emotional states and somatic correlates. For instance, in MS E (fol. 16r, col. b) l. 2732, 'De malvaiste se blame et rete', is immediately followed by l. 2737, 'Ker il de deust avoir comquis'; thus any reference to Lancelot's *ire* is completely absent.

MSS CTV use the noun *ire*, whereas MSS A (fol. 204v, col. a) and G (fol. 11v, col. a) offer different readings. MS A describes the emotion that shakes Lancelot's body as *mautalent* ('de mautalent li cuers li tranble', his heart makes him tremble with evil intent); the meaning of *mautalent*

---

[16] Chrétien de Troyes, *Le Chevalier de la Charrette (Lancelot)*, ed. A. Foulet and K. Uitti (Paris, 1989), p. 154. Reference to manuscripts will be based on Foulet-Uitti's abbreviations as follows: A = Chantilly, Musée Condé 472; C = Paris, Bibliothèque Nationale de France, fr. 794; E = Escorial, Real Monasterio de San Lorenzo M.iii.21; F = Paris, Bibliothèque Nationale de France, fr. 1450; G = Princeton, Firestone Library, Garrett 125; T = Paris, Bibliothèque Nationale de France, fr. 12560; V = Rome, Biblioteca Apostolica Vaticana Reg. 1725.

broadly overlaps with the noun *ire*.[17] MS G also gives *mautalent* instead of *ire* and employs the verbs *fremir* (shiver) and *ardre* (burn) rather than *trambler* ('de maltalent fremist et art'). Thus G does not directly refer to the protagonist's heart or body, but implicitly portrays these as 'shivering' and 'burning'; the somatic response is described on the basis of a widely lexicalised metaphor.[18]

The second relevant episode features Lancelot at the point of crossing the Sword Bridge, despite the anxieties expressed by the two young knights who are travelling with him (ll. 3046–54):

> Ce fesoit molt desconforter
> Les deus chevaliers qui estoient
> Avoec le tierz, que il cuidoient
> Que dui lÿon ou dui liepart
> Au chief del pont de l'autre part
> Fussent lïé a un perron.
> L'eve e li ponz et li lÿon
> Les metent an itel freor
> Qu'il tranblent andui de peor.[19]

> (The two knights who were travelling with the third were most concerned because they thought that a pair of lions, or perhaps leopards, were chained to a boulder on the far side of the bridge. The water, the bridge and the lions caused them to feel so much cold they both trembled with fear.)

The environmental description integrates features that evoke a combined sensory and emotional appraisal. A visual assessment allows the young knights to recognise the dangerousness of the river and the wildness of the lions. Fear and danger are described as integral parts of their experience of the environment. Indeed, the sight of 'l'eve et li ponz e li lÿon' (ll. 3052–4) directly causes Lancelot's young companions to experience 'fear' (*peor*). The somatic correlate of such an emotional response is 'cold' (*freor*), which causes 'trembling' (*tremblent*).

The verb *trembler*, which only occurs in these cases in the *Chevalier de la Charrette*, describes the two somatic responses to *ire* (anger) and *peor* (fear). The fact that *ire* causes Lancelot to tremble indicates an emotional state that directly affects the protagonist's body and spurs him into action. *Peor* freezes the hero's young companions, a pair of 'mirror characters'

---

[17] The meanings of *mautalant* range from 'Mißmut' (peevishness) to 'Unwille' (displeasure) to 'Ärger' (rage), 'Zorn' (anger) and 'Erbitterung' (exasperation): see A. Tobler and E. Lommatzsch, ed., *Altfranzösisches Wörterbuch* (Berlin and Wiesbaden, 1925–2002) V 1305). Subsequent references will be given in abbreviated form as TL.

[18] See TL I 507–9 and III 2232–4 (2233, in particular), for the specific contextual meaning of *fremir* ('erschauern') (shiver).

[19] *Chevalier*, ed. Foulet and Uitti, p. 172.

whose emotional response to specific circumstances most likely aims at influencing the audience to react accordingly.[20]

Somatic Correlates of Anger, Sadness and Fear

The cases discussed above present a variable correlation between bodily responses to environmental circumstances and affective states classified by different emotion words. On the one hand, the same verb contributes to the description of two very different affective states; these reflect the social conditions of the different characters. On the other, the same emotion word is associated with different bodily states, as shown by some further descriptions of *ire* and *peor*, analysed below.

The discussion takes into account all the cases in which descriptions of emotional states featuring *ire* and *peor* are complemented by a clear indication of somatic correlates experienced by the affected characters. Somatic correlates of *ire* are discussed first, since they occur more frequently. The first relevant case features *iriez*, the past participle of the verb *irier*, and appears at the very beginning of the romance, when King Arthur is grieved and saddened because he has conceded the battle against Meleagant to Keu, who is likely to be defeated (ll. 182–5):

> Au roi poise, et si l'an revest,
> Car einz de rien ne se desdist,
> Mes iriez et dolanz le fist,
> Si que bien parut a son volt.[21]

> (The king is upset, but his word had been given and he could not revoke it, even though his decision made him feel angry and sorrowful, as his countenance clearly showed.)

Chrétien combines the adjectives *iriez* and *dolanz* to describe the twofold emotional state the king is experiencing.[22] In this case the character affected by *ire* is not trembling as Lancelot is while fighting the arrogant knight later in the story. The description refers specifically to different somatic indices, stressing that grief and sadness show in Arthur's countenance.

A different somatic correlate of *ire* emerges when Lancelot is first portrayed as *iriez* in his battle with the Knight of the Ford (ll. 874–87):

---

[20] See Brandsma, 'Mirror Characters', in particular p. 284, and Brandsma, 'Arthurian Emotions', pp. 4–10.
[21] *Chevalier*, ed. Foulet and Uitti, p. 12.
[22] See TL II 1992–3 for the meaning of *dolent* (mainly 'schmerzerfüllt, traurig', painful, unhappy). Manuscript E (fol. 2r col. a) presents the unclear reading 'main' instead of 'dolant' ('Mais irriez et main le fist').

> Molt granz cos antredoner s'osent
> Tant que la bataille a ce monte
> Qu'an son cuer en a molt grant honte
> Li chevaliers de la charrete,
> Et dit que mal randra la dete
> De la voie qu'il a enprise,
> Quant il si longue piece a mise
> A conquerre un seul chevalier.
> S'il an trovast en un val hier
> Tex cent, ne croit il pas ne panse
> Qu'il eüssent vers lui desfanse,
> S'an est molt dolanz et iriez
> Qant il est ja si anpiriez
> Qu'il pert ses cos et le jor gaste.[23]

(The fighters dare to hit each other with hard blows, so that the fight escalates to the point that the *Chevalier de la Charrette* feels extremely ashamed deep in his heart and he says that he would hardly accomplish his mission, since it is taking so long to defeat a single knight. He thought and believed that if he could have met a hundred such knights in some valley just the day before, they wouldn't have had a single chance of resisting him. Hence, he feels very sorrowful and angry, his pride dramatically diminished after all the blows and the time he wasted.)

Lancelot feels ashamed: he senses that his knightly pride is being diminished because the fight is lasting longer than expected and that he is wasting precious time when he should be riding after the kidnapped queen. Lancelot's *honte* is described as a combination of sadness and pain: the emotion words *iriez* and *dolanz* describe his affective state just as they depicted Arthur's feelings when offering Keu the battle against Meleagant. Interestingly, if King Arthur's *ire* showed in his countenance, Lancelot's *honte* is rather embodied 'an son cuer', in his heart.

Facial expression is, however, mentioned in the description of Meleagant's sudden change of mood after the evil knight realises that Lancelot has crossed the Sword Bridge (ll. 3169–83):

> S'orent veü de la amont
> Le chevalier passer le pont
> A grant poinne et a grant dolor.
> D'ire et de mautalant color
> En a Meleaganz changiee;
> Bien set c'or li ert chalangiee
> La reïne; mes il estoit
> Tex chevaliers qu'il ne dotoit
> Nul home, tant fust forz ne fiers.
> Nus ne fust miaudres chevaliers,
> Se fel et deslëaus ne fust,

---

[23] *Chevalier*, ed. Foulet and Uitti, pp. 50–52.

> Mes il avoit un cuer de fust
> Tot sanz dolçor et sanz pitié.
> Ce fet le roi joiant et lié,
> Don ses filz molt grant duel avoit.[24]

(From their vantage point they had seen the knight cross the bridge with trouble and pain. Meleagant's colour changed with the rage and displeasure he felt; for he knows now that he will be challenged for the queen; but his character was such that he feared no man, however strong or formidable. If he were not base and disloyal, no better knight could be found; but he had a heart of wood, without gentleness and pity. What enraged his son and roused his ire, made the king happy and glad.)

King Bademagu and Meleagant observe Lancelot's successful attempt to cross the bridge from their privileged viewpoint on top of the tower. Father and son both sense the *poinne* ('sorrow') and the *dolor* ('pain') Lancelot experiences while gripping the blade of the sword bridge, but the same visual experience apparently triggers opposite emotional responses. Indeed, Melagant's emotional state is described as a combination of anger, discontent and sadness, whereas Bademagu is happy and glad.

The king and his son react to what they see according to their respective inclinations and temperaments. Bademagu is the mirror character who provides the audience with the appropriate affective response. Meleagant's attitude is described contextually in order to explain that his emotional response depends both on his distinctive character and the plot mechanics. Indeed, Meleagant is at the same time evil and concerned about the future implications of the event he has witnessed.

The description of Meleagant's emotional state also features a somatic correlate: the change of complexion.[25] The adjectives *joiant* and *lié* describe Bademagu's emotional state, which clearly contrasts with Meleagant's mood, restated by the noun *duel*. The contextual occurrence of the nouns *mautalant* and *duel* and the adjectives *joiant* and *lié* defines the elements of the lexical network that describes the episode's emotional dimension.

MS E (18v. col. a) presents a peculiar reading, one which implies a remarkable difference in Lancelot's emotional state while crossing the Sword Bridge (ll. 3169–75):

> S'orrent veu de la amont
> Le chevalier passer le pont
> A grant peinne et grant peor
> De maltalent out la color
> Meleogranz toute canchiee.

---

[24] *Chevalier*, ed. Foulet and Uitti, p. 180.
[25] TL II 573–4 mentions *color* as 'Gesichtsfarbe' (complexion).

(From their vantage point they had seen the knight cross the bridge
with pain and fear. Meleagant's colour changed with the displeasure
he felt.)

Instead of *dolor*, MS E gives *peor*, which inappropriately portrays Lancelot as being afraid, whereas the majority of manuscripts ascribe this emotional response to the young knights who have travelled with him (ll. 3052–4, as seen above). Moreover, Meleagant's change of complexion is only caused by *maltalent*: reference to *ire* is absent. This instance provides additional evidence that specific variant readings can perturb the romance's emotional dimension and its thematic implications.

An additional case in which the emotion word *peor* is indirectly associated with a somatic correlate occurs during the episode of the comb. Lancelot is leading the *damoisele avenant* through the wood when a natural spring appears in the middle of a meadow, near a rock, on top of which lies a comb. Strands of a woman's hair are caught in the teeth of the comb. (ll. 1356–68). The damsel leaves the main path so as to prevent Lancelot from noticing the presence of this object, which seems to be awaiting him on the rock (ll. 1369–76).[26]

When the knight clearly states that he will not escort the damsel further if she dares to venture on an unknown road (ll. 1377–95), she returns to the path leading to the rock, on which the comb is lying. As soon as Lancelot notices the object and marvels at its exceptional beauty, the damsel claims it. The knight becomes lost in contemplation when he picks up the comb, causing the damsel to laugh and to clarify the situation (ll. 1420–44):

> – Trop a certes m'an apelez,
> Fet ele, si le vos dirai,
> De rien nule n'an mantirai:
> Cist peignes, se j'onques soi rien,
> Fu la reïne, jel sai bien;
> Et d'une chose me creez,
> Que li chevol que vos veez
> Si biax, si clers et si luisanz,
> Qui sont remés antre les danz,
> Que del chief la reïne furent:
> Onques en autre pré ne crurent.'
> Et li chevaliers dit: 'Par foi,
> Assez sont reïnes et roi;
> Mes de la quel volez vos dire?'
> Et cele dit: 'Par ma foi, sire,
> De la fame le roi Artu.'
> Quant cil l'ot, n'a tant de vertu

---

[26] A. Combes, *Les Voies de l'aventure: réécriture et composition romanesque dans le Lancelot en prose* (Paris, 2001), p. 235, remarks that 'le peigne de la reine, posé (abandonné, oublié?) sur un perron' (the queen's comb, placed (abandoned, forgotten?) on a rock) is rather waiting 'que le récit le rejoigne' (for the narrative to catch up with it).

> Que tot nel coveigne ploier ;
> Par force l'estut apoier
> Devant a l'arçon de la sele
> Et quant ce vit la dameisele,
> Si s'an mervoille et esbaïst
> Qu'ele cuida que il cheïst;
> S'ele ot peor, ne l'en blasmez,
> Qu'ele cuida qu'il fust pasmez.[27]

('Your appeal is so strong,' she says, 'that I will tell you and keep nothing back. I am sure, as I am of anything, that this comb belonged to the queen. And you may take my word that those are strands of the queen's hair which you see to be so fair and light and radiant, and which are clinging to the teeth of the comb; they surely never grew anywhere else.' Then the knight replied: 'Upon my word, there are plenty of queens and kings; what queen do you mean?' And she answered: 'In truth, fair sire, it is of King Arthur's wife I speak.' When he hears that, he has not the strength to keep from bowing his head over his saddle-bow. And when the damsel sees him thus, she is amazed and terrified, thinking he is about to fall. Do not blame her for her fear, for she thought him in a faint.)

The discussion that takes place when Lancelot asks why the damsel is so amused concerns the identity of the lady whose fair hair is caught in the teeth of the comb (ll. 1407–22). The damsel, who is mysteriously informed about the lady's identity, reveals to Lancelot that both the comb and the hair belong to Queen Guenièvre, causing the knight to fall into a state of overwhelming emotional upheaval. The description focuses on somatic correlates and ensuing actions: after bending forward on the saddle, Lancelot grabs the pommel so as to avoid falling off the horse.

Chrétien directly addresses the audience when explaining that the emotional response of the damsel is completely understandable: her fear is caused by the fact that Lancelot has apparently fainted. Even though fear and fainting affect different characters, the noun *peor* and the verb *pasmer* are clearly part of the same empathic pattern that connects the emotional response of the damsel to Lancelot's undefined affective state.

The description of the tournament at Noauz presents a more direct association between *peor* and a somatic correlate, when Lancelot starts acting in accordance with the orders of Guenièvre, who commands his defeat and shame (ll. 5686–96):

> Et cil se met lors a la fuie;
> Ne puis cel jor vers chevalier
> Ne torna le col del destrier;
> Por amorir rien ne feïst
> Se sa grant honte n'i veïst
> Et son leit et sa desenor,

---

[27] *Chevalier*, ed. Foulet and Uitti, pp. 82–4.

> Et fet sanblant qu'il ait peor
> De toz ces qui vienent et vont.[28]

(Thereupon he took flight, and after that he never turned his horse's head towards any knight, and were he to die for it, he would never do anything unless he saw in it his shame, disgrace and dishonour; he even pretends to be afraid of all the knights who pass to and fro.)

Syntactic contiguity and semantic proximity connect the nouns *peor*, *honte*, *leit* and *desenhor* in a lexical network that sets the complex emotional tone of the episode.[29] Lancelot pretends to be afraid of all the knights who pass by and make fun of him, being eager to do whatever he can to draw shame, disgrace and dishonour on himself. Hence, *peor* refers to an emotion that the character is merely pretending to feel, so as to please his beloved queen, and the locution *fait samblant* describes the facial expression and/or attitude and/or posture he adopts for convincing his opponents that he is actually frightened.

Moreover, this very peculiar case shows that simulated emotions also lead to consequent actions, namely Lancelot's avoidance of combat. What is remarkable here is that the description of simulated affective states implies the adoption of a narrative strategy that entails multi-layered emotional perspective-taking. Indeed, the circumstance described implies a complex empathic pattern mostly based on the description of somatic correlates of emotions, according to which 'Lancelot thinks that his opponents think that he feels scared'.

Conclusion: The 'Emotional Community' of the Medieval Verse Romance

In conclusion, the noun *ire* shows a semantic spectrum that ranges from 'Zorn' (anger), to 'Verdruß, Gram, Kummer' (annoyance, grief, distress), 'was Kummer bringt' (that which distresses) and 'tätliche Feindseligkeit' (physical hostility).[30] The last definition best describes the majority of the word's occurrences in the *Chevalier de la Charrette*, where *ire* is typically an emotional response to specific events that directly lead to appropriate reactions. Somatic correlates often supplement the descriptions of *ire*, an emotional state that also clearly shows in facial expressions.

Occurrences of the emotion word *peor* in the *Chevalier de la Charrette* are somewhat limited in respect to *ire* and in many cases the noun rather means 'concern', 'worry', in addition to a primary meaning, 'fear'.[31] In all such cases the word occurs in direct speech, with the speaker guessing

---

[28] *Chevalier*, ed. Foulet and Uitti, p. 318.
[29] The *lectio singularis* of Manuscript V (26v col. b) repeats the noun *honte* at l. 5694 instead of *leit* ('et sa honte et sa deshonor').
[30] TL IV 1440–44.
[31] TL VII 691–5.

or being aware of the interlocutor's feelings, so that descriptions of worry or concern seem to be consistently based on the emotional perspective of a character who is decoding the affective state of someone else.[32] The rare descriptions of *peor* often emphasise mirror characters' emotional responses to specific events, and the more direct association between *peor* and a somatic correlate emerges from the description of a simulated emotional state, such as when Lancelot pretends to be frightened during the tournament at Noauz.[33]

An evaluation of the cases discussed here confirms that the emotional states described in medieval verse romances are typically attributed to specific characters in response to perceptual interaction with their natural and/or social environment. In the terms suggested by Damasio, Chrétien describes not emotions but feelings, providing readers and audiences with information on how characters feel the emotions arising from the situations in which they are immersed.[34] The fact that emotion-related descriptions are often complemented by somatic correlates is clearly a feature of this descriptive strategy, which is typical of fictional narratives.

Moreover, specific perceptual events are responsible for the change from one affective state to another, so that the development of character-specific affective states is regulated by meaningful transitions. In addition, descriptions of affective states and ensuing actions are typically related and often connected by the preposition *par* and the conjunction *ensi*. Hence, descriptions of perceptual events, emotional states and actions are closely related, supporting the idea that 'emotions provide a natural means for the brain to evaluate the environment within and around the organism, and respond accordingly and adaptively'.[35]

Hence, the role played by descriptions of emotional states in a medieval verse romance shows a striking congruence with current neuroscience. It is unlikely that a comparison with so-called realistic modern novels would evidence radical difference in this respect. These findings also suggest that emotion words are not intended to generate an empathic emotional response in the reader and/or the audience. In other words, it is unlikely that the words *peor* and *ire* actually trigger fear and rage or sadness by themselves. Rather, emotion words provide a means of labelling a specific environmental and/or social situation in a way that suggests an appropriate emotional response. Essentially, they describe some specific environmental circumstances or actions as frightening, enraging or saddening by describing the way characters respond to them. In doing so they contribute to the association of environmental

---

[32] Cf. ll. 3456–61, 5488–90, 6099–101.
[33] The cases in which *peor* affects minor characters are at ll. 898–902, 1420–44 and 5686–96, discussed above.
[34] According to Damasio's somatic marker hypothesis, feelings are the mental representation of emotionally dependent physiological changes. Cf. Damasio, *Looking*, pp. 88–133.
[35] Damasio, *Looking*, p. 53.

descriptions and/or vivid descriptions of actions with character-specific emotional responses.

The descriptions of emotion in Chrétien's *Chevalier de la Charrette* are crucial to the understanding of the romance because they make it possible to extract information about the individual motivations that make characters act the way they do. Essentially, emotions lead readers and listeners through the story, suggesting that everybody acts for a reason and everything happens for a reason, and defining a linear path of acceptable transitions from a proper beginning to a convenient end. Since the emotional involvement of characters is so crucial to the understanding of a story, it seems reasonable that descriptions of affective states based on emotion words should often be complemented by specific descriptions of somatic correlates.

The frequent association of emotion words and somatic states is likely to intensify the relevance of emotion-related situations, making descriptions more effective by facilitating the empathic response of the readers and/or the audience. Embodied responses to environmental circumstances may provide the audience with meaningful indications of emotion, especially when it comes to descriptions of emotional states that are too intense to be classified by specific emotion words. In some cases, somatic correlates of emotional states affecting specific characters may trigger descriptions of empathic responses in other characters.

Descriptions of affective states do not imply a fixed reference to specific somatic correlates. Indeed, the cases presented here have shown a variable correlation between similar bodily responses to environmental circumstances and affective states classified by different emotion words. Essentially, the same bodily states may correlate to different emotions, while on the other hand the same emotion can be associated with different bodily states. That is, there is no one-to-one correlative system.

Additional findings suggest that descriptions of affective states in the *Chevalier de la Charrette* are occasionally included in counterfactual and semi-factual descriptions of affective states; these imply frequent transitions from the emotional perspective of one character to that of another. Moreover, characters act and behave according to the particular emotions they feel, as conditioned by gender, age, social position and individual inclination. In some specific cases emotion-related descriptions also entail first-level theory of mind: the feelings of one character are presented from the emotional perspective of another.[36]

---

[36] On theory of mind, see the famous work of D. C. Dennett, 'Intentional Systems in Cognitive Ethology: The Panglossian Paradigm Defended', *Behavioral and Brain Sciences* 6 (1983), 343–90, which has been taken up by many scholars in the fields of animal and human ethology, cognitive science and neuroscience. Recent studies have introduced the idea that mirror neurons play a crucial role in the cognitive processes that allow mind-reading, as they do in simulation and imitation.

The adoption of these complex emotional perspectives adds a new dimension to Cesare Segre's remarks on the subject and to Norris Lacy's observation that 'Chrétien seldom tells us that a character does something; rather we learn that someone saw him do it'.[37] In essence, Chrétien de Troyes describes not only the various perceptual perspectives of different characters on narrated events, but also their specific individual emotional responses to these events.[38]

Moreover, the evidence presented here confirms that 'mirror characters' are described as reacting to specific environmental circumstances in ways that most likely aim at influencing the audience to react accordingly. Sometimes affective states manifested by mirror characters intentionally contrast with those manifested by leading characters, so as to qualify the latter as exceptional. In some cases similar environmental circumstances may trigger different or opposite affective responses in different characters or groups, responses that may also be shaped by gender, age and social status.

Thus certain subsets of emotional responses are ascribed to particular classes of characters. Recurrent descriptions of specific emotions seem to define linear paths that underlie the romance's main thematic directions. For instance, the description of *ire* and its somatic correlates in Chrétien's *Chevalier de la Charrette* plays a crucial role in the development of the conflict between the protagonist and his main antagonist. Some affective modulations are presented as part of a subset defining the specific emotional system of given characters or classes of characters.

This chapter suggests that the spectrum of emotional modulation indicated by *ire* in Chrétien's *Chevalier de la Charrette* typically affects male characters, mostly knights and especially the hero's main antagonist.[39] Indeed, specific emotional patterns emerge in less emotionally complex

---

[37] Cf. C. Segre, 'What Bachtin Did Not Say: The Medieval Origins of the Novel', *Russian Literature* 41.3 (1997), 385–409 [C. Segre, 'Quello che Bachtin non ha detto: le origini medievali del romanzo', *Teatro e romanzo: due tipi di comunicazione letteraria* (Turin, 1984), 61–84], and N. J. Lacy, 'Thematic Structure in the "Charrette"', *L'Esprit créateur* 12 (1972), 13–18.

[38] For descriptions of characters' perceptual perspectives in medieval romances, cf. Segre, 'What Bachtin Did Not Say'; S. Marnette, *Narrateur et point de vue dans la littérature française médiévale. Une approche linguistique* (Bern, 1998) devotes chapters 5 and 6 (pp. 137–59 and 169–84) to the focalisation of the point of view in medieval French narratives.

[39] Keu (two occurrences) in the introductory part of the romance (ll. 84–8 and 106–7); King Arthur (one occurrence), forced to offer the battle to Keu (ll. 182–5); all the knights of the Round Table when they realise that Keu was defeated by Meleagant and the queen has probably been abducted (ll. 259–69); Lancelot (four occurrences): feeling sad while fighting the knight of the ford (ll. 874–87), feeling angry during the combat against the arrogant knight, who is himself animated by anger (ll. 2702–5 and 2732–9), affected by sadness when he believes that the queen has died (ll. 4268–77) and angry again during the second combat against Meleagant (ll. 5024–8); the knight who contends for the damsel with Lancelot before the hero enters the kingdom of Gorre (ll. 1635–45); the captives while Lancelot is struggling in his combat against Meleagant and, conversely, Meleagant's people after the fight is postponed and the captives are released (ll. 3685–3705).

characters, such as Meleagant, whose decisions and actions are mainly driven by a consistent affective state.[40] The only case in which *ire* is described as an emotional state affecting a female character is reported by a male character, King Bademagu, who describes Queen Guenièvre as affected by this emotion (ll. 3972–4): 'Et de Meliagant mon fil / Vos a resqueusse et desfandue, / Qui molt iriez vos a randue' (and he has defended and rescued you from my son Meleagant who saddened you).[41]

Notably, three manuscripts present different readings of l. 3974, all of them describing Bademagu's awareness of Meleagant's emotional state while surrendering the queen to Lancelot. The readings 'ki sor som pois vos a rendue' of MS E (fol. 23r, col. a), 'ki a enuis vos a rendue' of MS G (fol. 16v, col. b) and similarly 'qui a enuis vos a rendue' of MS V (fol. 17v, col. a) might in fact reflect scribal concern about the propriety of ascribing such a strong emotion as *ire* to the queen.

Among the few cases in which *peor* is associated with somatic correlates, the most interesting presents fear as an affective state that seems to be affecting Lancelot. Indeed, it presents a simulated affective state, suggesting that fear is outside the emotional spectrum of a celebrated knight who happens to be the protagonist of a magnificent courtly romance. The presentation of the two young knights as frozen by *peor* at the sight of the Sword Bridge shows that fear is an appropriate emotion for a young *chevalier* but not for an older, brave and established one.

The whole array of occurrences of *peor* confirms the idea that the emotional system of given classes of characters is defined by a specific subset of affective modulations. Indeed, when *peor* indicates proper fear instead of concern or worry, it describes the affective state of young people, and mainly female characters. Not only are the best knights never described as experiencing fear, but also, when it seems they do, they are only feigning!

Moreover, close analysis shows that Chrétien tends to cluster emotion words and locutions in consistent textual segments describing emotion-related circumstances and events. Co-occurrence makes it possible, it may be argued, to appraise an emergent emotional system as underlying the thematic plan of the romance.[42] Indeed, the evidence here shows that a wide lexical range of emotion words co-occur with *ire*, *peor* or both.

The connections between *ire* or *iriez* and the nouns *despit*, *mautalant*,

---

[40] *Ire* describes Meleagant's emotional states on many occasions (seven occurrences), mostly while fighting against Lancelot or arguing with his father (ll. 3169–83, 3832–3, 3920–41, 5024–8, 6354–60, 6382–8, 7081–107).

[41] *Chevalier*, ed. Foulet and Uitti, p. 224.

[42] On thematic consistency in *Chevalier de la Charrette* see N. J. Lacy, 'Thematic Structure'. The ensuing study, N. J. Lacy, 'Spatial Form in Medieval Romance', *Approaches to Medieval Romance*, ed. P. Haidu, *Yale French Studies* 51 (1975), 160–69, reformulates the idea of 'spatial form' introduced by J. Frank, 'Spatial Form in Modern Literature', *Sewanee Review* 53 (1945), 221–40, 433–56, 643–53, and *The Idea of Spatial Form* (New Brunswick, 1998), to show that in medieval romances 'episodes are justified not as being necessary

duel, honte, joie, corroz, rage, the adjectives *dolant, pensif, mat, morne, joiant, lié* and the verbs *tranbler, adoler, peser, corrocier, esmaier, forsener, esperdre, enrager* have emerged from this investigation. Moreover, *peor* is found in combination with the nouns *freor, honte, leit, desenhor* and the verbs *pasmer, desconforter, trembler, criembre, esmaier*. Interestingly enough, the two groups combine to form twenty-seven words (ten nouns, six adjectives and eleven verbs); the noun *honte* and verbs *tranbler* and *esmaier* link the two groups, establishing an integrated lexical network.

Frequent co-occurring emotion words such as *iriez* and *dolanz* show that the lexical clusters underlying the emotional system of particular episodes may determine some recurrent patterns that Chrétien relies on when describing double or multiple affective states. Further emotion words emerge from the *variae lectiones* provided by the manuscript tradition, such as the adjective *mu* (l. 3941, MS E) and verbs *fremist* and *art* (l. 2736, MS G).

A typical problem arising from the investigation of a romance's emotional system concerns the definition of the parts of the lexical corpus considered pertinent. Indeed, the correlation between language and emotion is extremely variable from one given cultural context to another; since the very concept of emotion is historically determined, studies relying on a predetermined categorisation might easily miss the point.[43] The evidence presented here clearly supports the argument that the co-occurrence of emotion words in descriptions of character-specific affective states permits the identification of relevant lexical clusters.

The argument made in this article recommends the adoption of an emergent method based on the idea that syntactic proximity can be regarded as an indicator of semantic congruence, following Ludwig Wittgenstein's idea of *Familienähnlichkeit* (family similarity). Provided that at least one word can be considered as emotion-related *per se*, co-occurring words become part of an integrated lexical network defining the romance's emotional system. This lexical network reflects the conceptual system of an 'emotional community', which in this case completely coincides with a 'textual community'.[44]

The participants in this community, which originally revolved around the feudal court, share a common emotional system, permitting them to decode affective modulation as described and enabling them to empa-

---

or indispensable, but as being *appropriate*, because some aspect of the form, theme, or imagery reflects that of other episodes and relates one scene to another' (p. 169).

[43] On the categorisation of emotions in the Middle Ages see S. Knuuttila, *Emotions*, pp. 153–78.

[44] On the idea of 'emotional community' see Rosenwein, 'Worrying about Emotions', pp. 842–3, Rosenwein, 'Problems and Methods', p. 8, and cf. B. Stock, *The Implications of Literacy: Written Language and Models of Interpretation in the Eleventh and Twelfth Centuries* (Princeton, 1983), pp. 88–150, for the idea of 'textual community', which originally refers to the implications of oral and written culture for the interpretation of the Bible between the eleventh and twelfth centuries.

thise with affected characters. Indeed, the understanding of a story necessarily requires readers or listeners to recognise and properly process the emotional correlates of sensory experience and/or the affective modulations that underlie the planning of purposeful actions. This essay has demonstrated that the descriptions of emotions experienced by romance characters in response to environmental and/or social circumstances critically contribute to the understanding of the ensuing actions they perform.

Consequently, the emotional dimension of medieval verse romance must be a crucial component of its narrative system; such a system aims at integrating perceptual events, affective modulations and actions, just as actual human experience of nature and society does.[45] Moreover, the study of the *Chevalier de la Charrette*'s emotional system can illuminate the affective involvement of medieval courtly society in romance storytelling. Indeed, the emotional competence that underlies the understanding of a medieval romance is also that which supports courtly European culture in the twelfth and thirteenth centuries.

Emotional competence implies a direct correspondence between affective modulation and textual description, to the extent that the community's socially integrated emotional system will correspond in some way to the integrated lexical system on which Chrétien relied while planning and composing his romance. The variability of the lexical system from one manuscript to another reflects the textual and emotional communities who reshape the romance to their own needs and taste. The fact that the *variae lectiones* present peculiar readings of different manuscripts with respect to emotion-related textual circumstances shows that medieval redactors are likely to have adapted the emotional tone of specific episodes according to their own understandings of why characters might act as they do.

Of course, emotional communities have much in common with each other across space and time, nations, cultural systems and historical epochs. This explains why medieval romances are still comprehensible and incorporate features that have consistently characterised romance as a genre. For instance, the fact that the emotion word *ire* indicates an affec-

---

[45] Such isomorphism tends to be compromised by the typical narrative assumption that human experience of the world must essentially be characterised by logical (mainly temporal and causal) continuity. This is unfortunately false, since analogical connections between apparently unrelated events and items are far more prominent in our processing of the surrounding environment. S. Fleischman, *Tense and Narrativity: From Medieval Performance to Modern Fiction* (Austin, TX, 1990), pp. 131–5, presents and discusses the crucial idea of 'iconicity assumption', a diagrammatically iconic relationship between the sequence of narrated events and the sequence of clauses which narrate those events. Some remarks on the rhetoric of medieval romances drawing on that idea are offered in A. P. Fuksas, 'Selezionismo e *conjointure*', *Dal Romanzo alle reti* (Atti del Convegno Soggetti e territori del romanzo Università di Roma La Sapienza. Facoltà di Scienze della Comunicazione, 23–4 May 2002), ed. A. Abruzzese and I. Pezzini (Turin, 2004), pp. 152–84 [updated as A. P. Fuksas, 'Selezionismo e *conjointure*', *Rivista di Filologia Cognitiva* 1 (2003), http://w3.uniroma1.it/cogfil/selezionismo.html].

tive state close to those states described by the adjectives *pensif, mat, morne* and opposed to those indicated by the noun *joie* defines an emotional landscape so persistent that audiences can still easily envisage it in the twenty-first century.

Likewise, the association between *peor* and somatic states such as *freor* and *trembler* remains credible. At the same time, emotional communities have specific mindsets that characterise their peculiar *ethos* and are reflected in the stories they produce and listen to. For instance, the fact that *ire* typically affects celebrated knights or kings, and *peor* never does, adds new depth to Chrétien's courtly idealisation of knighthood.[46]

---

[46] E. Köhler, *Ideal und Wirklichkeit in der höfischen Epik: Studien zur Form der frühen Artus und Graldichtung* (Tübingen, 1956).

5

Kingship and the Intimacy of Grief in the Alliterative Morte Arthure

ANNE BADEN-DAINTREE

> Erec en pesa plus assez
> Qu'il n'en mostra semblant as genz;
> Mais duelx de roi n'est mie genz,
> N'a roi n'avient qu'il face duel. (*Erec et Enide*, ll. 6516–19)
>
> (This weighed upon Erec much more than he showed people outwardly, but grieving is uncourtly on the part of a king and it does not befit a king to show grief.)[1]

In the context of Chrétien de Troyes' twelfth-century romance *Erec et Enide*, it is clear that courtly, and specifically kingly, codes of conduct do not permit the outward expression of grief. But such behavioural codes, as Felicity Riddy has demonstrated, are common constraints on masculine behaviour in the romance tradition.[2] While men in romance settings often express grief and sorrow at bereavement with extravagant tears and gestures, there is a marked distinction between behaviours appropriate to the domestic setting and those which might be expressed publicly. This essay examines the way in which the behaviour of the grieving King Arthur exists in a liminal space where the emotions which are normally reserved for private situations can occur in a public setting, while still retaining a high degree of intimacy.

---

[1] Chrétien de Troyes, *Erec et Enide*, in *Romans*, ed. J. M. Fritz (Paris, 1994); trans. C. W. Carroll as *Erec and Enide* in *Chrétien de Troyes: Arthurian Romances*, ed. W. W. Kibler (London, 1991), p. 117.

[2] Riddy reads the expression of grief in the Alliterative *Morte Arthure* in the context of its narrative movement from 'public history' to 'family tragedy'. She observes that 'Kings and knights, participants in the great deeds of history, do not cry. In that impersonal public world from which women are excluded, weeping, clamouring and wringing the hands are seen as women's work. In the unhistorical sphere of the family, though, fathers do cry; Middle English romances have plenty of fathers distraught at the loss of their sons.' F. Riddy, 'Middle English Romance: Family, Marriage, Intimacy', in *The Cambridge Companion to Medieval Romance*, ed. R. L. Krueger (Cambridge, 2000), pp. 235–52, at p. 247.

There are a number of portrayals of grief in the course of the Alliterative *Morte Arthure*'s narrative.[3] Particularly detailed attention is given to Arthur's grief at Gawain's death, and this instinctive display of sorrow is problematised by the king's attendants and onlookers. Strong social pressures influence the expression of grief, and the response of others to such extreme emotion is a notable feature of this text. There is a tension between public and private responses to death, expressed in terms of gendered behaviours. Grief, and specifically weeping, is figured as feminine, but the enactment of revenge is considered 'manly'. However, the temporal gap between loss and revenge allows the opening up of a feminised space, enabling the expression of emotion as a precursor to vengeance. This is a feature of much heroic literature: on the medieval battlefield such private space is temporarily 'marked out' around a grieving king or warrior, allowing a pause in the communal enterprise where individual emotions take priority. In some texts this private space is acknowledged and accepted; in the *Morte Arthure* it is subject to severe critical scrutiny from Arthur's men. Furthermore, the movement from notionally private weeping to public revenge is marked by an intimate engagement with the dead body which is to be avenged. In the heroic tradition, battlefield deaths often involve a disturbing tactility whereby the bloodied corpse becomes not only an emblem for the enactment of vengeance but also the means of continued intimate interaction.

There are two distinct stages to Arthur's grief at his nephew's death. First there is an instinctive and dramatic expression of emotion, involving both speech and gesture, which receives a strongly worded critical response from those in attendance. This is followed by a series of apparently ritualistic actions, which seem to be accepted without comment. This movement from the instinctive to the highly considered and stylised arises, in part, from the text's merging of various literary traditions, but particularly its engagement with both heroic and romance conventions. The Alliterative *Morte Arthure* is a text which treads an uneasy path between genres: part epic, part history, part romance, its depiction of the expression of emotion draws on varied sources and traditions, including chronicles, *chansons de geste* and French prose romance.[4] However, as I shall demonstrate, similar dramatic patterning occurs in other heroic texts, where the expression of personal and private grief is swiftly followed by the public enactment of vengeance. In the first half of this essay I consider literary precedents for

---

[3] Most of these are clustered at the end of the narrative, but throughout individual deaths in combat are mourned, and there is also a close examination of female grief following the duchess of Brittany's death at the hands of the Giant of Mont St Michel. Gawain's death provokes three separate eulogies: from the narrator, from Mordred and from Arthur. It is the lengthy lament by Arthur which is the focus of this essay.

[4] *Morte Arthure: A Critical Edition*, ed. M. Hamel (New York and London, 1984), p. 34. All quotations from the Alliterative *Morte Arthure* are taken from this edition (cited as *MA*); translations from this text are my own.

the initial extravagant and emotional response to loss, and suggest that the text's apparent concerns about inappropriate behaviour are unjustified. Then, through interpretation of the more problematic second stage of Arthur's grief, I demonstrate that its ritualised processes in fact serve to legitimise the more openly expressive first stage.

The expression of grief in this text is noteworthy because of the enforced interaction between private and public that it brings about. The Alliterative *Morte Arthure* is an essentially public text. While Arthur speaks to individual knights during the course of the narrative and elicits individual responses, all takes place in a communal context. None of the issues of privacy, concealment, secrecy and enclosed spaces that so greatly trouble other Arthurian narratives intrudes. This text is concerned with matters of war, council, feasting; the actions on which the narrative is based are largely in the outward, political realm and involve Arthur's men moving as one body. The success of Arthur's endeavours depends upon this unity of thought and collective coherence of action, and the sense of communal identity is forged by and shared through participation in military exploits leading to multiple conquests of territory. But the bloody, destructive nature of the account is balanced by the sense of fellowship amongst surviving knights. There are moments of intimacy and personal revelation, although these, too, take place in public, in open spaces, specifically on the battlefield. This text is unafraid of showing us the physical consequences of military action; in common with other heroic or epic literature, the *Morte Arthure* is intimately concerned with the moment of death, with confrontation with the corpse and with the treatment of the dead body. It is obsessively interested in physicality, in physical prowess and wounding. The narrative involves extremes of violence and injury, but also superhuman achievement in overcoming the limitations of the human body. Blood is central to its operation, both in terms of the physical realities of the battlefield, and in terms of lineage, inheritance and loyalty.

The narrative of the *Morte Arthure* begins with Arthur as triumphant conqueror, celebrating his many victories across Europe. The Roman emperor, Lucius, apparently uneasy about the scale of these conquests, sends a message demanding that Arthur pay tribute to Rome, and the subsequent refusal triggers a state of war. Arthur eventually achieves victory over the Romans, and sends the enemies' bodies back to Rome as the 'tribute' that had initially been demanded. Arthur continues to conquer other lands; the following series of acts of military aggression are not, however, a response to political challenges but apparently indicate a desire for further acquisition of territory and power. In Arthur's absence his regent, Mordred, usurps his lands, and the remainder of the text is concerned with the civil war that this provokes. It is Arthur's final return to England, and the battle against Mordred and his allies, that concerns me in this essay. At the end of the text, after the lengthy account of warfare and conquest, Arthur is presented as a successful, although increasingly ruthless and acquisitive, leader, but for his men this entails a marked increase in loss of life by the final stages of the campaign. By the time Arthur reaches Cornwall, Gawain is already dead, his impulsive nature leading him to fight before all the ships have been able to land, and we see the king moving through the carnage, discovering the bodies of his own men:

> The riche kynge ransakes   with rewthe at his herte
> And vp rypes the renkes   of all þe Rownde Tabyll:
> Ses them all in a soppe   in sowte by them one,
> With þe Sarazenes vnsownde   enserclede abowte;
> And sir Gawayne the gude   in his gaye armes
> Vmbegrippede the girse,   and one grouffe fallen -
> His baners brayden down,   betyn of gowlles,
> His brand and his brade schelde   al blody beronen. (ll. 3939–46)

> (The noble king searches the battlefield, his heart filled with sorrow. He pulls up all the soldiers of the Round Table: he sees them all together in a group, with the dead and dying Saracen forces surrounding them. And brave Sir Gawain, too, in his bright armour, is fallen face down, holding onto the grass – his red banners cast down, his sword and his broad shield drenched in blood.)

The focus of Arthur's actions here is on finding Gawain. Although Arthur is fully aware of the implications of the slaughter of his troops, it is this one particular body that he seeks on the battlefield, this one particular loss that crystallises his pain:

> Was neuer oure semliche kynge   so sorrowful in herte,
> Ne þat sanke hym so sade   bot þat sighte one. (ll. 3947–8)

> (Our handsome king had never before been so sorrowful of heart. Nothing had ever sunk his spirits in such deep sadness as that sight alone.)

At this point the text is unusually reticent about the physical damage to bodies in battle; 'blody beronen' (l. 3946) refers not to Gawain's broken body but rather to his paraphernalia of battle, the material remnants of his military identity, which run with his blood. Arthur's gathering up of his men's bodies and the ritualistic quality of the placement of the knights in a grim tableau, visually imitative of the Round Table, underscore the relationship between particular and collective loss. Karen Cherewatuk suggests that the manner in which the men are found (in a huddled group, with the Saracen enemy surrounding them) is indicative of the manner of their death.[5] But it is not entirely clear whether, as Cherewatuk

---

[5] 'The architectural arrangement of their corpses reveals how they met their end. The small band had been driven off to the side and outnumbered by Mordred's troops,

suggests, the grouping of the knights reflects their position of death, or whether we should read 'vp rypes' as Larry Benson does, as meaning 'pulls up'.[6] Then 'ses them all in a soppe' could indicate that Arthur sets them in position, rather than just 'seeing' them, or finding them like this: in other words, their placement together might be seen as part of Arthur's ongoing care for their persons, even beyond death.[7]

Arthur's act of gathering up his troops prefigures his attention to Gawain's dead body, but also carries echoes of the descriptive terms in one of the *Morte Arthure*'s sources, indicating Arthur's habitual consideration for his knights. In Wace's *Roman de Brut* the equivalent scene of the battle's end is described as follows:

> Grant fud de ambes parz la perte,
> La plaine fud des morz cuverte
> E del sanc des muranz sanglente.
> Dunc peri la bel juvente
> Que Arthur aveit grant nurrie
> E de plusurs terres cuillie,
> E cil de la Table Roünde
> Dunt tel los ert par tut le munde. (*Roman de Brut*, ll. 13263–70)[8]

> (The losses were great on both sides, the plain was strewn with dead and bloody with the blood of the dying. Then perished the flower of youth, tended and gathered by Arthur from many lands, and those of the Round Table, famous throughout the world.)

Here the emphasis on Arthur's paternal tenderness refers to his having 'gathered' (*cuillie*) those young men as prospective knights whom the *Morte Arthure* later depicts being gathered up in death. The idea that Arthur has provided care, nurture and nourishment is encapsulated in the verb 'nurrir'.[9] In the masculine arena of the battlefield, Arthur provides care for his young warriors with maternal intimacy, as well as paternal safeguarding.[10] This sense of intimate physical care on the battlefield is

---

encircled by them, and cut down.' K. Cherewatuk, 'Dying in Uncle Arthur's Arms and at His Hands', in *The Arthurian Way of Death: The English Tradition*, ed. K. Cherewatuk and K. S. Whetter (Cambridge, 2009), pp. 50–70, at p. 50).

[6] Textual gloss to l. 3940 in *King Arthur's Death*, ed. L. D. Benson (Exeter, 1986).

[7] Where 'ses' carries the sense of taking heed, paying attention to, or ensuring that something is carried out: 'seeing to something', in modern terms. See *Middle English Dictionary*, s.v. *sen* v. 23 and 24.

[8] Text and translation: *Wace's Roman de Brut: A History of the British*, ed. and trans. J. Weiss, rev. edn (Exeter, 2002), pp. 332–3.

[9] A. Hindley, F. W. Langley and B. J. Levy, *Old French – English Dictionary* (Cambridge, 2000), s.v. *norrir*, 'Raise, bring up, nurture, foster; suckle, feed, nourish; maintain, provide for; keep in one's household, in one's service'. See also *OED*, s.v. *nourish*. This is also the term applied to Mordred, when Arthur justifies his decision to choose him as regent: 'Thowe arte my neuewe full nere, my nurree of olde/ That I have chastyede and chosen, a childe of my chambyre' (*MA*, ll. 689–90).

[10] As M. Bennett has demonstrated, the training for knighthood frequently began in childhood as part of the communal experience of service as a squire: 'A term frequently

also recorded in later literature of war, particularly the twentieth-century accounts of the Great War.[11] In such later literary accounts, although moments of close physical engagement often have erotic expression, the underlying sentiment is, nonetheless, one of feminised, often maternal, intimacy.

The actions and emotions represented in *Morte Arthure*, however, also have precedent in other medieval texts, particularly the *Chanson de Roland*. While there are specific correlations between Charlemagne's mourning of his nephew Roland and Arthur's grief at the death of his nephew Gawain (as various critics have noted), there are also several important parallels between the behaviours surrounding the deaths of Roland and Oliver and those of Arthur and Gawain, which may help to contextualise Arthur's actions.[12] In the *Chanson*, Roland is already dying as he enters the battlefield for the final time, and during the fight Oliver is mortally wounded. Roland's grief is great: he weeps, recalling their long companionship, and their interdependence. Without Oliver's companionship, he no longer wishes to continue living: 'Quant tu es morz, dulur est que jo vif!' ('Now that you are dead, it grieves me to remain alive', l. 2030). Left alone, he begins to search the battlefield for his companions, as we have seen King Arthur do. He lays them in a row, finding Oliver last, and 'clasping him tightly to his breast', brings him to be laid with the others:

> 'Noz cumpaignuns quë oümes tanz chers,
> Or sunt il morz; ne's i devuns laiser.
> Jo's voell aler e querre e entercer,
> Dedevant vos juster e enrenger.'
> [...]
> Rollant s'en turnet, par le camp vait tut suls,
> Cercet les vals e si cercet les munz.
> [...]
> Par uns e uns les ad pris, le barun,
> A l'arcevesque en est venuz atut,
> Si's mist en reng dedevant ses genuilz. (*Chanson*, ll. 2177–92)[13]

('Our companions, whom we loved so dearly,/Are now all dead; we must not leave them there./ I intend to go out and look for them and pick them out/ And place them here before you, side by side.' [...]

---

found in vernacular texts for boys brought up together is "*nurri*" (literally "nourished" in the same household). They formed close ties as they learnt their trade together.' M. Bennett, 'Military Masculinity in England and Northern France c.1050–c.1225', in *Masculinity in Medieval Europe*, ed. D. M. Hadley (London, 1998), pp. 71–88, at p. 73).

[11] See S. Das, *Touch and Intimacy in First World War Literature* (Cambridge, 2005), for a range of literary examples.

[12] The influence of the *Chanson de Roland* on this text has been noted by Hamel and Finlayson, amongst others. See Hamel, *Morte Arthure*, and *Morte Arthure*, ed. J. Finlayson (London, 1967). Some of the similarities of response lie in the fact that both Roland and Gawain are not just nephews but heirs (in the absence of sons to inherit).

[13] *La Chanson de Roland*, ed. I. Short, 2nd edn (Paris, 1990); *The Song of Roland*, trans. G. S. Burgess (London, 1990).

Roland sets off across the field alone;/ He searches the valleys and he searches the mountains.[...] One by one the brave man fetched them all;/He brought them right up to the archbishop/ And placed them in a row before his knees.)

Although Arthur, significantly, is absent during Gawain's final combat, many other aspects of these deaths in battle are similar: grief is expressed in tears, swoons and longing for death; the battlefield is searched, and the dead are laid out together; the closest companion is the last to be found, his body tenderly embraced before being placed with those of his companions. Many of these actions are repeated later in the *Chanson de Roland*, when Charlemagne finds Roland's body. Again there are repeated swoons, the vocalisation of loss, the clasping of the dead body in a gesture of intimate embrace:

> Sur l'erbe verte veit gesir sun nevuld.
> Nen est merveille se Karles ad irur;
> Descent a piéd, aléd i est pleins curs,
> Si prent le cunte entre ses mains ansdous;
> Sur lui se pasmet, tant par est anguissus. (*Chanson*, ll. 2876–80)

> (He sees his nephew lying on the green grass;/ It is no wonder that Charles is distressed./ He dismounts and [makes] his way swiftly to where he [lies];/ He takes him in both hands/ And, such is his anguish, faints upon him.)

Charles lies unconscious on the corpse of his nephew in a posture of grisly intimacy, and when he wakes, his companions draw him to his feet. He begins his lengthy eulogy, interrupted briefly by another faint. The parallels with the *Morte Arthure* are clear: the combination of physical embodiment of grief and stylised physical gesture indicates intimacy in a very public manner. In an echo of Roland's words over Oliver's death, Charles cries out:

> 'E! France dulce, cum remeins or deserte!
> Si grant doel ai que jo ne vuldreie estre!' (*Chanson*, ll. 2928–9)

> ('O, fair land of France, how bereft you are!/ My grief is so great that I no longer wish to live.')

In the *Morte Arthure*, the king's words express the same sentiment, the desire for death:

> 'Allas,' saide sir Arthure, 'nowe ekys my sorowe!
> I am vttirly vndon in myn awen landes.
> A, dowttouse, derfe dede, þou duellis to longe -
> Why drawes þou so one dreghe? thow drownnes myn herte!'
> (ll. 3965–9)

> ('Alas,' said King Arthur, 'now my sorrow increases. I am utterly undone in my own territory. Ah, cruel and fearful death, you linger

for too long. Why do you draw back? You drown my heart with grief!')

The response of Arthur's men to his grief, however, differs significantly in tone. When Arthur hears of Gawain's death, his initial response is both intensely personal and intensely physical, involving formulaic gestures of extreme emotion such as writhing and wringing of hands. He picks up Gawain's body, then voices his lament while still embracing the corpse. He then faints, staggers up again and repeatedly kisses the dead body until his beard is covered with his nephew's blood. This unseemly behaviour is roundly criticised by Arthur's shocked companions:

> 'Blyne,' sais thies bolde men, 'thow blodies þi selfen!
> Þis es botles bale, for bettir bees it neuer.
> It es no wirchipe, iwysse, to wryng thyn hondes;
> To wepe als a woman it es no witt holden.
> Be knyghtly of contenaunce, als a kyng scholde,
> And leue siche clamoure, for Cristes lufe of heuen!' (ll. 3975–80)

> (Stop, you stain yourself with blood,' say the brave men. 'This grief is hopeless, it cannot amend anything. Surely there is no honour in the wringing of your hands? To weep like a woman is without reason. Be knightly in your bearing, as befits a king, and for Christ's love of heaven, set aside such clamorous grief!')

It is the weeping and wringing of hands that leads Arthur's followers to criticise his 'womanly' weeping, and it is tempting to see this scene as central to the undermining of his masculine identity. But although mourning is often considered to be women's work, confined, as Riddy suggests, to the domestic sphere, John Burrow provides evidence that similar gestural patterns cross gender boundaries.[14] In situations of extreme distress, anger or grief, both men and women exhibit behaviours of weeping, writhing, swooning, wringing of hands and the tearing of hair and clothing. The smearing of Arthur's beard with his nephew's blood is an instinctive act, with the characteristic lack of self-consciousness that is part of the incoherence of grief:

> Than swetes the swete kynge and in swoun fallis,
> Swafres vp swiftely, and swetly hym kisses
> Till his burliche berde was blody berown,
> Alls he had bestes birtenede and broghte owt of life. (ll. 3969–72)

> (Then the beloved king breaks out in a sweat, and falls down in a swoon. Then he quickly staggers up again, and tenderly kisses him until his handsome beard is drenched in blood, as if he had butchered and slain wild beasts.)

---

[14] Riddy, 'Middle English Romance'; J. A. Burrow, *Gestures and Looks in Medieval Narrative* (Cambridge, 2002), pp. 39–41.

The word-play on 'swetes'/'swete'/'swetely' juxtaposes the physical response to distress and anguish with the tender emotional relationship between the two men. The incoherence of the king's movements (the swooning, the staggering up again) continues into the tender kissing of the corpse with little concern for decorum. But then the blood-drenched beard that results is disturbingly rendered in terms of the slaughter of beasts ('bestes birtenede'), bringing us back to the realisation that these men have been engaged in bloody combat on the battlefield.[15] Tenderness and intimacy are to be read in the context of extreme violence. Furthermore, this scene confirms that blood, in all its physical and figurative manifestations, is of central importance in this text, not only in the notoriously visceral battle scenes but as a connecting theme in the narrative. This bloodiness must, in a text so concerned with issues of inheritance and lineage, be read in terms of blood ties, of kinship, of affirming blood relationships: Arthur's messy act indicates a blurring or merging of physical selves that replicates the genetic identification between uncle and nephew. This passage also closely resembles an equivalent scene in *La Mort le Roi Artu*, where Arthur kisses the bloody face of his nephew Gaheriet, although in this text the inevitable 'bloodying' of Arthur is not emphasised.[16] In the *Morte Arthure*, Arthur's men, apparently shocked, call on him to cease his behaviour, for he 'bloodies' himself; deliberately allowing himself to be smeared with his nephew's blood is unbecoming according to royal standards of appearance. But the figurative sense of the term 'blodies' (tainting or staining) is also involved. This behaviour taints Arthur's reputation: it is damaging to his 'wirchipe'.[17] In the reactions of the spectators the text appears to indicate that the expression of grief is feminising, harmful, un-knightly and un-kingly. But the primary concern is that Arthur is not behaving 'als a king sholde'. Feminine mourning is set against male action, and the kingly response should be to make haste to seek reparation. Although the author does problematise Arthur's masculine identity in the poem's final stages, the king's eventual 'emasculation' is the result of multiple losses and failures; it does not simply arise from apparently feminised behaviours. Arthur's excesses of grief are, rather, the antithesis of womanly behaviour: they are demonstrative of an exaggeration of manly ideals and virtues.

---

[15] The MS spelling 'birtenede' clearly means 'brettenede' as used at l. 1067.
[16] See *La Mort le roi Artu: roman du XIIIe siècle*, ed. J. Frappier (Geneva, 1964), pp. 98–9; translation: *The Death of King Arthur*, trans. J. Cable (London, 1971), pp. 126–7. Although there are many verbal parallels in this description of the king's grief, this episode does not present an extended lament on one man's death, but presents the various elements (searching the field, swooning, longing for death, kissing the corpse) in response to the successive deaths of Agravain, Guerrehet and Gaheriet.
[17] *OED*, s.v. *bloody*, v. 1 (a) To make (a person, part of the body, etc.) bloody by drawing blood, esp. violently; to smear (a person or thing) with blood; (b) fig. To stain (a person, a person's hands, a country, etc.) with bloodshed; to taint.

It is Arthur's gestures, rather than his words, which inspire critical comment: the clasping of the bloodied body of Gawain, and the kisses which lead to the smearing of the king's beard with his blood, are the points of intimate contact which arouse concern. As I suggested above, this kind of act, the embrace of the corpse, is often problematised in later war literature as having clear homoerotic resonance, as if unspoken desire might only be enacted after death. But it helps our understanding of Arthur's actions to place them in the context of the wider epic and heroic tradition. The way in which Achilles responds to the death of Patroclos in Homer's *Iliad*, for example, has many useful points of comparison. Here the context is again death on the battlefield, followed by acts of tender intimacy accorded to the corpse, where the excesses of grief act as a prelude to vengeance.[18] In such accounts, the bodily embrace is not subject to comment or criticism; rather than suggesting a compromised masculinity, the emphasis is on the ensuing acts of vengeance.

In the *Morte Arthure*, however, while the expression of grief and loss does come under criticism, this is countered by an insistent continuation of mourning. For Arthur the loss of a nephew indicates both loss of companionship and loss of significant military strength, as well as carrying implications for inheritance. Confronted with the corpse of his beloved nephew, Arthur clasps the body in his arms, addressing it in a moving lament:

> Dere kosyn o kynde,   in kare am I leuede,
> For nowe my wirchipe es wente   and my were endide.
> Here es þe hope of my hele,   my happynge in armes;
> My herte and my hardynes   hale one hym lengede -
> My concell, my comforthe   þat kepide myn herte!
> Of all knyghtes þe kynge   þat vndir Criste lifede,
> Þou was worthy to be kynge, þofe I þe corown bare. (ll. 3956–62)

> (Dear cousin, I am left in sorrow, for now my honour has gone and my combat ended. Here lie my hopes of prosperity, my success in battle. My courage and my strength rested entirely in him. My counsellor, my comfort who maintained my heart! Of all the knights who lived under Christ the King, you were worthy to be king, even though I bear the crown.)

All Arthur's losses come together in this one moment. This is the final loss that signifies the end of his military campaigns; his 'wirchipe' is gone, and with it his well-favoured action on the field. All, in fact, was situated in Gawain: Arthur's well-being, his good fortune, his love, his courage. As he says, '*Here* es þe hope of my hele, my happynge in armes': the source of future as well as past success and happiness lies dead in his arms. This

---

[18] Homer, *Iliad*, Books 18–19. Here, the intimate physical attention to the dead body involves the cleaning and anointing of the body in preparation for the funeral, but Achilles is also found the following morning lying face down on his companion's body, weeping.

is an expression of concern about inheritance in the absence of an heir, but it is also a form of identification. In saying that Gawain was worthy to be king in his place, Arthur represents him as his 'better self'. This is rooted not merely in sentiment, but also in practical concerns; not only is Gawain his heir, but it is his skill and prowess that have won Arthur his kingdoms:

> My wele and my wirchipe of all þis werlde riche
> Was wonnen thourghe sir Wawayen and thourghe his witt one!
> (ll. 3963–4)
>
> (All my prosperity and honour in this great world were won through Sir Gawain, and through his abilities alone.)

Gawain's battle prowess is seen as fundamentally important to Arthur's reputation as a conqueror. The king's identity is forged by and through his knights; the dissolution of the Round Table occurs in parallel to the dissolution of Arthur's identity, and Gawain's death signifies the beginning of the decline of the king's realm.

King Arthur, however, is not to be swayed from his grief, echoing his men's phrasing of 'blyne' (cease or desist) and 'blode', such that '"Blyne," sais thies bolde men, "thow blodies þi selfen!"' becomes:

> 'For blode' said the bolde kynge 'blynn sall I neuer,
> Or my brayne to-briste or my breste oþer!' (ll. 3981–2)
>
> ('For blood,' said the noble king, 'I shall never cease, even if my brain or my heart should burst!')

His subsequent actions need to be read in terms of the emphasis on blood in the *Morte Arthure*, in both literal and figurative senses. Arthur defiantly expresses both guilt and sorrow at Gawain's death, and then embarks upon an ambiguous but apparently Eucharistic ritual. He begins by lamenting the blood spilt on the ground:

> Down knelis þe kynge and kryes full lowde,
> With carefull contenaunce he karpes thes words:
> 'O rightwis riche Gode, this rewthe thow beholde,
> Þis ryall rede blode ryn appon erthe!
> It ware worthy to be schrede and schrynede in golde,
> For it is sakles of syn, sa helpe me oure Lorde!' (ll. 3987–92)
>
> (Down kneels the king, and crying out loud with sorrowful demeanour he speaks these words: 'Oh just and splendid God, behold this pity: this royal red blood that runs on the ground. It would be worthy to be arrayed and enshrined in gold, for it is innocent of sin, so help me Lord.')

The pity of the situation, the pathos involved in the royal blood spilling out onto the soil, leads Arthur into a prayer of despair which imbues Gawain with, if not quite Christ-like, certainly saintly attributes. It is a cry which suggests that Gawain's blood embodies all his exemplary qualities. Arthur's assertion that this blood is 'sakles of syn' reinforces the association between guiltlessness and sinfulness, elevating Gawain to a level of moral purity that Arthur can no longer maintain. It adds emphasis to his comments on Gawain a few moments earlier that 'He is sakles, supprysede for syn of myn one' (l. 3986). Gawain, suggests the king, has been killed as a result of Arthur's sinfulness, not his own, and so Arthur indicates through this repetition that Gawain's innocent blood has been shed on his behalf.

Arthur then gathers up Gawain's spilled blood with his bare hands and places it in a kettle-hat, covering it and placing it by the corpse:

> Down knelis þe kynge   with kare at his herte,
> Kaughte it vpe kindly   with his clene handis,
> Keste it in a ketill-hatte   and couerde it faire,
> And kayres further with þe cors   in kythe þare he lenges.
> (ll. 3993–6)

> (Down kneels the king with sorrow in his heart, caught up the blood completely with his bare hands, then cast it into a kettle-helmet and completely covered it. He then journeys forth with the body to the country where he belongs.)

Again the descriptive terms have resonance with those employed elsewhere in the text. 'Kaughte it vpe kindly' might simply suggest 'completely', as indicated by most editions of the text, but 'kindly' also indicates consideration and gentle kindness. It verbally recalls the Priamus episode of the *Morte Arthure*, where both Priamus and Gawain are severely wounded after their hand-to-hand combat with one another, and Arthur's knights pay tender physical attention to their wounded bodies:

> With [the] clere watire a knyghte   clensis theire wondes,
> Keled theym kindly   and comforthed þer hertes (ll. 2711–12)

> (With the pure water a knight cleanses their wounds. He gently refreshed them and comforted their hearts.)

But on the battlefield any such gentleness shown by Arthur is short-lived. With Gawain's blood safely gathered up, Arthur vows revenge, and then allows the corpse to be borne to Winchester in his company, where it receives the appropriate funeral rites. The collecting and revering of Gawain's 'ryall rede blode' place emphasis on its value and purity, and the Eucharistic tone of Arthur's ritual over the corpse and its blood derives in part, as I have suggested, from the description of the blood as 'sakles of syn'. The implication, then, of Gawain's blood being worthy of being 'schrede and schrynede in golde' is that the 'ketill-hatte' then takes on the symbolic appearance of the Chalice.

However, it is not clear how far the text's readers are expected to understand an association between helmet and Grail or Chalice, as the quest for the Holy Grail is one of the key elements of the French Arthurian tradition that is absent from this Middle English text (the other being the adulterous relationship between Lancelot and Guenivere). And while we might draw a connection between the scooping up of Gawain's blood and the collecting of Christ's blood in the Grail, it is simply not the case that this text attempts to portray Gawain as a Christ-figure, however much Arthur wishes to preserve a fantasy of purity and sinlessness at his death.[19] Gawain in the *Morte Arthure* is a brave but flawed warrior, whose impulsive actions often lead to disastrous consequences.[20] And, as Hamel points out, any such Christianised reading must take into account the fact that Arthur appears to employ religious metaphor for secular ends.[21] We might also consider Arthur's actions in terms of the sacrificial associations of bloodshed, in that Gawain has given his blood for the defence of Arthur's kingship, although it is a sacrifice that roundly fails. Furthermore, it is unclear what happens to the gathered blood from Gawain's body, except that it appears to accompany his corpse. The act is perhaps, then, an attempt to restore the physical integrity of Gawain's dead body, to reunite its constituent parts in preparation for the physical resurrection of the body. But the difficulty here is that there is something distinctly un-Christian about the ritual. It is not simply a pre-funerary rite, but intimately connected with the vow for revenge, a battle action, where blood spilled requires a reciprocal blood spillage. The scooping up of Gawain's blood is followed immediately in the text by Arthur's vow to Gawain that all activity will pause 'till thi dede, my dere, be dewly reuengede' (l. 4006). It is a very specific list of activities (courtly, rather than heroic) that will have to wait, including deer-hunting with hounds, and falconry, as well as his duties as monarch and leadership of the Round Table. But mourning clearly places court life in stasis until the death is avenged.

---

[19] Matthews points out a parallel with the collecting of Christ's blood as recorded in the Vulgate *Estoire del Saint Graal*: W. Matthews, *The Tragedy of Arthur: A Study of the Alliterative Morte Arthure* (Berkeley and Los Angeles, 1960), p. 148; and Finlayson suggests that this episode 'emphasizes the dominant concept of Arthur and his men as Christian warriors', Finlayson, *Morte Arthure*, p. 111. Hamel, however, sees this allusion as being 'parodic rather than allegorical [...] he honors not Christ's teachings but chivalry – and revenge'; *Morte Arthure*, p. 385.

[20] J. O. Fichte suggests that, despite the positioning of Gawain as 'holy martyr' in Arthur's eulogy, the account of his actions (particularly when compared to the text's sources) presents him otherwise. Fichte emphasises Gawain's 'monomaniacal desire for revenge', 'arrogance and irascibility' and 'irrationality and blind obsession'. J. O. Fichte, 'The Figure of Sir Gawain', in *The Alliterative Morte Arthure: A Reassessment of the Poem*, ed. K. H. Göller (Cambridge, 1981), pp. 106–16, at pp. 107–9. It should be noted, however, that more recent criticism questions the various moralising readings by critics such as Fichte and Hamel. See, for example, J. A. Burrow, 'The Fourteenth-Century Arthur', in *The Cambridge Companion to the Arthurian Legend*, ed. E. Archibald and A. Putter (Cambridge, 2009), pp. 69–83, at p. 71.

[21] Hamel, *Morte Arthure*, p. 385. See also M. Nievergelt, 'Conquest, Crusade and Pilgrimage: The Alliterative *Morte Arthure* in its Late Ricardian Crusading Context', *Arthuriana* 20.2 (2010), 89–116, at p. 90, for a summary of criticism detailing the conflict between religious and chivalric ideals in the text.

A fuller understanding of the relationship between grief and revenge in operation here is to be found not in the French romance tradition but in heroic literature from other countries and traditions, particularly Icelandic sagas. Many of the values of kinship, loyalty and vengeance which preoccupy such texts are also present in the *Morte Arthure*, but it is the gestures and behaviours which accompany emotionally heightened situations which are of significance here. There is an episode in *Njáls Saga* which, although clearly not a direct influence on the *Morte Arthure*, certainly bears many points of similarity. This saga outlines a broad sweep of kinship, feuds and vengeance, with bonds of blood augmented by those of reciprocity, where kinship and loyalty are repeatedly tested and compromised in response to acts of violence and retribution. The story of Flosi and Hildigunnr has particular significance to the reading of *Morte Arthure*.[22] The episode begins with Flosi warning Höskuldr the chieftain of Hvítaness, of the dangerous ill-will that Njáll's sons bear towards him. As Höskuldr leaves, Flosi gives him a red embroidered cloak. Later, Höskuldr is wearing this cloak when he is wounded and killed by Skarpheðinn (one of Njáll's sons) and his men. Hildigunnr, Höskuldr's wife, finds that her husband is not in his bed, and, searching, finds his dead body. She accords it the kind of intimate attention that we have seen carried out by comrades in battle, specifically, Arthur's attention to Gawain's corpse:

> Hon tók skikkjuna ok þerrði þar með blóðit allt ok vafði þar í blóðlifrarnar ok braut svá saman skikkjuna ok lagði í kistu sína.
>
> (She picked up the cloak and wiped up all the blood with it and wrapped the clotted blood into the cloak and folded it and placed it in her chest.)[23]

That this retaining of the congealed blood from his body has a ritual or memorial function seems likely, but Hildigunnr's motives are not immediately explained by the text. While in the *Morte Arthure* the vocal expression of grief accompanies dramatic and symbolic gesture, here the acts of cleaning the dead body and retaining the blood appear to replace the overt expression of emotion. Hildigunnr later receives Flosi (her uncle) into her home with great honour; she presses him to help her gain vengeance, and he is prepared to act accordingly. But it is clear that Hildigunnr demands a reciprocal loss of life and, like Arthur, she uses a physical engagement with the bloody remnants of slaughter to make her point clear. She produces the bloodied cloak from the chest, and uses Flosi's return to press it into action. When the meal is finished, she silently

---

[22] I am grateful to Dr Sif Rikhardsdottir, of the University of Iceland, for bringing this episode to my attention.

[23] *Brennu-Njáls Saga*, ed. E. Ó. Sveinsson (Reykjavik, 1954), Chapter 112 (p. 282). All quotations from this text are taken from this edition. Translations are from *Njals Saga*, trans. R. Cook (London, 2001).

fetches the cloak and places it on his shoulders so that he is covered in the flakes of dried blood that fall from the cloth, then she explains its symbolic significance:

> 'Þessa skikkju gaft þú, Flosi, Höskuldi, ok gef ek þér nú aptr. Var hann ok í þessi veginn. Skýt ek því til guðs ok góðra manna, at ek sœri þik fyrir alla krapta Krists þins ok fyrir manndóm ok karlmennsku þina, at þú hefnir allra sára þeira, er hann hafði á sér dauðum, eða heit hvers manns niðingr ella.'
>
> ('This cloak, Flosi, was your gift to Hoskuld, and now I give it back to you. He was slain in it. In the name of God and all good men I charge you, by all the powers of your Christ and by your courage and manliness, to avenge all the wounds which he received in dying – or else be an object of contempt to all men.')[24]

In response, Flosi throws back the bloodied cloak and curses Hildigunnr, aware that this challenge will lead to much bloodshed. Hildigunnr has retained the congealed blood in his cloak as evidence of Höskuldr's murder, as a memorial token, but also as an emblem of the need for vengeance that clearly implicates Flosi in its attainment. The bond is reinforced by the gift of the cloak, and the covering of Flosi in Höskuldr's blood symbolically recalls the blood ties and the bonds of loyalty. In recalling acts of violence, such tokens act as indicators of honour, and as a signposting of the appropriate action to follow. Bloodied war-tokens, then, are an important component in determining the course of masculine honour, or 'wirchipe' as the Arthurian tradition describes it.

In this way, the *Morte Arthure*'s use of symbolic action complicates any sense we might have gained of the apparently spontaneous expression of emotion. From the point at which the king scoops up Gawain's spilt blood, grief seems temporarily subsumed by purposeful action, unless the 'ritual' itself is a means of holding on to grief. In its literary context, Arthur's collecting Gawain's blood might be seen as having a memorial function as well as being a signifier of honour and revenge; in contemporary medieval religious texts that figure Christ as warrior the memorial function of bloodied battle relics is also evident. Such figurative tokens occur in texts as diverse as the *Ancrene Wisse*, the fifteenth-century *Dives and Pauper*, Henryson's *The Bludy Serk* and a number of Franciscan lyrics. The bloodied war token similarly performs a dual function in a Christian context: its materiality is intended to provide an ongoing memorial to Christ's sacrifice at the same time that it represents, through its power to shock and visually recall the violence of death, a call to action. Of course, the action demanded of Christians is repentance rather than vengeance, and the reward salvation rather than honour, and this is where Arthur's adoption of this motif becomes problematic. But the image of Christ

---

[24] *Brennu-Njáls Saga*, Chapter 116, p. 291.

as knight sending a message or memorial article to man in the form of blood-stained letter or garment clearly relates to the kind of actions we have seen in *Njáls Saga*. In both contexts the bloodied battlefield memento is treasured in its power to recall the sacrifice of love, but it also exists as material relic in order to stir either reciprocal love or reciprocal action.

Such literary precedents for the association of bloodied mementoes of battle with Christ's sacrifice render it unlikely that the only impulse for the depiction of Arthur's ritualistic actions is Eucharistic symbolism. The intention, in representing Gawain as 'sakless', and an exemplary warrior, is to imply a moral authority that justifies reciprocal action. Gawain's death is a sacrifice that demands reparation. Arthur's physical reverence of Gawain's spilled blood is clearly an act that, in a similar manner to the examples above, engages with the physical horror of death in order to commemorate that death appropriately, and acts as a visual signifier for the necessity of vengeance. But in addition to exploring the figurative associations and the underlying intent of such action, we might also consider the response of Arthur's men to the bloodied embrace and the scooping up of congealing blood. While the initial response to Arthur's grief is condemnatory –'Blyne,' sais thies bolde men, 'thow blodies þi selfen!' – comment on his 'Eucharistic' ritual is notably absent; further expressions of opinion are confined to the necessity for military action.

While such ritualistic actions appear to retain some continuities of interpretation across the range of literary examples detailed above, the ambiguity in the *Morte Arthure* resides not in the contextual understanding but in the interpretation by onlookers. In his highly influential study *The Ritual Process*, Victor Turner emphasises the separation of ritual activity from everyday life.[25] The crossing of a symbolic threshold (*limen*) in order to enact the ritual processes removes the actor from the constraints of social and cultural boundaries. King Arthur, then, might be seen as temporarily setting aside his kingship to observe personal (yet publicly observed) mourning rites. Having temporarily moved into this liminal space, the king then returns to the social setting of the battlefield. In other words, having scooped up Gawain's blood, he enters the final 'phase' of ritual, which, according to Turner, is 'reaggregation or reincorporation', whereby

> [The] ritual subject [...] is in a relatively stable state once more [...] [and] is expected to behave in accordance with certain customary norms and ethical standards binding on incumbents of social position in a system of such positions.[26]

This suggests that, as I indicated at the beginning of this essay, Arthur temporarily inhabits a distinct 'private' space in the wider context of its

---

[25] V. Turner, *The Ritual Process: Structure and Anti-Structure* (New York, 1969; repr. 1995).
[26] Ibid., p. 95.

public setting in which he might express his grief. But this is complicated by the way in which the king brings material traces of his actions with him beyond the temporal space of his ritual acts; his blood-smeared beard and the kettle-hat full of Gawain's congealed blood both extend their influence outside the liminal space of ritual to intrude on his identity as monarch.

An alternative way of viewing Arthur's actions is through Catherine Bell's consideration of ritual as 'a strategy for the construction of [...] power relationships'.[27] Rather than trying to uncover the 'meaning' of Arthur's actions, we might consider their significance in terms of power relations. His 'bloodying' and the gathering of blood could then be seen as a reassertion of Arthur's royal right to grieve in accordance with his own personal standards and parameters. We see here the authority of medieval kingship: the power to determine what is, and is not, appropriate behaviour, beyond the established social norms. It is important to remember, however, that the ritualistic actions involving Gawain's spilled blood meet no resistance (unlike Arthur's relatively conventional, if feminised, mourning behaviours seen earlier).[28] Indeed, as I have indicated, these acts fail to elicit any comment, either positive or negative. We have no way of knowing whether Arthur's actions have been fully understood, or if the silence simply means an acceptance of his authority (now without challenge). Whether the king's assertion of authority, the reclaiming of the right to mourn and the symbolic nod to vengeance are clearly understood by Arthur and his followers, his actions are both 'instrumental' and 'symbolic' (to adopt Christina Pössel's terminology).[29] As well as having symbolic significance, the gathering up of body remnants has practical application in terms of restoring the physical integrity of the body for burial; the contents of the kettle-hat accompany the corpse for the enactment of funeral rites. We might further see this restoration of bodily integrity as having figurative associations: at a time of political division and weakness, the symbolic restoration of Gawain's body carries particular weight.

---

[27] C. Bell, *Ritual Theory, Ritual Practice* (Oxford, 1992; repr. 2009), p. 197. Bell develops Foucault's analysis of ritual and power as 'an alternative to the view that ritual is a functional mechanism or expressive medium in the service of social solidarity and control'. Bell further suggests (p. 206) that 'The deployment of ritualisation, consciously or unconsciously, is the deployment of a particular construction of power relationships, a particular relationship of domination, consent, and resistance.' This is in opposition to the approach of Phythian-Adams, who sees public ritual as performing an important social function, intensifying the 'bonds of belonging'; C. Phythian-Adams, 'Ritual Constructions of Society', in *A Social History of England, 1200–1500*, ed. R. Horrox and W. M. Ormrod (Cambridge, 2006), pp. 369–82, at p. 382.

[28] Bell concludes that 'the resistance [ritual] addresses and produces is not merely a limit on the rite's ability to control; it is also a feature of its efficacy' (p. 218). We might then question the effectiveness of Arthur's ritual actions on the basis of the lack of response, and particularly the lack of resistance.

[29] C. Pössel, 'The Magic of Early Medieval Ritual', *Early Medieval Europe* 17.2 (2009), 111–25, at p. 117.

The intimate attention to the physical body of Gawain after his death, with its dual suggestions of memorialising and vengeance, is not so much a compromise of masculinity (as appears on first reading to be suggested by Arthur's knights), but rather an extravagance of gesture that might be deemed unseemly. However, this enactment of ambiguous ritual is also an enactment of power, and, specifically, kingship. The extravagances of personal grief in the *Chanson de Roland* and the *Morte Arthure* may share characteristics of female mourning behaviours, but, more importantly, they demonstrate masculinity writ large. In these texts, men in positions of power enact the performance of large, even exaggerated gestures, in accordance with their social and political stature. While the romance tradition may generally prohibit the expression of grief in the public arena, the *Morte Arthure* challenges this position. It draws on gestures and formulaic expressions of lament from the French Arthurian tradition as well as *chansons de geste*, but increases the stakes by concentrating mourning tropes from a wider context into the expression of grief for one man's death. This text problematises the king's lament by superimposing a religious metaphor without presupposing associated religious sentiment or action. The blood ritual on the battlefield then brings this text closer in intention to the broader heroic tradition of blood feud, as evidenced in the Icelandic saga. Extravagant grief precedes military action and vengeance. By exhibiting 'feminised' behaviours, warriors such as Arthur are taking responsibility for grief and appropriate ceremony away from the female, domestic, sphere and reconstituting the right to mourn as part of the ceremony and ritual of combat. Excessive weeping is the precursor to excessive violence and vengeance in accord with the compass of chivalric and martial ideals that inform the complex and divided purposes of the Alliterative *Morte Arthure*.

6

Tears and Lies: Emotions and the Ideals of Malory's Arthurian World

RALUCA L. RADULESCU

'You who subdue others, strive to conquer yourself.'[1]

Extreme emotions are a common feature of medieval romance, be they swooning at the sight of the beloved or tears shed by knights at the death of their fellows. In this respect Thomas Malory's *Morte Darthur* is no exception. Yet the emotions expressed both at the individual and the collective level in the *Morte* bring out, as this chapter will demonstrate, an essential tool in the interpretation of Malory's politically astute rewriting of the Arthurian story.

Malory uses a specific phrase, 'oute of mesure', in a number of places in the *Morte*; as I have demonstrated elsewhere, his use of the phrase leads to a direct connection between emotions of an extreme nature and violence, itself the trigger for the demise of the Arthurian fellowship.[2] On the basis of my earlier analysis I concluded that displays of extreme emotion in the final books or tales of the *Morte* reveal excesses of passion, or lack of temperance, the virtue praised in numerous tracts, from the fathers of the Church and Christian theologians to writers of mirrors for princes and chivalric manuals. This chapter directs attention to another, related, area: displays of extreme emotion intended to affect public events and others' emotions. The case study used here is the highly charged and dramatically complex episode in the last book of the *Morte* when Lancelot returns Guenevere to Arthur at the pope's request. In this decisive moment, Lancelot displays the very ideal of nobility – or so Malory seems to want his readers to see it – as he relinquishes Guenevere and professes his continuing loyalty to Arthur. Lancelot's attitude stirs the

---

[1] John Gower, *The Major Latin Works of John Gower*, trans. Eric Stockton (Seattle, 1962), p. 234 (Epistle to King Richard, Book VI).

[2] R. L. Radulescu, '*oute of mesure*: Violence and Knighthood in Malory's *Morte Darthur*', in *Re-Viewing 'Le Morte Darthur': Texts and Contexts, Characters and Themes*, ed. K. S. Whetter and R. L. Radulescu (Cambridge, 2005), pp. 119–31.

emotions of all the audience apart from Gawain, who stands unmoved. All the bystanders – that is, the entire court, male and female – weep copiously: 'all the knyghtes and ladyes that were there wepte *as they were madde*, and the *tearys felle* on kynge Arthur hys chekis'.[3] Modern critics tend to accept these public tears (Lancelot's, Arthur's and the court's) as testimony of a public recognition of Lancelot's nobility despite all other evidence of his affair with Guenevere. This chapter explores the context in which a medieval audience would experience and understand these emotions. I suggest they form part of a well-defined and sophisticated response to a charged *political* moment, governed by established codes of interpretation which can be traced to educational treatises popular with Malory's contemporaries. By means of a re-examination of Malory's episode and its close sources, the Old French Vulgate *Mort Artu* and the Middle English Stanzaic *Morte Arthure*, I propose to investigate whether the episode presents a tragedy of virtue[4] or whether there is a particular cultural context in which Lancelot's words and the emotions they elicit among the courtiers can be read. The central focus of the analysis will be the precarious balance between Lancelot's dismay at his impending exile while protesting his loyalty to Arthur and the calculated nature of his words and actions, especially his repeated emphasis on calling 'liars' those close to Arthur. In particular I will examine Lancelot's speeches and self-renunciation in his offer of reparation for the accidental killing of Gawain's brothers, since these two actions trigger extreme reactions from the court.

Lancelot's return to the court with Guenevere marks the moment when he and Arthur should be reconciled. Prior to this, the affair between Lancelot and the queen has been exposed by Aggravain and Mordred, who, with twelve Scottish knights, have surprised Lancelot in Guenevere's chamber. Lancelot has fought back, killing Aggravain and the other twelve knights. When Guenevere is sent to the stake for her role in the death of the Scottish knights, Gawain's brothers Gareth and Gaheris refuse to wear armour at her execution, so as to show their disagreement with the manner in which she is to be punished. Lancelot saves the queen from the fire and, in the mêlée, accidentally kills Gareth and Gaheris, for which

---

[3] All references will be to *Sir Thomas Malory: Le Morte Darthur*, ed. P. J. C. Field, 2 vols (Cambridge, 2013), cited parenthetically in the text by page and line number from vol. I: *The Text*. The quotation is from p. 901.9–10.

[4] This view is common among a host of critics. C. D. Benson summarises the situation in the last tale of the *Morte* as a 'tragedy of virtue', or rather of Arthurian ideals: 'The Arthurian ideal of fellowship is destroyed by the Arthurian ideal of honour' (C. D. Benson, 'The Ending of the *Morte Darthur*', in *A Companion to Malory*, ed. E. Archibald and A. S. G. Edwards (Cambridge, 1998), pp. 221–37, at p. 231). Following Derek Brewer's earlier analysis of honour and shame in the last tale of the *Morte*, in the Introduction to his edition of *Le Morte Darthur: Parts Seven and Eight* (London, 1968), M. Lambert states that 'it is Malory himself, not just his characters, for whom honour and shame are more real than innocence and guilt. *Le Morte Darthur* is *of* rather than *about* a shame ethos.' M. Lambert, *Malory: Style and Vision in 'Le Morte Darthur'* (New Haven and London, 1975), p. 179.

Gawain swears eternal vengeance. In the episode under discussion here, Lancelot returns to the court with Guenevere in order to make peace with Arthur, but Gawain does not allow it. Gawain's attitude is evidently in opposition to that of the entire court. The depiction of the court, therefore, seems to suggest Malory intends it to act as a channel by which feelings that could or should be felt by the main protagonists are induced in the audience outside the text: 'Wyte you well, than was there many a bolde knyght wyth Kynge Arthur that wepte as tenderly as they had seyne all theire kynne dede afore them!' (898.10–12).[5]

First, Malory's Arthur shows no signs of emotion: he 'sate stylle and seyde no worde' (898.13). He may be cautiously waiting for Lancelot's words and wanting to show a stern countenance. Indeed Arthur's attitude is experienced via Lancelot's perception, as the authorial comment registers:

> So the kynge sate *stylle* and *seyde no worde*. And when sir Launcelot saw hys countenance he arose up and pulled up the quene wyth hym, and thus he seyde full knyghtly:
>
> [...] 'But, sir, lyars ye have lystened, and that hath caused grete debate betwyxte you and me. For tyme hath bene, my lorde Arthur, that [y]e were gretly pleased with me whan I ded batayle for my lady, youre quene; and full well ye know, my moste noble kynge, that she hathe be put to grete wronge or thys tyme. And sytthyn hyt pleased you at many tymys that I shulde feyght for her, therefore mesemyth, my good lorde, I had more cause to rescow her from the fyer whan she sholde have ben brente for my sake.
>
> For they that told you tho talys were lyars, and so hit felle uppon them ...'
>
> (898.13–15; 22–31)

Lancelot's words are those of a political ally who exposes his hurt now that he is given a chance to show his loyalty one more time by returning Guenevere to Arthur.[6] Lancelot uses the word 'liars' and appeals not only to Arthur, so that the latter exercises wisdom in judging how the present situation has arisen from the initial rumours spread by Mordred and Aggravain, but also to two other audiences: the court within the text, and the readers of Malory's text. Lancelot's use of the word 'liars' is to be understood in this context; he lays the claim of treason at the feet of those who stirred trouble in the first place. At this point in the narrative Lancelot realises he will leave the country as a traitor, albeit accused not

---

[5] For an examination of courtly emotions in other contexts, see F. Brandsma, 'The Court's Emotions', in *Cultures courtoises en movement*, ed. I. Arseneau and F. Gingras (Montréal, 2011), pp. 74–82, and, by the same author, 'Mirror Characters', in *Courtly Arts and the Art of Courtliness*, ed. K. Busby and C. Kleinhenz (Cambridge, 2006), pp. 275–84, and 'Arthurian Emotions', *Actes du 22e Congrès de la Société Internationale Arthurienne* (Rennes, 2008), http://www.uhb.fr/alc/ias/actes/index.htm, 15 July, session 2 L2: '*Conte de Graal* et émotions'.

[6] I discuss this elsewhere; see R. Radulescu, *The Gentry Context for Malory's 'Morte Darthur'* (Cambridge, 2003), p. 136.

of adultery with the queen but of killing Gawain's brothers. Lancelot's nobility may still be preserved in the eyes of the court and those of the text's audience, yet this becomes more problematic when we consider his appeal to Arthur to regard Mordred and Aggravain as '[liars]'. After all, Aggravain and Mordred are Gawain's brothers, and Arthur's natural closest royal counsellors, being of his kin. As Aggravain points out at the beginning of the last tale in the *Morte*, he and Mordred and are '[Arthur's] syster sunnes, [and] may suffir hit no lenger' (872). A medieval audience could interpret their actions as motivated by concern over their lord's honour and hence, in that context, in the spirit of avoiding shame. Thus they can say they were right to inform the king of that which the king himself knew, but was reluctant to acknowledge publicly. Yet of course they only *purport* to be motivated by concern for Arthur's honour.[7] The same audience would also be aware of the fact that counsellors to the king could be covetous and envious, and Arthur should beware those who might want to serve their own interests before his own, despite their flattering words regarding their concern over his reputation and worship. Therefore Lancelot here displays knowledge of and makes full use of well-known advice to princes found in advice texts such as Lydgate and Burgh's translation of the *Secrees of Old Philisoffres*, in which a good king wisely avoids flatterers:

> Atwen trouthe / And forgyd fflaterye [in between]
>   Ther is a straunge / vnkouth difference,
> Contraryous poysoun / I dar wel certeffye,
>   To alle Estatys / of Royal excellence:
> Wheer double menyng / hath ony existence,
>   Ther growith ffrawde / And Covert fals poysoun,
>   And sugryd galle / honyed with Collusyoun.[8]   [sugared gall]

The topic of the king's counsellors might appear unconnected to the emotions displayed in the episode of Lancelot's return to court.[9] However, the court's judgement of and reaction to Lancelot's words about the role of counsellors do matter. In particular, there seems to be no sign of interest in the actual nature of Lancelot's allegations. No comment is recorded when he utters strong words ('liars'), nor is there any sign of a potential challenge to his words from anyone except Gawain, who is singled out for his stubborn refusal of Lancelot's ensuing (noble) offer of reparation. One

---

[7] In that same earlier episode Aggravain also says: 'hit ys shamefully suffird of us all that we shulde suffir so noble a kynge as kynge Arthur ys to be shamed' (870.21-3). Malory's Arthur deliberately ignores the affair out of his love for Lancelot and the service done by him: 'for the kynge had a demyng of hit' (872.24).

[8] Lydgate and Burgh's *Secrees of Old Philisoffres*, ed. R. Steele, EETS ES 66 (London, 1894), p. 28, ll. 876–82 (glossed as 'the evils arising from flatterers'). I thank Dr Megan Leitch for exchanges on the topic of books of nurture relevant to my topic.

[9] For a discussion of counsellors in Malory's *Morte*, see Radulescu, *The Gentry Context*, ch. 4, esp. pp. 122–6, 131–2 and 134.

might expect some form of comment on either Lancelot's earlier actions or those of Aggravain and Mordred – from Arthur's other counsellors or from a figure of the Church, such as the archbishop of Canterbury, since, after all, this public event comes as a result of the direct command of the pope that Arthur and Lancelot be reconciled. All we witness is Gawain's vehement rebuttal, which, as in the Stanzaic *Morte*, seems to suggest an implicit condemnation of his rash and vengeful nature, as will be discussed below, by the audience within and outside the text. This is surprising, given the high emotional loading of the episode, and the length and content of Lancelot's speeches, which, in contrast, appear to be polished *political* speeches.

Turning to the two main sources for this episode can help illuminate how Malory shaped his innovative approach to the story. In the Stanzaic *Morte*, there is no comment on Arthur's countenance: 'fair wordes' were exchanged at Lancelot's arrival, and many knights stood weeping. Feelings do not seem to run as high as in Malory's version; this may be dictated as much by metrical constraints as by authorial decision:

> The king then salues he full soon,
>   As man that was of muche might;
> Fair wordes were there fone,   [taken]
>   But *weeping stood* there many a knight. (ll. 2376–9; my emphasis)

Arthur's emotional state is, however, conveyed through his words, reported to be 'keen and thro' (l. 2389: 'keen and fierce'); he refers to the close friendship he had enjoyed with Lancelot and his dismay at how it has been broken by Lancelot's actions (ll. 2390–95). Lancelot responds:

> Launcelot then answerd he,
>   When he had listened long:
> 'Sir, thy wo thou witest me,
>   And well thou wost it is with wrong;
> I was never fer from thee
>   When thou had any sorrow strong;
> *But liers listenes thou to lie,*
>   Of whom all this word out sprong.' (ll. 2396–404; my emphasis)

Before Lancelot can explain his view of the past situation, Gawain intervenes to make his own position known. Yet in the stanzaic poem Lancelot's emotions are emphasised early on in the exchange, framing as they are his first brief response to Gawain:

> Launcelot answerd with *herte sore*,
>   Though he were nothing afrought:
> 'Gawain', he said, 'Though I were there,
>   Myself thy brethern slogh I nought;
> Other knightes fele there were
>   That sithen this war dere han bought.'

>   Launncelot sighed *wonder sore;*
>   The *teres of his eyen* sought. (ll. 2412–19; my emphasis)[10]

The exchange continues, in brief sentences, between Gawain and Lancelot, with Arthur merely deploring the start of the war twice, displaying his own emotions ('The teres from his eyen ran', l. 2437; 'He said, 'Alas!' with sighing sore / 'That ever yet this war began!', ll. 2442–3).

Here, as in Malory, the blame is placed on Gawain, whose influence over Arthur is too great, and whose revenge overshadows Lancelot's attempt to invoke (political) wisdom. In this episode the audience of both the stanzaic *Morte* and Malory's text would also identify Arthur as the foolish king placing everything in one man's hands (something Arthur will also do later, when he leaves Mordred as regent):

>   Be sad of cheer / play nat the Enfaunt,
>   In answere prudent / wys nat chaungable,
>   Oon singuler man / to make thy leyf tenaunt,   [your life]
>   To the ne thyne / is not a-vayllable;
>   ffor yif he be wood / and vntretable,
>   He may in his / furyous Cruelte
>   Thy pepil, thy Reem / destroye, and also the.[11]

A long time before Mordred shows his true colours Gawain can be seen to be a dangerous counsellor since his blind vengeance (in the *Secrees* 'furyous cruelte') will eventually lead Arthur, his people and his realm to ruin. In other words, the excessive emotions that guide Gawain's response to Lancelot in this scene are to be blamed for what follows.

On the evidence of the Stanzaic *Morte*, therefore, Malory's text builds up both the public context of the encounter and Lancelot's speeches. The poem is, however, itself based on the Vulgate *Mort Artu*, the other main source for Malory's episode. The anonymous author of the equivalent episode in the French text does not seem to condone extreme reactions at all. There Lancelot approaches the king, then dismounts, taking the queen by the reins of her horse to present her to the king:

>   Sire vez ci madame la reïne que ge vos rent qui fust pieça morte *par la desloialté de ceus de vostre ostel* … […]

---

[10] Indeed, as in the Vulgate *Mort Artu* (of which the stanzaic poem is a translation), Lancelot is correct to say he did not slay Gawain's brothers in quite the way that is implied. In the *Mort* Lancelot only kills Gaheriet (Gareth) unwittingly, but this is due to the fact that Hector has already struck Gaheriet's helmet off his head (hence, unlike in Malory, Gaheriet has gone armed to Guenevere's execution) – while Guerrehet is killed by Bors. Aggravain also dies in this moment, not earlier, when he and the Scottish knights surprise Lancelot in Guenevere's chamber. Thus the circumstances of who killed whom in the *Vulgate* and the stanzaic poem are rather different and render Gauvain more unreasonable than Malory's Gawain.

[11] *Secrees*, ed. Steele, p. 69, ll. 2192–8 (glossed as 'Do not trust your power into one man's hands').

Lancelos, fet li rois vos en avez tant fet [Sommer: por moi] que ge vos en sei bon gré; et ce que vos en avez fet vos porra [Sommer: encore tant] valoir en aucun tens. (158)

(Sir, here is the queen, whom I am returning to you. Members of your household would have killed her treacherously long ago ...
'Lancelot', said the king, I'm very grateful to you for what you have done, and it may well stand you in good stead some day.') (132)[12]

In the *Mort Artu* Gawain does repeat that Lancelot's past service is appreciated but also stresses that Lancelot must now leave the court, to which Arthur acquiesces. Lancelot replies by making a point-by-point case for his past service and its value to Arthur and the kingdom. Unlike in Malory, Lancelot's speech refers to the early part of Arthur's reign, and thus to the crucial role Lancelot played in securing Arthur's crown. The wording is stronger than in Malory, and more political in nature, since Lancelot refers to his vital place in the hierarchy of the Round Table and Arthur's lack of gratitude for past service at a critical time in his reign. Malory's Lancelot too alludes to past service, but his examples are both more general, lacking reference to any particular time in Arthur's reign, and yet more pointedly specific. He spells out details of how he personally saved Gawain and his brothers from certain death in past encounters with enemies. The Lancelot of the *Morte Darthur* thus appears as a shrewd and measured speaker, whose appeals first to personal ties, then to his public service, and then back to personal service are carefully balanced in his speech.

No narratorial comment is present regarding the manner in which Arthur greets Lancelot, nor what the court's reaction might be at the sight of Lancelot's approach. The 'liars' of Malory's Lancelot are, in the original French, 'li desloial de vostre ostel' (158).[13] This charge is not quite equivalent to the framing in either the Stanzaic or Malory's *Morte*. On the basis of these two main sources it seems evident Malory developed his storyline by amplifying both the emotional displays and the calculated nature of Lancelot's appeals in his speeches. In Malory, Lancelot continues, making a compelling case for his past service to the king, queen and other knights at the Round Table, in particular Gawain and his faction, and showing how his efforts have helped maintain the fellowship's unity. He displays his full understanding of how intertwined personal and public service is in the Arthurian court. In other words, he displays a mature grasp of politics and an awareness of the application of the Round Table oath to

---

[12] All quotations are from *La Mort le Roi Artu: roman du XIIIe siècle*, ed. J. Frappier, 3rd edn (Geneva, 1964), pp. 157–8, with translations from *Lancelot-Grail: The Old French Arthurian Vulgate and Post-Vulgate in Translation*, trans. N. Lacy et al., 5 vols (New York and London, 1992–6), vol. IV, both sources cited by page number.

[13] O. Sommer glosses the phrase as 'evil tongues' – or the disloyal (see *The Vulgate Version of the Arthurian Romances*, ed. H. O. Sommer (Washington, 1908–16; repr. New York, 1979), vol. 7, p. 311.9).

the situation in hand. His words are carefully crafted, showing him to be an eloquent speaker, and a genuine competitor with the Gawain of the insular romance and chronicle tradition, known for his wisdom and fair speech:

> 'My lorde,' seyde Sir Launcelot, 'so ye be nat displeased, ye shall undirstonde that I and myne have done you oftyntymes bettir servyse than ony othir knyghtes have done, in many dyverce placis; and where ye have bene full hard bestadde dyvers tymes, I have rescowed you frome many daungers; and ever unto my power I was glad to please you and my lorde Sir Gawayne. In justis and in turnementis and in batayles set, bothe on horsebak and on foote, I have oftyn rescowed you, and you, my lorde Sir Gawayne, and many mo of youre knyghtes in many dyvers placis.'[...] 'And I take God to recorde, I never was wrothe nor gretly hevy wyth no good knyght and I saw hym besy and aboute to wyn worship; and glad I was ever whan I founde a good knyght that myght onythynge endure me on horsebak and on foote. (899.9–17; 23–7)

In Malory's version Lancelot's words stir greater emotions than in either of the two main sources discussed above. Arthur keeps his silence, and only his tears are reported, while the court's emotions become extreme, escalating swiftly from 'as they were madde' to 'as people oute of mynde':

> Than all the knyghtes and ladyes that were there wepte *as they were madde*, and the *tearys felle* on kynge Arthur hys chekis.
> [...] Than sir Launcelotte syghed, and therewith the *tearys felle* on hys chekys, and than he seyde ...
> [...] And therewith he brought the quene to the kynge, and than Sir Launcelot toke hys leve and departed. And there was nother kynge, duke, nor erle, barowne nor knyght, lady nor jantyllwoman, but all they wepte as *people oute of mynde*, excepte Sir Gawayne. And whan thys noble knyght sir Launcelot toke his horse to ryde oute of Carlehyll, there was *sobbyng and wepyng* for pure dole of hys departynge.
> (901.9–10; 902.1–2; 903.10–16; my emphasis)

Lancelot's speech has no equivalent in either the stanzaic poem or in the *Mort Artu*. The length of his exposition is significant, especially as the others present are given neither as much to say nor any arguments to counter Lancelot's claims. In the event it even seems as if (Malory's) Lancelot's lengthy rehearsal of the services he had provided to the king and the queen, and, by association, to the fellowship, the court and the country, erases his allegation about the 'lies' and 'liars'. The word 'liars' can be traced back to the stanzaic poem (see above), though in that context it does not get an explanation. In the *Mort Artu*, the same concept is more politically loaded, thanks to Lancelot's extensive explanation of his role in maintaining Arthur's position during the early challenges to his crown. The Vulgate Arthur also thanks Lancelot for past service. But in Malory Arthur remains silent.

This is interesting, since Malory's Lancelot now contradicts himself. In the earlier episode of the Poisoned Apple, Lancelot famously said that he rescued the queen because 'y ought of ryght ever [to be] in youre quarrel and in my ladyes the quenys quarell to do batayle, for ye ar the man that gaff me the hygh order of knyghthode, and that day my lady, youre quene, ded me worshyp' (802.13–17). In relation to this earlier episode, Eugène Vinaver notes that the explanation comes from the *Prose Lancelot*, not from the *Mort Artu*, but the wording is so similar to the *Lancelot* that it suggests Malory must have read it.[14] Now, when he returns Guenevere to Arthur, Lancelot says all his service has been to the king all along, not in response to something done by the queen. His structured speeches seem to suggest not a lack of consistency in Malory's approach to Lancelot's character, but rather a broader, overarching design which governs Lancelot's actions and his words in both episodes. In fact a political reading of Lancelot's words in these two episodes and the emotions they elicit gives more coherence to his character and the trajectory Malory seems to envisage for him in the *Morte Darthur*.

In the Stanzaic *Morte* the courtly display of sorrow is described in powerful, but minimal phrasing: 'There was *dole and weeping sore, / At the parting was little pride*' (2458–9). It is in Malory's *Morte* that we encounter the most moving description of the reaction of the court, and the pervasive feelings of sadness suggest that boundaries between involvement and non-involvement collapse. In other words, the court is an active participant in a highly charged political transaction, but its members conform to pressures dictated by conventional modes of behaviour, and thus become mere spectators. The courtiers' reactions are restrained by hierarchy – they do not intervene – but their emotions are both conventional and represent a statement: they endorse Lancelot's plea and his nobility of purpose. On the other hand, the boundaries between King Arthur's court and Malory's medieval audience have also collapsed, since it becomes evident that a clear invitation to sympathise with Lancelot and his cause is extended outside the narrative to the audience of the *Morte*. How are, therefore, the phrases 'as they were madde' and 'as people oute of minde' supposed to influence the audience? The specificity of the linguistic choices Malory makes is relevant: he names each social rank among those present, male and female: 'nother kynge, duke, nor erle, barowne nor knyght, lady nor jantyllwoman, but all they wepte as *people oute of mynde*, excepte Sir Gawayne'. He bars from the list the ranks below the aristocracy, and the list is comprehensive and clear. By implication, even more attention is drawn to Gawain, as the only unreasonable member of the upper echelons in Arthur's society who chooses not to conform and ignores what appears to become a universal call for shared

---

[14] Vinaver, Commentary, in *Works*, p. 1599.

sadness in view of Lancelot's situation. Hence Gawain actively refuses to follow accepted rules of noble behaviour.

The gravity of the situation and the controversial aspect of the court's attitude when faced with Lancelot's justification of past actions warrant further investigation into how Malory's contemporary audience would have received the text. A medieval audience's understanding of emotions and acceptable public displays of emotion was guided by norms of behaviour and lived experience of similar events. Correspondences between events in Malory's narrative and the political reality of his time have been sought by many critics. Some have chosen to look for literal correspondences, for example, identifying political actors in Malory's Arthurian universe as fifteenth-century figures. Like any fictional text, Malory's goes beyond the simple correlation of this kind; reading the *Morte* as a *roman à clef*, as if intended to point to particular events or historical persons in Malory's time, would limit our understanding of what the work itself might have meant for its original audience.

Without suggesting any simplistic parallels between fifteenth-century political actors and Lancelot, we can agree with a scholar writing nearly a century ago. In 1933, Nellie Slayton Aurner suggested that Malory's episode may reflect the demise of William de la Pole, duke of Suffolk, in 1450, following allegations related to his presumed role in the loss of the French territories, and rumours about his presumed affair with Henry VI's queen, Margaret of Anjou.[15] In his commentary to his edition of Malory's *Morte*, Vinaver notes:

> It has been suggested that Lancelot's defence bears some resemblance to Suffolk's address to the Commons before his banishment, and that the whole story offers analogies with Suffolk's trial. The analogy may be tempting, but there are unhappily no verbal similarities between Lancelot's speech and Suffolk's as reproduced by Turner (*History of England*, vol. iii, p. 69), while all the other traits that the two characters have in common (the banishment and the slander concerning the favour by the Queen) are traceable to M[alory]'s French source [*Mort Artu*] and to *Le Morte Arthur* [the Stanzaic poem].[16]

Vinaver's traditional approach to the study of this episode is unsurprising; he, like other critics of his generation, asked for evidence of close 'verbal similarities' between the literary work and recorded historical speeches and events. In fact the echo may well have been intended to cover a broader range of events experienced by Malory and his contemporaries, including both Suffolk's trial and banishment and, later in the century, the disgrace faced by another over-mighty subject, Richard Neville, earl of Warwick, in his relation to the Yorkist Edward IV. Warwick 'the King-

---

[15] See N. S. Aurner, 'Sir Thomas Malory – Historian', *PMLA* 48.2 (1933), 362–91.
[16] Vinaver, Commentary, p. 1639, referring to Malory's text at p. 1198.

maker' had supported Edward while the latter was only a young man, eighteen years of age; if a loose comparison may be made, then Warwick's role in Edward's ascent to the throne and early reign may be echoed in Lancelot's reproach to Arthur about support throughout his reign. While Warwick has been vilified both in his own time and by modern historians, his personality and trajectory have enjoyed a renewal of interest in recent decades.[17] No verbatim records survive of a verbal confrontation between Edward IV and Warwick, but there is plenty of evidence to show how the older earl's support of Edward was essential during the early days of Yorkist rule. In the highly charged political atmosphere in the late 1460s when popular opinion turned against Edward, Warwick himself had grounds to believe himself betrayed, to feel estranged and ultimately exiled from among those advisors closest to the king. The audience of the *Morte*, medieval or modern, this remains at liberty to imagine either Suffolk or Warwick in Lancelot's position.

Malory's depiction of the atmosphere at the court in this episode may also have been influenced, indirectly, by propaganda produced to support the Yorkist cause during the Wars of the Roses. Yorkist propaganda manipulated highly charged political events, such as Edward's return to rule, using theatrical devices in the form of so-called 'miracles'. One such event took place when Edward was praying in Daventry on Palm Sunday in the church of St Anne, where, the anonymous author of the chronicle says, 'God and Seint Anne shewyd a fayre miracle', while Edward prayed to God, the Blessed Virgin Mary, St George and St Anne in gratitude for having helped him to return to England from exile. The wooden case of the alabaster statue of St Anne, which was boarded up, according to tradition, during Lent, 'gave a great crack, and a little openyd, whiche the Kynge well perceyveyd and all the people about hym'.[18] It is easy to imagine the effect of the miracle, not only on its original witnesses, but also on the audience who heard reports of it; the powerful combination of high politics and apparent divine confirmation of Edward's right to rule would likely produce strong emotional responses. As Peter Field has demonstrated, there are evident influences from prose chronicle writing in the period on Malory's style.[19] Was Malory channelling similarly strong feelings among his own contemporaries with regard to unrewarded service, and the ingratitude of kings? Was he inviting his audiences to read between the lines more than just despair at the breakdown of the Arthurian fellowship? And in what ways is the gender of those involved in the weeping and 'mad' tears to be taken into account, if at all?

---

[17] Indeed, two leading modern historians have published book-length studies of his career: see M. A. Hicks, *Warwick the Kingmaker* (Oxford, 2002), and A. J. Pollard, *Warwick the Kingmaker: Politics, Power and Fame during the Wars of the Roses* (London, 2007).

[18] *Historie of the Arrivall of King Edward IV*, in *Three Chronicles of the Reign of Edward IV*, ed. K. Dockray (Gloucester, 1998), pp. 13–14.

[19] P. J. C. Field, *Romance and Chronicle: A Study of Malory's Prose Style* (London, 1971).

A theoretical framework for this discussion may take as its starting point the 2001 issue of *Early Medieval Europe*, part of which was dedicated to emotions. In her contribution to this debate Barbara Rosenwein notes:

> emotions are part of human communication; [...] they, like thoughts, have an appraisal function and thus cannot be considered primarily 'irrational'; ... they are expressed within socially constructed narratives, both imaginary and unfolding in the real world.[...] being non-verbal and complex, they resist formulation. That's part of what's so interesting about them: they are continually in the process of being shaped. In their very expression they are social products. Nor is this just because they are verbal expressions of the non-verbal.[20]

In the same issue Carolyne Larrington emphasises that various expressions of emotion such as tears, laughter or anger are expressed in ways that are controlled or at least mediated by cultural rules.[21] Further work on emotions helps contextualise the present discussion of public displays of emotion in Malory's text. Exploring anger in a number of medieval texts, Stephen D. White reminds modern scholars that:

> Emotions are often performed *publicly* instead of being shared among intimates or experienced in isolation. Those who show grief by weeping weep openly. Those who are angry sooner or later broadcast their anger to others, enacting their enmity before audiences. [...] Public displays [here, male displays of anger, but the same applies to any strong emotions] occur in a limited number of predictable settings. The settings are predictable because displays of anger can usually be read as conventionalized responses to certain kinds of past political acts, as political acts in themselves, and as motives for future political acts of certain kinds.[22]

The gender and socio-political dimension of these displays of emotion are also important. According to Pierre Bourdieu:

> the use of language, the manner as much as the substance of discourse, depends on the social position of the speaker, which governs the access he can have to the language of the institution, that is, to the official, orthodox and legitimate speech. It is the access to the *legitimate instruments of expression* that makes *all* the difference.[23]

It is therefore crucial, in our reading and understanding of Malory's

---

[20] B. Rosenwein, 'Writing without Fear about Early Medieval Emotions', *Early Medieval Europe* 10.2 (2001), 229–34, at p. 231.

[21] C. Larrington, 'The Psychology of Emotion and Study of the Medieval Period', *Early Medieval Europe* 10.2 (2001), 251–6.

[22] S. D. White, 'The Politics of Anger', in *Anger's Past: The Social Uses of an Emotion in the Middle Ages*, ed. B. H. Rosenwein (Ithaca and London, 1998), pp. 127–52, at p. 139; author's emphasis.

[23] P. Bourdieu, 'Authorized Language: The Social Conditions for the Effectiveness of Ritual Discourse', in *Language and Symbolic Power* (Cambridge, 1991), p. 109 (Bourdieu's emphasis on 'all'; mine on 'legitimate instruments of expression').

choice to intensify the display of emotion in this episode, to explore the extent to which his precise listing of those present by gender and social status is not fortuitous, but rather a calculated measure intended to give weight to the situation in hand. Everyone is behaving in a manner appropriate to their status, apart from Gawain, who keeps a stern countenance. In White's analysis (of different texts) this translates into a 'display of emotion [that] is mediated by an appraisal of the appropriateness of an emotion to a given political situation'.[24] White's observations are based on his analysis of a chronicle passage which focuses on anger and goading and the political dimension of an outburst of anger (and what caused it) as well as its highly staged 'cooling' period. Yet his conclusions are apposite here; in Malory's episode it is also true that, in White's words, 'displays of emotion are *highly conventionalized* and *socially generated*, and they are associated with *collective* political processes'.[25] Further, presenting certain types of emotion in a negative light 'was often part of a *political strategy*' (such emotions might be hot temper, hot anger, hence violence).[26] Are we to understand, from this complex perspective, that the court's reaction is similarly 'highly conventionalised' and 'socially generated', since it is associated with 'collective political processes'?

Against this rich theoretical background we can read the reactions of the court in Malory's episode as both political strategy and an invitation to the audience outside the text to empathise with the tears shed by the characters. How might the gender of the double audience, within and outside the text, and their social status, be relevant to this evaluation of the situation? A clue to this is to be found in the circulation and use of literature meant to shape behaviour (personal and public) among the upper classes in Malory's time. Among such literature, mirrors for princes and derivative texts played a crucial role in shaping both principles of education and those of political action.[27] Usually considered as general widely shared educational material, whether for kings, princes or other rulers, mirrors for princes are often dismissed by many critics on the grounds of the generality of advice contained in them: they do not appear to focus on particular socio-political or economic conditions.

---

[24] White, 'The Politics of Anger', p. 148.
[25] White, 'The Politics of Anger', p. 150.
[26] Ibid. T. Reuter also discussed the political nuances of emotions; see his 'The Symbolic Language of Medieval Political Action', part II of *Medieval Polities and Modern Mentalities*, ed. J. L. Nelson (Cambridge, 2006), esp. 'Symbolic acts in the Becket dispute', p. 173 ff. Reuter stresses, once again, the importance of considering reports on the display of emotions in highly politicised contexts; he uses the example of Thomas Becket and Henry II, and the relationship described in contemporary documents and chronicles to show that nothing can be taken to be true to the situation, but rather as part of a larger contexts of accepted behaviour.
[27] See the extensive work by N. Orme on medieval education; also N. Orme, 'Gentry Education and Recreation', in *Gentry Culture in Late Medieval England*, ed. R. Radulescu and A. Truelove (Manchester, 2005), pp. 63–83.

Two other popular tracts which contain advice on how to judge a person's actions by studying their behaviour (in addition to the commonplace advice given to princes and kings, as in the *Secrees* cited above) are the thirteenth-century *De regimine principum* of Giles of Rome (Aegidius Romanus or Egidio Colonna) and the independently written *Secreta secretorum* (also known as the 'Letter of Aristotle to Alexander the Great'). Translations of both texts were produced throughout the fifteenth century in England and were enormously popular in the upper social strata, from the king to the gentry and merchant classes.[28] Giles wrote his treatise in the late thirteenth century and by the fifteenth many manuscripts were in circulation; about sixty (out of 350) extant manuscripts survive of English origin or circulation, the majority from the late fourteenth and early fifteenth century.[29] Giles's treatise was owned across social classes, including by the fifteenth-century English gentry. The appeal of Giles's tract among the aristocracy and kings of England is well documented, and Charles Briggs notes that the Lancastrian king Henry VI appears to have been educated by means of 'some instruction in the doctrines of Giles's', since he was the recipient of an anonymously composed text titled *Tractatus de regimine principum ad Regem Henricum Sextum*.[30] Copies of Giles's *De regimine principum* were held in high esteem and used across generations. The paucity of manuscripts of the text specifically produced in England in the fifteenth century merely confirms that the market had been saturated, and that the manuscripts already imported or produced continued to be treasured and thus survived in sufficient numbers for the needs of those who required them.

The verse and prose versions of the other mirror-for-princes text, the *Secreta secretorum* or *Secret of Secrets* (the only other real competitor to Giles, with over 600 Latin copies surviving, and numerous vernacular translations in languages of medieval Europe), were so widely disseminated as to warrant no fewer than nine independent prose translations into English alone.[31] The *Secreta* had the advantage of being a much shorter text than either Giles's *De regimine principum* or any of the court

---

[28] See John Trevisa, *The Governance of Kings and Princes: John Trevisa's Middle English Translation of the 'De regimine principum' of Aegidius Romanus*, ed. D. C. Fowler, C. F. Briggs and P. G. Remley (New York, 1997), and *Three Prose Versions of the 'Secreta secretorum'*, ed. R. Steele, EETS ES 74 (London, 1898), vol. I.

[29] C. F. Briggs, *Giles of Rome's 'De regimine principum': Reading and Writing Politics at Court and University, c. 1275–c.1525* (Cambridge, 1999).

[30] Ibid. The tract is edited in *Four English Political Tracts of the Later Middle Ages*, ed. J.-P. Genet, Camden 4th series 18 (London, 1977).

[31] See *Secreta secretorum: Nine English Versions*, ed. M. A. Manzalaoui, EETS OS 276 (Oxford, 1977). The *Secreta* had an even longer transmission history than *De regimine*, having been translated from Arabic into Latin in the twelfth century, long before Giles's tract, while a second translation was made in the first half of the thirteenth century.

poets' comparable works such as instructional poems by Lydgate and Hoccleve. It was also a popular work in the modern sense of the word.[32]

With as many as sixty manuscripts of Giles's *De regimine principum* and many more of the *Secreta secretorum* in use in fifteenth-century England, it is reasonable to assume that Malory's first audiences would have been at least aware of the advice contained in these tracts, even if they did not in fact shape their behaviour in accordance with the precepts advocated in them. Evidence from this type of literature can, therefore, be used to contextualise not only Lancelot's behaviour but also the court's reaction to it in the episode under discussion. This context assists us with reading the ways in which public (here political) behaviour is learned, and reactions are and can be orchestrated or manipulated. Yet these responses are experienced as completely embedded in the natural course of social life, proving how cultural norms discipline even the emotions presumed to be 'uncontrollable', as in Larrington's analysis.

These tracts contain an average of three to four chapters on governance of the self and guidance on temperance, but also three to four chapters on the properties, choice, and conditions of a good counsellor and the tests to which a good lord or king should subject his counsellor. The *Secreta* also contains extensive guidance on physiognomy, as well as ways in which one can tell a well-wisher or good lover (of the same sex), by keen observation of his behaviour and, above all, his tearful aspect when looking on his friend:

> And thou se a man that is glad laughyng, and whan he lokith on the is dredy and ashamyd, and his visage wexith reed and sigheth, and the teeres fallen in his eyene when thou blamyst him, wite welle that he doutith and lovith moche thi persone.[33]

A comparison with Malory's *Morte* reveals that the emotions experienced by both Arthur and Lancelot are depicted as genuine in the episode under discussion, and would be perceived as such by the two protagonists, by the court witnessing the event, and by Malory's audience.[34]

Other detailed aspects of physiognomy and voice also correspond with the episode, in particular Lancelot's sadness and tears. In the *Secreta* a 'rightful' man is to be recognised by his voice and manner of address:

> … who-so hath the voyce grete and plesaunt, and wel hardyn, he is chyualerous, plesaunt and eloquente. Who-so hath the voyce meene betwen grete and smale, he is wise, Purueyaunt, veritable, and ryghtfull.[35]

---

[32] See J. Scattergood, 'Peter Idley and George Ashby', in *A Companion to Fifteenth-Century English Poetry*, ed. J. Boffey and A. S. G. Edwards (Cambridge, 2013), pp. 113–25.
[33] *Three Prose Versions*, ed. Steele, p. 38.
[34] Another relevant example is when Bors has an opportunity to kill Arthur and 'make an ende of thys warre' and Lancelot stops him (1192.14–15). There Arthur sheds tears at the sight of Lancelot's gesture, being reminded of the great nobility of his friend (1192.28–31).
[35] *Three Prose Versions*, ed. Steele, p. 234.

For those present, therefore, irrespective of the truth value of Lancelot's words, his chivalrous and noble nature, his pleasant and eloquent exposition, and his well-crafted speeches, show him in the best light, as a 'ryghtfull' man, whose voice should be heard (and whose arguments credited). In this context the personal (in terms of friendship with Arthur) and public assessments of Lancelot's speeches, and his present and proposed actions (returning Guenevere to Arthur and offering to do penance for his accidental killing of Gareth and Gaheris) seem to push the issues of truthfulness in his allegations beyond the framework of debate. The courtiers' tears now stand as a reminder that Lancelot may be seen to conform to accepted rules of conduct when he appeals to past service and his accepted position at the Round Table by virtue of service to the king, queen, and fellow knights.

By contrast, Gawain appears as the very embodiment of haste and anger, both triggers of violence and vengeance, and thus as a symbol of intemperance easily recognised by a medieval audience within and outside the text. Despite the debatable nature of the truth value of Lancelot's words, Malory seems to suggest that Arthur and the court accept Lancelot's behaviour on the terms proposed in the *Secreta*. His nobility is recognised within these parameters, and the tears may be understood as a confirmation of the clash between the ideals of the Arthurian world and the impossible task of stopping their imminent demise. From this perspective they can be seen to have little to do with the semantic content / illocutionary aspect of Lancelot's utterances.

Interestingly, the author of the *Secreta* gives no details about other methods to discern a man's truthfulness, but only his 'rightfulness'. An accepted code of behaviour and the key to its interpretation are both stipulated here, suggesting ways in which one should conduct oneself in society and judge others. By contrast, regarding the man who displays haste and anger, the *Secreta* says:

> Who-so hath the worde hasty, yf he haue a smale voyce, he is angri, fole, Enuyous, *and* a liere: And yf his voice be grete, he is angri and *hasty*.[36]

If read from this perspective, Aggravain and Mordred's plot (to expose Lancelot and Guenevere), as it is conducted in private and motivated by envy, with 'small voice', reveals them as angry men, envious of others and eager to lie in order to achieve their ends. The comparison also helps identify Gawain as one who used to be the voice of wisdom, when he advised Arthur not to be over-hasty in judging the queen, but who then became an anti-hero himself, by behaving with haste and anger.[37]

---

[36] Ibid. Gawain and later Arthur repeatedly lament the rupture of this friendship, a result of Aggravain's and Mordred's initial 'noise', seen as the opposite of the 'small voice' a loyal friend would possess.

[37] See discussion in Radulescu, *Gentry Context*, ch. 4.

In conclusion, Lancelot's, Arthur's, and indeed the court's tears would have been assessed against the relevant literature which stated rules of public engagement, including the tacit acceptance of inclusive public displays of emotion in highly politicised moments. The medieval cultural framework can be expressed, moreover, in modern terminology. The reactions and emotions explored in Malory's *Morte* display a sophisticated form of 'strategic social intelligence' that, neuropsychologists tell us, represents the ability to perform internal cognitive modelling of social relationships, in order to understand, predict, and manipulate the behaviour of others. Malory's Arthuriad transcends any such conscious or unconscious modelling of behaviour, however: the ideals it is governed by elicit emotions that transcend the boundaries of time and criticism.

7

Mourning Gawein: Cognition and Affect in Diu Crône *and Some French Gauvain-Texts*

CAROLYNE LARRINGTON

In Heinrich von dem Türlin's romance *Diu Crône*, dated to the early thirteenth century and composed in Austria, the knight Gigamec rides to Arthur's court with the head of Gawein's physical double, Aamanz, whom he has just slain. His claim to have killed Arthur's most eminent knight provokes a series of emotional displays and utterances from Keii, from Arthur, from Gawein's wife, Amurfina, and from the rest of the court. Heinrich's audience, however, knows that Gawein is alive and well and is on a quest elsewhere, as the narrator has related the death of Aamanz and thus accounted for the deception in advance. This essay investigates this elaborate scene of mourning and its function within a highly complex Arthurian text. It will also consider two other episodes in contemporary French romances – *Le Chevalier aux Deux Épées* and *L'Atre Périlleux* – in which Gawain is falsely believed to be dead: the 'Gawain als Scheintoter' (Gawain as apparently dead) topos.[1]

At the most fundamental level, texts depict the emotions of characters as responses to the vicissitudes and successes that they experience in pursuit of their goals within the plot. Psychologists (in particular, Keith Oatley, Ed Tan and T. J. Scheff) have analysed literary emotion episodes as producing identificatory or empathetic emotion in their audiences or as triggering autobiographical memories of similar emotion.[2] Literary texts can contain mimetic simulations of real-world emotion scripts: the events

---

[1] On Gawein as Scheintoter, see B. Schmolke-Hasselman, *Der arthurische Versroman von Chrestien bis Froissart: zur Geschichte einer Gattung* (Tübingen, 1980), pp. 100–6, or B. Schmolke-Hasselman, *The Evolution of Arthurian Romance: The Verse Tradition from Chrétien to Froissart*, trans. M. and R. Middleton (Cambridge, 1998), pp. 122–9.

[2] See K. Oatley, 'A Taxonomy of the Emotions of Literary Response and a Theory of Identification in Fictional Narrative', *Poetics* 23 (1994), 53–74; K. Oatley, 'Why Fiction May Be Twice as True as Fact: Fiction as Cognitive and Emotional Simulation', *Review of General Psychology* 3 (1999), 101–17, and, most recently, R. A. Mar, K. Oatley et al., 'Emotion and Narrative Fiction: Interactive Influence before, during, and after Reading', *Cognition and Emotion* 25 (2011), 818–33; further, E. S.-H. Tan, 'Film-Induced Affect as a Witness Emotion', *Poetics* 23 (1994), 7–32, and T. J. Scheff, *Catharsis in Healing, Ritual, and Drama* (Berkeley, 1979).

represented in literary texts are those which produce emotion in real life, and hence the running of the simulation within the text evokes emotions in the audience or reader.[3] Emotional engagement with the mourning emotions and behaviour in *Diu Crône* on the part of its audience may thus be predicted. But what happens when, as is the case in *Diu Crône* and the two French romances that are discussed below, the audience knows from the outset that Gawein/Gauvain is not dead at all?[4] In these cases the 'mirror characters', as Frank Brandsma terms them, encourage an audience response which, although socially congruent with the situation within the text, is at odds with the audience's cognitive assessment of the episode.[5] This calls for, as I shall argue below, a different audience understanding and response than is produced by other episodes of high emotion.[6]

Tan's analysis makes a useful distinction between A-emotions and F-emotions. A or 'artefact-based' emotions are related to audience appreciation of the work of art, while F or 'fiction-based' emotions are stimulated by elements of the fictional world within the artefact.[7] An audience may thus experience pleasure, wonder or annoyance at *the way* in which the fiction is presented, while simultaneously responding – through identification or empathy – to events in the artefact's fiction. Miall and Kuiken refine Tan's A- and F-emotion model to distinguish between feelings (their term) at four levels: 1) the satisfaction produced by an already interpreted text (A-emotion); 2) empathetic or sympathetic feelings elicited by figures within the fiction (F-Emotion); 3) feelings of fascination produced in response to the formal qualities of the text (A-emotion); 4) finally, feelings produced by an *interaction* of fictional and aesthetic feelings, self-modifying feelings 'that restructure the reader's understanding of the textual narrative and, simultaneously, the reader's sense of self'.[8]

---

[3] Oatley, 'Why Fiction', derived from Tan, 'Film-Induced Affect' and Mar, Oatley et al., 'Emotion and Narrative Fiction', pp. 822–6.

[4] Tan argues that characters' appraisal of their situations is crucial to the empathy produced in the audience. In addition to effects of dramatic irony, audience emotions such as pity, *Schadenfreude* or, as I argue below, anticipation depend on the audience employing theory of mind to extrapolate what the character is thinking, especially where the audience itself has a different perspective, a fuller understanding, and thus a different appraisal of the situation; see 'Film-Induced Affect', pp. 18–19.

[5] F. Brandsma, 'Mirror Characters', in *Courtly Arts and the Art of Courtliness*, ed. K. Busby and C. Kleinhenz (Cambridge, 2006), pp. 275–84, and cf. F. Brandsma, 'Arthurian Emotions', *Actes du 22e Congrès de la Société Internationale Arthurienne* (Rennes 2008), http://www.uhb.fr/alc/ias/actes/index.htm, 15 July, session 2 L2: Conte du Graal et émotions.

[6] For example, where audience members can suppress emotional responses either by reminding themselves that the characters are fictional constructs, or by speculating that the romance genre would not permit the death of a major protagonist in the individual work or in the larger Arthurian intertext. Here it is worth noting the difference between the oral narrative, where the audience has no particular sense of how much more of the work remains after the supposed death of the character, and the reader's clear apprehension of how many pages of the literary work remain to be read.

[7] Tan, 'Film-Induced Affect', p. 13.

[8] D. S. Miall and D. Kuiken, 'A Feeling for Fiction: Becoming What We Behold', *Poetics* 30

A final consideration relevant to medieval audiences is the social nature of emotion, as recently highlighted by Brian Parkinson.[9] Unlike the modern solitary reader, medieval audiences consumed texts – particularly romance texts, postulated as appealing to socially varied audiences – in group settings, where social appraisal, the cues given by the reactions of others within the audience, becomes critical to the activation of individuals' emotions. For, as Parkinson argues,

> emotions are active and embodied modes of engagement with the social and practical world. They reconfigure relations between people and objects in the shared environment as well as responding to, and conveying information about, these relations.[10]

What happens then when the audience's emotional connection with 'narrative truth' is severed, when audience appraisal contradicts the appraisals of the characters within the text? How might the audience's empathic response to the performance of grief be affected when that grief is premised on error, rumour or a fantastic coincidence? I will focus my discussion and argument on the extended episode in *Diu Crône*, and the two French episodes, but I will also consider briefly the place of these mourning scenes in the larger Arthurian intertextual universe, suggesting some ways in which the death of Gawein/Gauvain is treated as a kind of 'thought-experiment' for Arthurian writers and anticipating the moment where, within the many iterations of the *Mort Artu* in English and French, Arthur's nephew does – finally – die.

Diu Crône

The sequence in *Diu Crône* opens at an outdoor scene of feasting at the court.[11] The court has been hunting the white hart, that epitome of collective aristocratic activity, when Gigamec rides up and arrogantly announces: 'sehent hie daz houbt an, / daz ich hie in der hant hân: / daz ist Gâweins gewesen' (ll. 16767–9) (look at the head that I have here in my hand: it was Gawein's). Dropping the head, covered with a cloth, on the table, Gigamec rides away, anticipating that some court champion will

---

(2002), 221–41, at p. 223. For the neuropsychology of anticipation, see D. S. Miall, 'Anticipation and Feeling in Literary Response: A Neuropsychological Perspective', *Poetics* 23 (1995), 275–98.

[9] B. Parkinson, 'How Social is the Social Psychology of Emotion?', *British Journal of Social Psychology* 50 (2011), 405–13.

[10] Parkinson, 'How Social', p. 409.

[11] This episode: Heinrich von dem Türlin, *Diu Crône: Mittelhochdeutsche Leseausgabe mit Erläuterungen*, ed. G. Felder (Berlin and Boston, 2012), pp. 265–73, ll. 16713–17313. Translation: *The Crown*, trans. J. W. Thomas (Lincoln, NE and London, 1989), pp. 189–95. All further references are cited from this edition, with line-numbers given parenthetically. Translations are from Thomas's *The Crown*, though in places I have adapted them.

pursue and challenge him in vengeance for Gawein. The court's reaction is perhaps unexpected: assuming that Gigamec is either very angry (expressing *etelîchen zorn*) or else playing a joke (*spot*), the whole court – except Keii – bursts into laughter. Keii, however, maintains that this could be a punishment for the court's sins and that Gigamec may be telling the truth. He uncovers the head; its back is turned towards the king so only Keii can see the face. The seneschal reacts powerfully to the sight, with *jâmer*, *klagen* and *weinen* (misery, complaining and weeping). He weeps, kisses the head many times, wails, falls silent and then repeats this series of reactions before falling to the ground in a swoon. Other courtiers now loudly lament; no one can take the head from Keii who, even unconscious, is clutching it tightly. Keii revives, and utters a formal lament, 'diu sô senlîch was / daz von ir ein adamas / gar möhte sîn zerkloben' (ll. 16937–9), (so distressing it could have cloven a diamond). Chrétien (*meister Cristian*) is identified as the source for Keii's lament, perhaps with reference to the reaction of king and court to the absence of Gauvain at the Pentecost feast at the very end of the *Conte del Graal*.[12] Here Artus is described as *mornes et pansis* (l. 8946) (gloomy and pensive); when he surveys the assembled court and fails to see his nephew, 'si chiet pasmez par grant destrece' (l. 8949) (he faints from great distress). Heinrich makes frequent, often disparaging, reference to Chrétien throughout the poem, and this remark seems likely to be part of an intertextual joke about the *Conte*'s abrupt and incomplete ending. The first *Continuation*, which starts at exactly this point in a number of manuscripts, speedily puts the king and court's minds at rest by showing the arrival of Gauvain's messenger, who had, before the end of the *Conte*, been dispatched with the news of his lord's continuing good health. General rejoicing breaks out at the news.[13]

In his extended lament, Keii challenges God's will, and, astonishingly, suggests that Arthur should relinquish the crown:

> künic Artûs, ir sollent ûf seln
> daz rîch und die krône
> und gebent ime daz ze lône
> das iuwer vröud an ime stuont,
> alsô vriunden vriunde tuont. (ll. 17026–30).
>
> (King Arthur, you should relinquish the realm and the crown and give them as a reward to him on whom your joy depended, as a friend does with friends).

---

[12] G. Felder, *Kommentar zur >Crône< Heinrichs von dem Türlin* (Berlin and New York, 2006), p. 462. *Le Conte du Graal*, in *Les Romans de Chrétien de Troyes*, ed. F. Lecoy, 6 vols (Paris, 1972–5), here V. 8946–60; my translation.

[13] *The Continuations of the Perceval of Chrétien de Troyes*, ed. W. Roach, 6 vols (Philadelphia, 1949), I: ll. 1–92.

The tense is not a past conditional (Arthur, you should have ...), but it nevertheless attends to an unreal condition – an extraordinary, and apparently illogical, demand. Renouncing the throne in favour of a dead man can scarcely amount to practical politics, and we might wonder whether mourning creates a space in which uncomfortable truths can be uttered. Keii now exhorts all knights, squires and ladies to join him in his mourning and directs how this should be done: knights must wail and lament, ladies put aside their finery. He thus leads and cues the court in appropriate mourning behaviour, as indeed a seneschal should.[14] And now the rest of the court join in, rending their clothes and tearing at their bodies. Ladies kiss the head, tears rolling down their cheeks; they lacerate their robes and disarrange their hair, wring their hands and beat their breasts. Gawein's wife, Amurfina, and her sister Sgoidamur approach. Amurfina takes up the head and kisses it, then utters a lament in which she celebrates Gawein's virtues and courage and pitifully laments her own plight. She curses Amor, wishing that she had never fallen in love with Gawein, curses the day and the place where her husband fell and finally faints into her sister's arms. Amurfina's collapse marks the climax of the mourning scene. Even had he time, Heinrich notes, to describe how each individual lamented Gawein, the story drives him onward, 'die mære mich vürbaz jeit' (l. 17311). The court itself remains, as it were, in a vacuum, 'quasi im luftleeren Raum', as Matthias Meyer notes.[15] Heinrich leaves behind 'die grôze klage' (l. 17312) (the great lament), and turns to the further adventures of Gawein, who is making his way through the forest, quite unaware of the distress and uproar at Arthur's court.

Critics have taken widely differing views of this episode. For Lewis Jillings, the court's emotional display, in particular Keii's astonishing demand that Arthur relinquish the throne to Gawein, is of a piece with his general argument that Heinrich's intention is primarily parodic.[16] The audience ought to find the scene 'grotesque[ly] comic' and there are 'numerous levels of irony' in Keii's words. Meyer argues to the contrary: that *Diu Crône* is engaged in a re-evaluation (*Umwertung*) of Keii's character and role.[17] The multiple aspects of Keii's lament demonstrate both a reversion to his earlier role as Arthur's representative and an appropriate reaction which contrasts sharply with Arthur's and the rest of the

---

[14] Personal communication with Matthias Meyer; see also M. Meyer, *Die Verfügbarkeit der Fiktion: Interpretationen und poetologische Untersuchungen zum Artusroman und zur aventiurehaften Dietrichepik des 13. Jahrhunderts* (Heidelberg, 1994), pp. 136–9, for insightful discussion of this scene.

[15] Meyer, *Die Verfügbarkeit*, p. 139.

[16] L. Jillings, *Diu Crone of Heinrich von dem Türlein: The Attempted Emancipation of Secular Narrative* (Göppingen, 1980), pp. 91–2. He argues that Keii's role as chief court performer of grief discredits the emotional display in itself, for Keii's judgement is consistently wrong and his performance is generally inept in Arthurian romance.

[17] Meyer, *Die Verfügbarkeit*, p. 137.

court's apparent paralysis.[18] Arno Mentzel-Reuters also denies the ironic effect, taking the episode, despite its mistaken premise, at face value within its context, as reflecting 'die Explizierung der ideellen Verbindung zwischen Herrschaft und höfische Lebenformen' (the making explicit of the idealized connection between lordship and courtly ways of life).[19] For Menzel-Reuters, Keii's example and verbal direction to the court to display appropriate mourning behaviour confirm the intuition that this is the correct emotional reaction both within and beyond the fiction to the death of a major heroic character. That he is not in fact dead should not disturb the expected emotional response.

Gudrun Felder suggests that Keii's demand that Arthur relinquish his rule is an 'übersteigerter Trauergestus' (exaggerated manifestation of sorrow), which serves to confirm Gawein as Arthur's heir.[20] More plausibly, Keii's proposition gestures towards a hypothetical condition: one which explores an alternative possibility that, given the apparent narrative situation, is already closed off. In the Middle English *Sir Gawain and the Green Knight* (second half of the thirteenth century) a comparable alternative scenario is sketched in order to express the court's grief when Gawain departs to seek the Green Chapel and to withstand the return blow. Instead of allowing Gawain to set out to be 'britned to noȝt, / Hadet wyth an aluisch mon' (ll. 680–81) (smashed to nothing, embroiled with an elvish man), the courtiers complain, Arthur should 'warloker ... haf wroȝt .../ And haf dyȝt ȝonder dere a duk to haue worþed' (ll. 677–8) (have acted more cautiously and have promoted that good man to be a duke).[21] The court's criticism is predicated on an impossible and unfulfillable condition, for Gawain has already ridden away. Moreover, given Gawain's understanding of his chivalric obligation to keep his promise to the Green Knight, the king's perception that his nephew must fulfil his oath and the poet's own warning at the end of Fitt 1 that Gawain should think well about the adventure he has undertaken, the king could never have prevented Gawain's departure. The contrast between promotion to greater and well-deserved honour and the desperate fate that the court fears will overtake the knight parallels Keii's imagining of an alternative

---

[18] Meyer, *Die Verfügbarkeit*, p. 138.
[19] A. Mentzel-Reuters, *Vröude: Artusbild, Fortuna- und Gralkonzeption in der >Crône< des Heinrich von dem Türlin als Verteidigung des höfischen Lebensideals* (Frankfurt and Berlin, 1989), p. 132; cf. Felder, *Kommentar*, p. 463. See Fritz Peter Knapp's objection to importing our own modern emotional reaction – to view the court's behaviour as ridiculous and excessive – into the text. F. P. Knapp, *Chevalier errant und fin'amor: das Ritterideal des 13. Jahrhunderts in Nordfrankreich und im deutschsprachigen Südosten* (Passau, 1986), p. 93, n. 171.
[20] Felder, *Kommentar*, p. 468. Cf. Mentzel-Reuters, *Vröude*: 'sein Tod ... macht auch Reich und Herrschaft obsolet' (his death ... moreover makes kingdom and rule obsolete), p. 134.
[21] *Sir Gawain and the Green Knight*, in *The Poems of the Pearl Manuscript*, ed. M. Andrew and R. Waldron, 5th rev. edn (Exeter, 2007). My translation.

universe in which Gawein is not only restored to life, but also exercises royal rule.

Felder, among others, notes the extensive range of emotional behaviours displayed by the court, identifying them as belonging to a repertoire of thirteenth-century 'exaltierte' *Trauergestus*.[22] Since important protagonists rarely die in Arthurian romance, parallels to the court's performance here are not altogether easy to find. Nevertheless, Gawain himself is stricken by a comparable grief when he learns of the death of his brothers at the hands of Lancelot and his allies in the *Mort Artu* (and, in a slightly more moderate fashion, in Malory).[23] The king shows Gauvain the dead body of Gaheriet and

> li faut touz li cuers, si chiet a terre pasmez ... Quant messire Gauvains revint de pasmoisons, si se dreça et cort la ou il voit Gaheriet mort ... et l'estraint contre son pis et le commence a besier; en cel besier li faut li cuers; si chiet a terre ... en pasmoisons.
>
> (his heart failed him and he fell to the ground in a faint ... When sir Gawain regained consciousness, he leapt up and ran to the body of Gaheriet ... he embraced it against his chest and started to kiss it. Thereupon his heart failed him, and he fell to the ground ... in a faint.)

When he has recovered his senses, Gauvain utters a lament for Gaheriet, remonstrating with Fortune and vowing vengeance. After sitting a while in grief-stricken silence, Gauvain becomes aware of the corpses of his other brothers. He flings himself upon their bodies, faints once again, and Arthur's barons, fearing for his life, advise that he be put to bed, while the brothers – whose bodies provide a stimulus for renewed grief – are buried.

The collective mourning of the court in *Diu Crône* then, despite its mistaken premise, is not out of line with Gauvain's grief reactions when his brothers are demonstrably dead. Interpreting this episode as modelling an 'exaltierte *Trauergestus*' seems thus to be justified. Heinrich himself approves the collective performance with a sententious comment:

> von reht michel klage geschiht,
> swâ ein guoter ververt,
> der sich an êren hât gewert,
> daz den der tôt niht enschert! (ll. 17169–72)

---

[22] Felder, *Kommentar*, p. 463, cf. Mentzel-Reuters, *Vröude*, p. 132.
[23] *La Mort le roi Artu: roman du XIIIe siècle*, ed. J. Frappier (Geneva, 1964), pp. 127–33, at p. 131; *Lancelot-Grail. The Old French Arthurian Vulgate and Post-Vulgate in Translation*, trans. N. J. Lacy et al., 5 vols (New York and London, 1992–6) (hereafter *L-G*), IV.125. Sir Thomas Malory, *Le Morte Darthur*, ed. P. J. C. Field, Arthurian Studies LXXX, 2 vols (Cambridge, 2013), I: 887–8.

> (It is right that there should be great lamenting when such a good man passes away, one who has gained honour for himself, so that death does not cut him off entirely!)

The functional effect of Gawein's 'death' within the plot is liberating for Arthur's nephew, notes Almut Suerbaum: 'Gigamec's lie has made Gawein a non-person, he is free to pursue adventures which take him into the realm of the Other World.'[24] Suerbaum also draws attention to Heinrich's deliberate manipulation of the audience's cognitive appraisal and emotional affect. 'The aim of these narrative interventions is to give profile to the role of the narrator, and to highlight the difference between the knowledge and insight of the narrator and his audiences, and the knowledge and insight of the figures within the narrative.'[25] As in the French romances discussed below, the mistaken assumption permits, as Mentzel-Reuters terms it, a kind of 'Gedankenexperiment' (thought-experiment) – what might Arthurian courtly life be without Gawein?[26]

Brandsma has recently argued that the Arthurian court can itself function as a distinct emotional entity, vividly expressing basic emotions, such as joy and sorrow, and more cognitively complex ones: for example, shame.[27] Brandsma considers an episode in the *Lancelot* in which Lancelot is erroneously assumed by king, queen and court to have been killed.[28] In this episode, as in the examples discussed in this essay, the audience knows perfectly well that the mourners are mistaken. The emotions displayed by the court there, as in this self-contained *Diu Crône* sequence, might be regarded as excessive, given the hypothetical nature of the situation, though Brandsma prefers to interpret the episode as ironic rather than parodic. These gaps between the audience's instinctive empathy with stricken mourners and their superior knowledge open up interesting questions about their affective and cognitive engagement with the texts they consumed. I return below to these questions, after discussing two further parallels to Gawein's supposed death.

Gawain as 'Scheintoter' in French Romance

When Gauvain is falsely assumed to be dead in the French romance *Le Chevalier as deus espees* (probably 1215–30, thus broadly contemporaneous

---

[24] A. Suerbaum, '"Entrelacement?" Narrative Technique in Heinrich von dem Türlîn's *Diu Crône*', *Oxford German Studies* 34.1 (2005), 5–18, at pp. 13–14.
[25] Suerbaum, '"Entrelacement?"', p. 14.
[26] Menzel-Reuters, *Vröude*, p. 133.
[27] F. Brandsma, 'The Court's Emotions', *Cultures courtoises en mouvement*, ed. I. Arseneau and F. Gingras (Montréal, 2011), pp. 74–82, in particular, pp. 80–81.
[28] *Lancelot: roman en prose du XIIIe siècle*, ed. A. Micha, 9 vols (Geneva, 1978–83), II: LIII: 1–13. Translation: *L-G*, III: 82–3. The episode continues in *Lancelot*, ed. Micha, II, LX, 1–14; *L-G*, III: 84–5.

with *Diu Crône*), the emotional outcomes are very different from those we have seen in the Austrian text.[29] Gauvain's supposed death comes about because of his superlative reputation, a reputation that he particularly enjoys in the estimation of women. The Queen of the Isles has promised to wed Brien, who loves her, only if he can show that he is a better knight than Gauvain by killing him (a motif and motive shared by *L'Âtre Périlleux*).[30] When he encounters Gauvain roaming about near the court on a beautiful spring morning, Brien elicits his name, attacks him (despite his lack of armour) and leaves him for dead.[31] He is overjoyed when he realizes that his blade has pierced Gauvain's stomach, '[s]'en est a demesure liés' (l. 3055) (he was overjoyed about this); 'il a de la joie grant' (l. 3064) (he had great joy). Pausing only to thank God for his victory, and noting that to behead Gauvain would be 'vilains' since the king's nephew is so well known, Brien departs into the forest, clapping his hands with joy and declaring the whole episode the most wonderful adventure ('la plus biele aventure', (l. 3094)).[32]

Gauvain meanwhile staggers back to his lodgings, where he takes to his bed. The king and queen come to visit him when he does not appear at court; when they see how seriously injured he is, they are extremely upset. The king faints and grieves; the queen, whose sorrow is indescribable (*nus hons ne pooroit retraire*) tears and pulls out her hair. So do the other ladies, while the knights are filled with rage; the court's unhappiness is a communal emotion, publicly performed: 'Ja n'ert huiseus, je vous plevis, / Nus de duel faire, ne de plourer' (ll. 3288–9) (they were by no means averse to displaying their sorrow, nor to crying). Only when Gauvain begs them to stop lamenting and to send him some doctors does their sorrow diminish. The king makes a speech praising his nephew and vowing vengeance; though he does not go so far as to suggest that Gauvain is worthy of his kingdom, he confirms that his nephew is indispensable, wondering how he might protect his lands if Gauvain were to die. The public performance of sorrow is less extreme than in *Diu Crône*; for, although Gauvain is seriously injured, his wounds are not critical. The poet's description of the court's grief is not perfunctory, but neither does it verge on excess.

Later, when a recovered Gauvain sets out on the quest to find Mériadeuc (the *chevalier as deus espees*) and to achieve vengeance for the attack

---

[29] *French Romance: III: Le Chevalier as deus espees*, ed. and trans. P. V. Rockwell, Arthurian Archives XIII (Cambridge, 2006). All citations and translations from this edition, henceforth noted by line number in text.
[30] See S. Atanassov, *L'idole inconnu: le personnage de Gauvain dans quelques romans du XIIIe siècle* (Orléans, 2000), on the development of the motif in the thirteenth century.
[31] Gauvain's consistent habit of refusing ever to withhold his name does him a disservice here.
[32] Atanassov notes the comic speed with which the elated Brien hastens to spread the word of Gauvain's demise: *L'idole inconnu*, p. 91.

on him, he soon encounters an elderly pilgrim, who enquires whether he knows where Gauvain is buried:

> 'Gist?' dist il, 'Comment?' Et cil dist:
> 'Mors.' 'Mors n'est il encore pas,'
> Dist mesire Gauvains. 'C'est gas.' (ll. 3618–20)

> ('Lying?' he asked, 'How so?' And he replied: 'Dead.' 'He is not dead yet,' said my lord Gawain. 'This is a joke.')

The unwelcome news that Gauvain is still alive causes the pilgrim to turn livid with anger (*il norcist de corous*) (ll. 3632–3); on learning that his interlocutor is indeed Gauvain he faints dead away. The pilgrim is revealed to be Brien's father, whose hopes for his son's promotion to the rank of King of the Isles are thereby dashed; he curses Gauvain as he departs. The knight seeks lodging in a nearby hermitage where a courtly knight-turned-hermit and his churlish servant offer hospitality. But the hermit recognizes his guest as Gauvain, the man whom his nephew Brien had bragged of killing. *Tous mautalentis et iriés* (l. 3815) (full of hatred and anger), the hermit orders the churl to murder the sleeping knight. The servant is on the verge of striking Gauvain with his axe when the hermit recalls his religious duty (and indeed the obligations of a host) and realizes that it is Brien who is in the wrong. The next day Gauvain meets in the forest a youth who is on his way to invite the hermit to Brien's wedding; thus he learns the identity of his assailant and determines to reveal the truth about their encounter to the public who will be present at the ceremony.[33]

En route, Gauvain pauses to take part in an adventure which wins him the hand of a beautiful girl, the Damoisele du Castiel du Port. At a critical moment in their love-making, disappointingly for Gauvain, she suddenly remembers that she has previously vowed her virginity to the distant idea of Gauvain, and cannot love another now that he is dead. The very improbability of the situation, suggests Atanassov, suggests that 'une nouvelle logique de répresentation' is at work, pointing up the ways in which the romance's characters are interested only in the *idea* of Gauvain, not his embodied form.[34] For Brien, all that mattered was the *récit* of his victory over his enemy; he fails to engage with the 'real' Gauvain sufficiently closely to seal his victory by taking his head. Just so, the Damoisele's emotions are so invested in her idea of Gauvain that she cannot recognize the desirable – and desiring – body of Gauvain

---

[33] Gauvain subsequently spends the night in a castle belonging to Brien's cousin; the lord challenges him when he learns his identity: he is furious and the blood drains from his face (*si fu iriés et li fuï / li sans*) (ll. 4112–13). Gauvain defeats him, breaking his collar-bone, and rides on.

[34] Atanassov, *L'idole inconnu*, p. 97. See also on Gauvain/Gawan's character in the wider context, M. Meyer, 'It's hard to be me, or Walewein/Gawan as Hero', *Arthurian Literature* 17 (1999), 63–78.

in her bedchamber. The Damoisele's passion for a knight she has never met chimes with that of the Queen of the Isles, whose *amour lointain* for Gauvain first provoked Brien to try to prove his superiority through his unchivalric attack.

The amorous knight feels sure that the news that *he* is Gauvain will resolve the girl's sorrow satisfactorily, but she flatly refuses to believe him and their night of passion terminates abruptly. Next day she insists on departing to Arthur's court, where, discovering the truth, she remains to await the return of her lover. At last Gauvain arrives at the grand public ceremonies accompanying Brien's wedding to the Queen of the Isles: a formal reading of the queen's agreement that her marriage to the knight is conditional upon his having vanquished or slain Gauvain in single combat. Brien declares publicly, 'Gauvains est ocis voirement / Je sui cil ki l'ocist sans faille' (ll. 5526–7) (Gawain is truly dead / I am the one who killed him). When Gauvain openly contradicts him, '[h]onteus fu Brïens et dolens' (l. 5757) (Brien was ashamed and distressed). The supposed corpse soon proves the truth of his account in combat with the unhappy bridegroom. The marriage is called off, while Brien is sent to render himself as a prisoner at Arthur's court. The intended bride falls more deeply in love with Gauvain now that she has seen him in the flesh, though, like the Damoisele du Castiel du Port, she first failed to recognize him. Many more partings and battles ensue before Brien is rehabilitated (though he never wins back the queen he had hoped to marry, nor does he gain the title of King of the Isles). Gauvain is reunited with his sceptical Damoisele at the wedding of the knight with the two swords and his bride.

In this text, the supposed death of Gauvain is never reported to the court and thus it excites no profound emotional reactions, although the knight's injuries are sufficient grounds for a display of grief when the king and queen come to visit him. Brien's misapprehension about the success of his attack on Gauvain functions to set up a series of testing encounters for the minor characters who belong to his family. The comic fury of his father and uncle, pilgrim and hermit, draws a pointed contrast between their social aspirations for Brien and their religious callings, while Gauvain's encounter with Brien's cousin follows the usual trajectory of knightly challenge and combat.[35] Emotional expectations are reversed for these characters: instead of rejoicing at the news that Arthur's great knight is alive and well, Brien's partisans fiercely deplore Gauvain's survival. The elderly pilgrim curses him, while the hermit comes within a hair's breadth of having the apparently sleeping knight murdered. Long before the poem's climax Brien's social inadequacy is confirmed by his relatives' horribly uncourtly behaviour when they come face to face with

---

[35] See footnote 33.

a live Gauvain. Thus the lowly son of a vavasour gets his comeuppance: justly punished for his overweening pride in his accomplishments and appearance, his unchivalric attack on Gauvain (apparently motivated as much by social ambition as by jealousy of a rival for his lady's affections) and his pretensions to the hand of a queen, far above him in lineage and status.

For the audience then, *Le Chevalier as deus epees* produces literary pleasure through both artefact-effects and fiction-effects, to revert to the terms suggested by Tan. The effects at work here are as much intertextual as intratextual. Familiar tropes from earlier romance – the *amour lointain* felt for Gauvain by women who have never met him, but who are impressed by his reputation, his well-attested habit of never concealing his name, his prowess as lover when he meets attractive young ladies and his habitual courtesy and modesty – animate a plot which makes play with, even ironizes, Gauvain's celebrity status. Gauvain's expectations of sexual success, his pride in his name and ancestry and his popularity with high and low alike are characteristics deployed with unexpected results. Within the fiction, the audience seems likely to enjoy various comic high points: when Gauvain cuts off the court's extravagant mourning for his plight with a brisk demand for doctors, when his serial revelations that he is in fact alive produce rage rather than relief, and finally when his sexual advances are baulked at the *moment critique* by a troubling doubt about his identity, a motif which recurs elsewhere in Gawain-narratives.[36]

The assumption of his non-existence unsettles Gauvain's understanding of himself, ironically and comically developed when his revelation of identity has the effect of bringing to a halt his erotic activity rather than allowing the damsel to yield her virginity to the man for whom she had always intended it. When the couple are reunited at the court, the Damoisele explains that she could not believe he was Gauvain, because the 'real' Gauvain would not have desisted in his love-making as he so courteously had. Play is made with Gauvain's 'ironic identity' as Rockwell terms it, just as *Sir Gawain and the Green Knight* switches between English and French traditional, and in context equally ironic, construals of Gawain's character.[37] If the poem were, as Rockwell suggests, composed in England for Norman and Breton exiles, it seems likely that the author of *Sir Gawain and the Green Knight* may have known the romance [38] For *Sir Gawain and the Green Knight* shares suggestive themes with the earlier text: it investigates Gawain's status as representative of the Round Table in his acceptance of the Beheading Game and it pitches Gawain's erotic

---

[36] Compare, for example, Lady Bertilak's challenges to Gawain in *Sir Gawain and the Green Knight* at ll. 1293 and 1481: 'Sir, ȝif ȝe be Wawen, wonder me þynkkez' (Sir, if you are [indeed] Gawain, it seems to me a wonder).

[37] See C. Larrington, '*Sir Gawain and the Green Knight* and English Chivalry', in *The Blackwell Companion to Arthurian Literature*, ed. H. Fulton (Oxford, 2009), pp. 252–64.

[38] *Le Chevalier*, ed. Rockwell, pp. 3–5.

reputation against his actual performance in the bedchamber. In *Le Chevalier* the audience's F-emotions are satisfied when, as it anticipates, justice is done: Brien's treachery is revealed; at the poem's end reconciliation is achieved between Brien and Gauvain; and Gauvain finally becomes the Damoisele's lover.

In *L'Atre Périlleux*, a probably mid-thirteenth-century text, Gauvain rides out from the court in shame, having failed to prevent the abduction of a lady placed under his care.[39] Almost his first adventure is an encounter with three damsels, all mourning loudly.[40] The first damsel faints after claiming that her grief is inexpressible; the second announces the death of all chivalry at that very spot before fainting in her turn, while the third explains that the doyen of knightly virtue, Gauvain himself, was set upon and murdered there by three knights a little earlier. His death had been witnessed by a squire who was blinded by the assailants and who is lying near by. The ladies resume their lamentations, 'si fors / Que nus nel vous porroit retraire' (ll. 578–9) (so powerful that no one could describe them to you).[41] Their grief is not, however, accompanied by the tearing of hair or rending of clothes that is conventional in other descriptions.

When Gauvain learns the murdered knight's identity, he assures the mourners that he has just come from court where he saw Gauvain alive and well. But the squire asserts that Gauvain was slain and dismembered: the body taken away by the killers so that it cannot now be inspected.[42] The young man's blindness means that he cannot be made to account for the appearance of the real Gauvain. For the audience, the main emotional focus of the scene is aligned with Gauvain's perspective. They empathize with the knight's bafflement, and with his new dilemma: should he continue the adventure for which he left the court or should he try to investigate the maiming of the squire and his own apparent death? And, as Matthias Meyer notes of the titular hero in *Walewein*, who expresses fear of death in an interior monologue, he thus becomes 'a character ... assailed by doubts regarding his own standing which are obviously at odds with the actual importance he has within the "world" of the romance'.[43]

As in *Le Chevalier as deus espees*, Gauvain's supposed death has no impact on the court as a community, for the news never reaches the king.

---

[39] *L'Atre Périlleux*, ed. B. Woledge (Paris, 1936). All citations from this edition with line numbers given in text, with my translation. The abductor is Escanor, whose kidnap functions simply as a provocation to the court, for the lady is his *amie* and loves him, as he her.

[40] See Atanassov, *L'idole inconnue*, pp. 111–14, for analysis of the mourning scene, 'une rhapsodie à quatre voix' (a rhapsody for four voices), at p. 111.

[41] My translation.

[42] The murderers, unlike Brien in *Le Chevalier*, make sure that they have physical, though not conclusive, proof of their exploits.

[43] Meyer, 'It's hard to be me', p. 71.

And, as in *Diu Crône*, the hero finds himself 'dispossessed of his reputation as an exemplary knight and of his name', a state which allows him to embark on a particular set of adventures to recuperate his previous failure to protect the maiden from her abductor.[44] Gauvain's quest involves vigorous engagement with the supernatural in the romance's eponymous adventure, and with a series of doubles of himself, before his identity is finally re-integrated and his existence reinstated on the social plane.[45] Towards the end of the tale, Gauvain's death is narrated to him once again by Tristan-*qui-jamais-ne-rit* (Tristan who never smiles). Tristan is able to explain the motivations of the antagonists who fabricated Gauvain's death: as in *Le Chevalier*, the Orgueilleux Faé, a malevolent knight with magical powers, is frustrated by his *amie*'s preference for the king's nephew. Like the Queen of the Isles, the girl believes that she is stipulating an impossible condition when she promises her love to her suitor if he can overcome Gauvain in combat: 'Mais ja se Dix plaist n'avenra, / Car ce seroit trop grant damage' (ll. 5154–5) (But please God that will never happen, / For it would be too great a loss). Her sister likewise loves Perceval. Tristan reports that matters are now at a stand-off; the damsels rightly refuse to believe that the corpse is Gauvain's, the Orgueilleux Faé and his associates have declared that the girls must make good their promise unless a challenger can refute their assertions through trial by combat, and the sisters have sworn to commit suicide if they are forced into the murderers' arms. Gauvain and his companion Espinogre of course defeat the miscreants and force the Faé to admit the truth. Retracing his course back to Caerlion, Gauvain reveals the name he has recovered to all the knights he previously met. The Faé is magically able to restore to life the pseudo-Gauvain, significantly named 'Cortois de Huberlant' (Courteous of Huberlant), and to heal the blinded squire, Martin.[46] The mourning maidens, who still have 'le cuer tristre et noir, / Del doel de monsegnor Gavain' (ll. 6494–5) (a sad and gloomy heart in mourning for my lord Gauvain), accompany the party back to court, where great rejoicing (*joie molt grant*) (l. 6547) breaks out. The various couples are united in marriage and Gauvain is restored to his position of honour and esteem at the heart of the court. As Elizabeth Kinne has argued for *L'Atre Périlleux*, and as Felder notes of *Diu Crône*, the counter-factual exploration of the consequences of the premature loss of Gawain

---

[44] L. Morin, 'Le Soi et le double dans *L'Âtre périlleux*', *Études françaises* 32 (1996), 117–28, at p. 120 ('dépossédé de sa réputation de chevalier exemplaire et de son nom'). See also K. Busby, 'Diverging Traditions of Gauvain in Some of the Later Old French Verse Romances', in *The Legacy of Chrétien de Troyes*, ed. N. J. Lacy, D. Kelly and K. Busby, 2 vols (Amsterdam, 1988), II, pp. 93–109.

[45] See A. Combes, '*L'Atre périlleux*: cénotaphe d'un héros retrouvé', *Romania* 113 (1992–5), 140–74.

[46] Morin, 'Le soi et le double', p. 125. Gauvain's dilemma of courtesy – whether to leave the king's table to pursue Escanor or to politely wait until the end of the feast – initially gave rise to the adventure.

to the Arthurian world demonstrates his centrality as an embodiment of chivalric values.[47]

Similar A-emotion effects to those described above for *Le Chevalier as deus espees* are at work in *L'Atre Périlleux*; the text is a 'tissu de références intertextuelles', as its modern French translator observes.[48] As a result of his apparent erasure, Gauvain takes on the pseudonym of 'Cil sans Nom', the Man with no Name: witty play is made with the convention that Gauvain is the knight who always reveals his name. Although, as Atanassov comments, '[l]'intrigue de ce roman donne l'impression que plus Gauvain est aimé, moins il s'intéresse à l'amour' (the plot of this romance gives the impression that the more Gauvain is beloved, the less interested he is in love), this story is once more driven by the regard in which women hold the knight whom they have never met.[49] The variation here, in a text which surely responds to *Le chevalier as deus espees*, is the provision of a fraudulent body. This almost backfires on the malefactors when their ladies threaten to commit suicide on account of Gauvain's demise. The key emotion within the fiction, however, in contrast to the earlier romance, is suspense: how can Gauvain's supposed death be accounted for? And how can it be undone? When the Faé achieves the magical resurrection of Courtois, casually explaining that he gained the gift of magic the night that he was born, both Gauvain and his companion the Laid Hardi bless themselves against this incursion of the uncanny.[50] The resolution of the suspense through magic may be experienced as anti-climax; the villains are reformed and their victims reconstituted, but the court's joy at the end of the text provides sufficient closure to content an audience who has all along shared Gauvain's appraisal of his own situation.

Thinking about Emotion through Gawain's 'Death'

The three Arthurian texts discussed above represent and evoke emotion on different levels. Characters within the texts express a mourning which is consistently represented through a series of individual behaviours: weeping, the utterance of formal laments, fainting, the tearing of hair and clothing. They also display broader and more enduring social mourning practices such as the silencing of music, the abandonment of courtly entertainments and dressing in dark-coloured clothes without ostentatious displays of jewellery or elaborate head-dresses. The kinds of

---

[47] E. Kinne, 'Waiting for Gauvain: Lessons in Courtesy in *L'Âtre périlleux*', *Arthuriana* 18.2 (2008), 55–68; Felder, *Kommentar*, pp. 461–2.

[48] M.-L. Ollier, in *La légende arthurienne; le graal et la Table Ronde*, gen. ed. D. Régnier-Bohler (Paris, 1989), p. 608.

[49] Atanassov, *L'idole inconnue*, p. 108; compare A. Putter, *'Sir Gawain and the Green Knight' and French Arthurian Romance* (Oxford, 1995), p. 111.

[50] Presumably the Faé was endowed with his *destinee* (l. 6397) by a fairy godmother.

mourning behaviour evidenced by both court and other characters within the texts suggest that – apart from Keii's extraordinary disparagement of Arthur's rule in *Diu Crône* – the fictional figures' reponses and actions are not out of line with the mourning behaviour performed elsewhere in Arthurian texts when the narrative circumstances thoroughly justify it.

The audience, though, is not invited to empathize fully with the court's emotional display: to weep along with the noble mourners and to experience the kind of empathy famously evoked and criticized by Ælred of Rievaulx in his *Speculum caritatis*.[51] The space opened up in *Diu Crône* and *L'Atre Périlleux* by the audience's superior knowledge that there is no need to lament for a thoroughly alive Gawain produces a kind of alienation effect, allowing the emergence of a distinctively dramatic, but not necessarily morally critical, irony. Thus Heinrich's listeners are positioned as relatively disengaged spectators of the grief displays, while the poet's anatomization of mourning behaviour allows a detachment which facilitates complex emotional effects, both within the text, such as the topsy-turvy reactions to the news that Gauvain is alive in *Le Chevalier as deus espees*, and exterior to it.

The audience of each text would experience, we may hypothesize, varying kinds of complex emotions. Nevertheless, the audience's response would not, I think, be solely or even primarily ironic; as suggested above, pleasurable A-emotions derive from the audience's appreciation of the poet's skilled deployment of Gawain-related tropes. F-emotions are both stimulated and unsettled by the emotion scripts of death and mourning which the plot invites its audience to run in simulation within their own minds. The court and characters' reactions *could* be read as modelling exemplary reactions to extreme grief: culturally determined behaviour which conditions the audience's own views of the appropriate expression of mourning within a courtly context, contributing to the construction of the kinds of courtier-personas discussed by C. Stephen Jaeger.[52] Despite the false appraisals at work within the scene, emotional modelling would be a possible audience response. This would be congruent with the arguments advanced by Felder, Menzel-Reuters and others, who take the view that the mistaken premise does not matter and that the exemplary effect is paramount. As the court weeps, so the audience's mirror neuron functions would, in this light, be activated and it would find itself impelled to weep in sympathy. Whether the feeling of sorrow is (as Tan would argue) produced by the emotion script of the text (that is: a beloved knight has died) or is triggered by autobiographical memories of loss (as Scheff and others suggest) is not important here.

---

[51] Ælred of Rievaulx, *Speculum caritatis*, PL 195, col. 565D. II, 17; see on this passage, J. Tahkokallio, 'Fables of King Arthur: Ælred of Rievaulx and Secular Pastimes', *Mirator* 9:1 (2008), 19–35.

[52] C. S. Jaeger, *The Origins of Courtliness: Civilizing Trends and the Formation of Courtly Ideals, 939–1210* (Philadelphia, 1985).

Although the court's behaviour is entirely normative, according to romance genre conventions – as the comparison with the *Mort Artu* indicates – the audience's divergent cognitive appraisal (that Gawein is in fact alive) seems likely to inhibit an empathic reaction, and to open up instead different emotional possibilities. Among these might be Miall and Kuiken's type 4, self-modifying feelings, produced by an interaction between the text-internal emotion conditions and the aesthetic and intertextually inflected audience response: a hybrid of A- and F-emotions. The self-modifying feeling most crucially at stake in *Diu Crône* is, I suggest, the audience's joyful (and self-congratulatory) anticipation, produced as listeners imagine how the court will react when it learns the truth. '[F]eeling, with its script-like qualities, leads us to act as if certain contingent events were anticipated – even if not explicitly expected – in the immediate or near future', note Miall and Kuiken.[53] So, while the court mourns extravagantly, the audience looks forward to the sequence, much later in *Diu Crône*, when a squire brings the news that Gawein is still alive. The court had apparently remained frozen in grief since the revelation of the head.[54] Now Arthur kisses the squire thirty times, while the ladies busy themselves in preparing their fine clothing and courtly adornment once more; a formal 'before and after' sequence explicitly contrasts the two emotional states.[55] There may well be a satirical point in the women's joyfully speedy resumption of their fine clothing, but the joy, like that evinced in the various romance episodes related to Chrétien's 'Joie de la Cort' adventure, the *joie molt grant* at Caerlion at the end of *L'Atre Périlleux* and the extended and multiple joyful climaxes of *Le Chevalier as deus espees*, produces a powerful pleasure that is both aesthetic *and* empathic. As David Bordwell observes, 'When we bet on a hypothesis, especially under the pressure of time, confirmation can carry an emotional kick; the organism enjoys creating unity ... The mixture of anticipation, fulfilment and blocked or retarded or twisted consequences can exercise great emotional power'.[56] J. R. R. Tolkien identified the joy generated by the restoration of order and the resolution of the vicissitudes endured by the protagonist, as the singular transcendent quality of fairy-tale: 'Joy, joy beyond the walls of the world', with the assurance of 'goodness, stability and order eventually prevailing', and which is, perhaps, an emotion particularly stimulated by the successfully narrated romance.[57]

---

[53] Miall and Kuiken, 'A Feeling', p. 227.
[54] See footnote 15.
[55] *Diu Crône*, ll. 21792–22215; before – and – after, ll. 22042–83; cf. Felder, *Kommentar*, pp. 568–9.
[56] D. Bordwell, *Narration in the Fiction Film* (Madison, 1985), pp. 39–40.
[57] J. R. R. Tolkien 'On Fairy Stories', in *Tree and Leaf*, ed. C. Tolkien (London, 1992), p. 62; for 'the vicissitudes of human intentions' as generating empathy, see first J. Bruner, *Actual Minds: Possible Worlds* (Cambridge, MA, 1986), p. 16, and Oatley, 'A Taxonomy', especially pp. 69–70.

The unifying communal experience of shared emotion, and its consequent amplification through the social performance contexts is, as noted above, now alien to the individual reader, but the romance audience, like modern film or theatre audiences, would have derived greatly increased positive affect (on both A- and F- levels) from participating in a shared emotional experience.

Conclusion: Gawain's Death

Piquancy is added to the joyful resolution of these emotion episodes by the intertextual knowledge that one day Gawain's death will not be a false report.[58] As I have suggested elsewhere, the defeat of Morgan le Fay's plot to kill her brother and put her lover Accolon on the throne in the Post-Vulgate *Suite de Merlin* and in Malory refers proleptically to the later success of Mordred, even if the episode's immediate resolution is emotionally satisfying.[59] Just so, these 'thought-experiments' about Gauvain/Gawain's death serve on a metatextual level to foreshadow his ultimate fall, whether he is hacked down in battle against the usurper Mordred on Dover Beach (in the chronicle tradition) or subjected to a painful and lingering death which gives him time to reflect on his own vengeful folly in the *Mort*/Malory versions. In the larger narrative pattern of the cycles, Gawain's death is so closely followed by the final catastrophe of the Arthurian polity that there is barely time to mourn him properly. Nevertheless, suggestively enough, in the *Mort Artu* we find the curious episode of the Dame de Beloé, murdered by her husband for mourning Gauvain too greatly, her reaction motivated by the sight of Gauvain's actual corpse, brought by chance to her castle.[60] Once again, Gauvain's death has a disproportionate and hyperbolic effect on a lady who has loved him from afar, with 'une sorte d'absolu pervers dans un amour *post-mortem*' (a sort of perverse absoluteness with a love beyond death), as Atanassov characterizes the Dame's cousins in the verse romances.[61] The Dame de Beloé's grief performance, one which is, at last, elicited by a genuine death provides a prose tradition counterpart to those multiple ladies in French verse romance, whose heteronormative feelings for Gauvain motivate, through the false death motif, romance plots exploring large questions of real and symbolic identity, of truth and rumour and of vengeance and chivalric excellence.

---

[58] See Meyer, 'It's hard to be me', p. 75. 'If the death of the hero is a possibility, then the basis for Arthurian literature is threatened.'

[59] C. Larrington, *King Arthur's Enchantresses: Morgan and Her Sisters in Medieval Tradition* (London, 2006), pp. 37–8; Malory, *Le Morte*, ed. Field, I: 120–22.

[60] *La Mort*, ed. Frappier, pp. 222–4.

[61] Atanassov, *L'idole inconnue*, p. 119.

'[E]motional expression has an exploratory and a self-altering effect in the activated thought material of emotion', observes William Reddy.[62] When a romance audience responds to a narrative's emotion script, something happens, even when the simulation is running under a deviant cognitive premise. The popularity of the false death topos – and its consistent association with Gawain – suggests that it offered medieval Arthurian poets something good to think with, whether they aimed to model appropriate mourning behaviour in the maintenance of a courtly persona or for the court as a collective, or to consider the significance of the outstanding individual within chivalric society. The audience's cognitive and emotional detachment from the hero's death permits the literary pleasure of observing, perhaps critically, courtly emotional display, but the dramatic irony of its superior knowledge allows a highly pleasurable empathetic anticipation of the comeuppance and defeat of Gauvain's/Gawein's enemies, the hero's vindication and indeed his joy-filled return to courtly life and the arms of his lady. Yet, be that joy never so *molt grant*, it is inevitably shadowed by its nostalgic and proleptic function: to rehearse and anticipate the time when Gawain's actual death will herald the catastrophic downfall of the Arthurian empire. '[L]iterary works ... provide us with multiple and complex instances of differentiated emotional responses', observes Patrick Colm Hogan, defending the interrogation of literature to answer questions about human emotions, both in the past and in the present.[63] Gawain's false death instantiates just such a series, offering a literary effect of such emotional complexity as to defy – or at least to challenge – psychological analysis.

---

[62] W. Reddy, *The Navigation of Feeling: A Framework for the History of Emotions* (Cambridge, 2001), p. 128.
[63] P. Colm Hogan, *What Literature Teaches Us about Emotion* (Cambridge, 2011), pp. 64–75, at p. 68.

8

Emotion and Voice: 'Ay' in Middle Dutch Arthurian Romances

FRANK BRANDSMA

T. H. White's *The Once and Future King* is one of the most popular and enduring retellings of the Arthurian legend, in the Netherlands as well as in the Anglophone world. In his March 2011 column, on speed skating, Utrecht's city poet Ingmar Heytze refers to the Dutch translation of White's work as the most beautiful book he knows. He uses the description of Lancelot's superior way of jousting to present his admiration for the ease and commitment with which a famous Dutch skater tackles the 10,000 metres. According to White's narrator, spectators and opponents would always recognize Lancelot's style:

> The riding was the whole thing. If a man had the courage to throw himself into the fullest gallop at the moment of impact, he generally won. Most men faltered a little, so that they were not at their best momentum. This was why Lancelot constantly gained his tilts. He had what Uncle Dap called *élan*. Sometimes, when he was in disguise, he would ride clumsily on purpose, showing daylight at his seat. But at the last moment there always was the true dash – so that onlookers, and frequently his wretched opponent, could exclaim, 'Ah, Lancelot!' even before the lance drove home.[1]

The Dutch translation gives the exclamation as: 'Ai, Lancelot!'[2] *Ah* and *Ai*, the shared words of the onlookers and opponent, express a mixture of fear and admiration and perhaps even curiosity – where does *he* come from? – as well as sadness about the inescapable fall. Words do not come much smaller than *Ay*, yet the mini-word may give voice to a whole range of emotions, and the same goes for its medieval equivalents.

Words like *ha* and *hélas* in Old French, and, in Middle Dutch, words like *ay*, *owi*, and *acharmen*, are quite common in Arthurian romance. By means of these exclamations, characters, and sometimes also the narrator, give voice to sorrow, joy, fear, or curiosity. Their emotion is presented as

---

[1] T. H. White, *The Once and Future King. Book III. The Ill-Made Knight* (New York, 1987), ch. 7, p. 352.
[2] T. H. White, *Arthur, koning voor eens en altijd*, trans. M. Schuchart (Utrecht, 1998), p. 361.

strong and spontaneous, as in the following example from the translation of the *Suite-Vulgate du Merlin* by Lodewijk van Velthem, made in 1326. When the kings Ban and Bohort visit Logres to support King Arthur, Merlin takes them to the castle of King Agravadain. Since the king's beautiful daughter and King Ban only have eyes for each other, Merlin casts a love spell to bring them together. That night, the smitten damsel reflects on her longing for Ban:[3]

> Maer Agravadeins dochter, lude ende stille,
> Hadde haer ogen altoes opten koninck Ban.
> Sine konde daer niet gekeren van,
> Si wart dickewile roet ende blanc.
> Detentijt dochte haer veel te lanc,
> Si stont als ene dien vaket:
> 'O wi,' dachte si, 'ocht ic nu al naket
> In sinen arme lage! Ach, my!
> Wanen quam my dese gedochte? O wi,
> Dat ic optesen gedinc nu achte!'
> Des leide si daer nu al haer gedachte
> An den koninck Ban, sonder waen,
> Ende dit hevet Merlijn al gedaen.

(Agravadain's daughter kept her eyes on King Ban all the time; she could not keep herself from doing so and often turned red and white. The dinner took far too long for her, she stood there as if she were asleep: 'Oh no,' she thought, 'if only I could lie naked in his arms! Oh my! Where did this idea come from. Oh no, that I should give heed to these thoughts!' Thus she was thinking only of King Ban, without a doubt. And this was all Merlin's doing.)

The damsel does not voice her erotic thoughts aloud, yet they are presented as spoken words in a monologue. In her mind, she speaks to herself and reacts to her own ideas with apparent apprehension and reproach. Comparison with the French original shows that the Middle Dutch translator has deliberately chosen to insert direct discourse here: the French prose has the same content in indirect phrases, without the exclamations.[4] The use of direct speech, combined with the repeated exclamations in rhyme position and the unusual elliptical syntax, turns

---

[3] Cf. Jacob van Maerlant, *Merlijn, naar het eenig bekende Steinforter handschrift uitgegeven*, ed. J. van Vloten (Leiden, 1880), ll. 33378–90; I have corrected the punctuation in the passage to clarify the sentence structure (van Vloten often placed a semi-colon where we now would use a full stop) and translated the passage.

[4] *The Vulgate Version of the Arthurian Romances*, ed. H. O. Sommer (Washington, 1908–16; repr. New York, 1979), II: 404, ll. 25–7: '& moult li estoit tart que les napes fuissent ostees car moult uoldroit uolentiers ester couchie entre ses bras toute nue si ne sauoit dont cele uolentes li uenoit'; translation by R. T. Pickens in *Lancelot-Grail: The Old French Arthurian Vulgate and Post-Vulgate in Translation*, trans. N. J. Lacy et al., 5 vols (New York and London, 1992–6), I: 390: 'She could hardly wait for the tablecloths to be taken away, for she very much would have liked to lie naked in his arms, yet she did not know where this yearning came from.'

the already rather exceptional description of female desire into a 'special effect' in this episode. The emotions remain silent and internal, yet are foregrounded far more clearly than in the original. As the girl speaks to herself, she also addresses the listeners/readers of the tale, who thus become connected to her emotions. Merlin's enchantment will lead to her sharing Ban's bed and conceiving Hector.

The clustering of three exclamations (*O wi, Ach my, O wi*) in this passage is exceptional, as is their role as 'oral fireworks', yet the exclamations in themselves are not. These and similar phrases appear quite frequently in Arthurian romances, in different forms and contexts, with different functions and different represented emotions, but they have not yet been studied as carriers of emotions. Surely, a closer look at exclamations and emotions is in order!

Theoretical Framework

In 2008, Minne de Boer published a survey of the roles assigned to interjections and exclamations in traditional and modern grammar.[5] As a starting point, he quotes Longman's *Grammar of Spoken and Written English* (1999), which proposes a class of 'inserts' (characterized as 'emotional sounds'!) with nine subcategories:

> Interjections (*oh! wow! oops!*), greetings and farewells (*Hi, See you*), discourse markers (*well, right, you see*), attention signals (*Hey you*), response elicitors (*eh? okay?*), response forms (*yes, no okay, uh huh*), hesitators (*uh, erm*), various polite speech-act formulae (*You're welcome*) and expletives (*shit, bloody hell*).[6]

De Boer then focuses on the interjections and, in his overview of their role in grammars through the ages, mentions time and again their emotional aspect, described as *affectus animi*, 'sentiments' or 'Affekte'.[7] Of the nine subclasses, the emotional impact is felt most strongly in the interjections and in the expletives, and that may explain the recent interest in them in Dutch linguistics and lexicography.[8] To start with the latter: there is a Dutch dictionary of exclamations, listing no fewer than 850 modern

---

[5] M. G. de Boer, 'Tussenwerpseltheorieën', *Voortgang, jaarboek voor de neerlandistiek* 26 (2008), 221–52; De Boer refers to an English article on the same topic, which I have been unable to consult: M. G. de Boer, 'Talking about Interjections', *Bulletin of The Henry Sweet Society for the History of Linguistic Ideas* 50 (2008), 31–44.

[6] De Boer, 'Tussenwerpseltheorieën', p. 223.

[7] Although De Boer takes into account grammars of Classical Greek and Latin, he does not discuss medieval texts or words, apart from one example from the *Roman de Renart* ('huilecome' > 'willekome', trans.: welcome) to indicate perspectives for future diachronic research (p. 244). For the impact of the interjections, sometimes even a musical metaphor is used: De Boer (p. 237) quotes L. Spitzer: 'Die Interjektionen wirken wie absolute Musik [...] Posaunentöne' ('The interjections function like absolute music [...] sounds of the trombone').

[8] Cf. P. G. J. van Sterkenburg, *Woorden van en voor emotie* (Leiden, 2007).

examples. There has been little investigation into their medieval equivalents, however.[9] Swear words and insults, the former category, are studied in modern language use, and even in Middle Dutch. In December 2013, Martine Veldhuizen defended her Ph.D. thesis on 'The Untamed Tongue: Middle Dutch Notions of Sinful, Unethical and Criminal Words (1300–1550)', discussing medieval ideas about the use of bad language.[10] Modern swear words are studied, for instance, morphologically and syntactically: they may seem very flexible and personal, yet they closely follow the linguistic rules for making and combining words, as well as for the placement of the words in the sentence. Researchers working on language and the brain are fascinated by the fact that when people are allowed to swear aloud, they are able to keep their hand in ice water far longer than when they only use neutral words like 'wood'. There is something in swear words that gives them 'right of way' in the brain, overruling other sensations (such as the tactile experience of cold).[11]

The study of medieval exclamations and their emotional function will no doubt profit from these new insights, as it has from the results of studies of interjections, dialogue structure, and theatricality in French medieval texts. In 2006, the linguistic journal *Langages* devoted a special issue to 'L'interjection: jeux et enjeux', edited by Claude Buridant.[12] Buridant's overview, like De Boer's, reveals that interjections form a rather strange category syntactically, since they do not belong to the standard components of the (modern) sentence and may be found in different positions. An important feature of the category is the modal multi-functionality of the words: they may express an emotion, an appeal, a consent or denial, a question or an insult. In the same issue, Jean-Jacques Vincensini demonstrates how, in medieval texts, interjections play an important role in dialogues, especially at the beginning of speeches.[13] As highly audible signal words, they signpost the start of a new speaker's words. This is a very important function in the oral delivery of a text, read aloud before an audience without modern punctuation to alert the reader to the start

---

[9] T. den Boon, *Van Dale modern uitroepenwoordenboek: van aanvalluh tot Ziezo en 848 andere uitroepen* (Utrecht, 2009).

[10] M.Veldhuizen, 'De ongetemde tong: opvattingen over zondige, onvertogen en misdadige woorden in het Middelnederlands (1300–1550)', dissertation, Utrecht University, 2013. Cf. also, on the sins of the tongue, E. D. Craun, *Lies, Slander, and Obscenity in Medieval English Literature: Pastoral Rhetoric and the Deviant Speaker* (Cambridge, 1997).

[11] The fact that often taboo words are used seems quite relevant here, cf. T. Jay, 'The Utility and Ubiquity of Taboo Words', *Perspectives on Psychological Science* 4 (2009), 153–61. The findings described above have led Jos van Berkum (Communication Studies, Utrecht University) to study what happens in the brain when a person is insulted, in comparison to being complimented. The insult yields a far stronger and immediate reaction, clearly visible on fMRI read-outs. This is work in progress (spring 2014); no publications are available as yet.

[12] C. Buridant, 'L'interjection: jeux et enjeux', *Langages* 161.1 (2006), 3–9.

[13] J.-J. Vincensini, 'Formes et fonctions structurantes: à propos de quelques interjections en ancien et en moyen français', *Langages* 161.1 (2006), 101–11.

of a new speech or speaker.¹⁴ I will come back to this issue at the end of this section.

Evelyne Opperman-Marsaux also works on medieval interjections and has recently compared romances to dramatic texts in the use of exclamations, demonstrating that these words flourish in the theatre: she found three times more instances in the plays she analysed than in the romances.¹⁵ Even when they are less prominent than in the real theatre, the role of exclamations in romance dialogues may also be explained by what Evelyn Birge Vitz has called 'the theatricality of dialogue' in her discussion of the art of the sublime storyteller Chrétien de Troyes.¹⁶ Vitz cites a splendid example, from Chrétien's *Conte du Graal*, of the girl who yells at the townsfolk who have come to 'rescue' her from an amorous moment with Gauvain:¹⁷

> 'Hu, hu!' fait ele, 'vilenaille,
> Chien enraigié, pute servaille!
> Quel deable vos ont mandez?
> Que querez vos? Que demandez?
> Que ja Deux joie ne vos doint'

> ('Be off with you!' she said, 'rabble, mad dogs, filthy wretches! What devils called you together? What do you want? What are you after? I hope God doesn't hear your prayer!')¹⁸

Her insults are accompanied by giant chess pieces which she throws at the commoners, which must also have invited a theatrical and comical performance. The example also shows how exclamations (*'Hu, hu'*) may be combined with expletives, longer phrases, and questions, to enliven both speeches and the whole narrative. In the first example given above, of King Agravadain's daughter, the use of direct discourse also allows for the oral delivery to become a performance. The oral performer, reading from the manuscript to a (small) audience, may have used a special tone of voice for the phrases that reveal the girl's internal emotional turmoil.

---

¹⁴ Cf. F. Brandsma, 'Medieval Equivalents of "Quote-Unquote": The Presentation of Spoken Words in Courtly Romance', in *The Court and Cultural Diversity: Selected Papers from the Eighth Triennial Congress of the International Courtly Literature Society (Belfast, 26 July–1 August 1995)*, ed. E. Mullally and J. Thompson (Cambridge, 1997), pp. 287–96.

¹⁵ E. Opperman-Marsaux, 'Les interjections en discours direct: comparaison entre fictions romanesques et fictions dramatiques en moyen français', in *De l'oral à l'écrit: le dialogue à travers les genres romanesques et théâtral*, ed. C. Denoyelle (Orléans, 2013), pp. 283–300.

¹⁶ E. B. Vitz, 'Theatricality and Its Limits: Dialogue and the Art of the Storyteller in the Romances of Chrétien de Troyes', in *De l'oral à l'écrit*, ed. Denoyelle, pp. 27–44. Vitz discusses the passions and gestures that the text suggests to the performer in his roleplaying, but also stresses that the storyteller is a 'one man band' (p. 39).

¹⁷ Chrétien de Troyes, *Le Conte du Graal*, in *Romans*, ed. C. Méla (Paris, 1994), ll. 5881–5.

¹⁸ Chrétien de Troyes, *Arthurian Romances*, trans. W. W. Kibler (Harmondsworth, 1991), p. 454. The older translation by D. D. R. Owen gives the first line as 'hey, hey, you rabble'; cf. Chrétien de Troyes, *Arthurian Romances*, trans. D. D. R. Owen (London, 1987), p. 453.

The role of interjections/exclamations as emotion signals, which modern linguistic research has corroborated, may – to round off this section – also be demonstrated by a brief discussion of the activities of an exceptional participant in the medieval textual communication system. The contemporaneous corrector of the Middle Dutch *Lancelot Compilation* makes use of exclamations to clarify and intensify dialogues. In the margins of the manuscript of the compilation in the making, the corrector added words (like *ende*, 'and') that help the reader recognize the beginning of a new sentence or a change of speaker. Most probably, he was preparing the text for reading it aloud (himself) by signposting tricky passages and correcting textual mistakes. Discourse markers like *ja* (yes), and interjections like *ay* (ah) and *entrouwen* (on my honour) belong to his repertoire of signals. In the following monologue of the desperate queen, the words in the margin were added by the corrector. The queen has dreamt about finding Lancelot in a young woman's bed and sending him away. Waking up, she laments her actions:

>   'Ay, wel soete mine Lanceloet,
>   U scoenheit es noch also groet
>   Alse mi dochte dat icse sach
>   Als ic in minen drome lach.
> ay   Vergave God, wel lieve minne,
>   Dat gi nu wart hier inne
>   Gesont ende ic nu ter stonde
>   Die joncfrouwe hier liggende vonde,
> ja   Op die vorwarde oft ic mi
>   Daer af vererrede, dat ic daer bi
>   Mijn hoeft verliesen moeste dan,
>   Dat ic niet en woude nochtan
>   Om al dat es in erderike.'[19]

(Ah, my sweet love Lancelot, your handsomeness is as great as I think I saw it as I lay dreaming. *Ah*, if only God, my dear love, would allow you to be here in good health, even if I would then find the damsel lying here with you ... *yes*, [if only that could be so] even on the condition that I would lose my head if I became angry, which I would not want for everything in the world.)[20]

The corrector's additions strengthen the emotional tone of the queen's complaint, as *ay* repeats the exclamation already used by the scribe of the original translation. *Ja* is far less emotionally charged: it functions mostly as an affirmative insert to clarify the sentence structure. This is in line with the idea that the corrector was preparing the text for oral delivery, signposting passages that were problematic, but also tweaking

---

[19] *Lanceloet*, ed. Brandsma, ll. 11245–57, cf. note 22.
[20] My translation is somewhat free, since the Middle Dutch phrases are complex and concise here, even with the help of the corrections.

passages – like this one – that would allow the reader to make his performance more lively.[21] There are thousands of (marginal) corrections in the over 31,000 lines of the compilation that have been published in the new edition (up to 2013). This gives the corrected text and shows exactly what the corrector added. Sixty-nine of the marginal corrections are exclamations: 31 times the corrector has added *ja*, 22 times *ay*, and 16 times other words, like *entrouwen*.[22]

This is a special case, however, a kind of reception document showing the hand (and voice?) of a medieval reader/performer rather than an author. Still, this editor obviously saw the interjections as a natural textual element with a specific role in the narration of Arthurian romance. This role will now be explored further by looking at words like *ay*, *o wi* and *acharmen* (oh dear) in all the Middle Dutch Arthurian romances. The focus in the analysis will be on these words' connections to emotions, on the narrative situations in which they occur (narrator's text, monologue, or dialogue), on the different kinds of emotions represented, and on the possibility that the exclamations are a special signal for the transfer of these emotions to the audience by means of the so-called mirror effect.

Corpus, Cases, and Emotional Connotation

Sixteen Middle Dutch Arthurian verse romances containing instances of *ay* and its variants formed the corpus for the analysis. The texts date from the second half of the thirteenth to the fourteenth century, and were analysed through the digital text collection in the CD-ROM version of the *Middelnederlandsch Woordenboek*.[23] In general, the editions in this collection represent the medieval material adequately, with one exception: the material from the *Lancelot Compilation*, especially for *Lanceloet*, *Perchevael*, *Queeste*, and *Arturs doet*, does not make the insertions by the corrector available. His activities have therefore been analysed separately and, because of his special 'non-authorial' status, were also discussed separately above.

---

[21] Cf. F. Brandsma, 'Doing Dialogue: The Middle Dutch Lancelot Translators and Correctors at Work', in *De l'oral à l'écrit*, ed. Denoyelle, pp. 69–84, for a discussion of recent work on this subject.

[22] Cf. *Lanceloet: de Middelnederlandse vertaling van de Lancelot en prose overgeleverd in de Lancelotcompilatie. Pars 1 (vs. 1–5530, vooraf gegaan door de verzen van het Brusselse fragment)*, ed. B. Besamusca and A. Postma (Hilversum, 1997); *Pars 2*, ed. B. Besamusca (Assen and Maastricht, 1991); *Pars 3*, ed. F. Brandsma (Assen and Maastricht, 1992); *Pars 4*, ed. A. Postma (Hilversum, 1998), and also *De Middelnederlandse 'Perceval'-traditie: inleiding en editie van de bewaarde fragmenten van een Middelnederlandse vertaling van de 'Perceval' of 'Conte du Graal' van Chrétien de Troyes, en de 'Perchevael' in de 'Lancelotcompilatie'*, ed. S. Oppenhuis de Jong (Hilversum, 2003).

[23] *Middelnederlandsch Woordenboek* (The Hague and Antwerp, 1998) [CD-ROM]. For the up-to-date database of all European Arthurian texts, manuscripts, and editions, see http://www.arthurianfiction.org (consulted January 2014).

This table gives the texts and the numbers of cases for *ay* and its variants; the following diagram visualizes the numbers.

Text	Number of cases	Total number of lines	Frequency per 1,000 lines
Ferguut	12	5604	2,14
Walewein	20	11202	1,79
Merlijn	6	10408	0,58
Merlijncontinuation	20	25810	0,78
Lantsloot	9	6073	1,48
Lanceloet	246	36947	6,67
Perchevael	12	5598	2,15
Moriaen	4	4716	0,85
Queeste	31	11154	2,79
Wrake	25	3413	7,35
Ridder metter mouwen	10	4021	2,49
Walewein & Keye	19	3664	5,21
Lanc. & hert Witte voet	1	856	1,17
Torec	11	3853	2,86
Arturs doet	50	13054	3,83
Total	**476**		

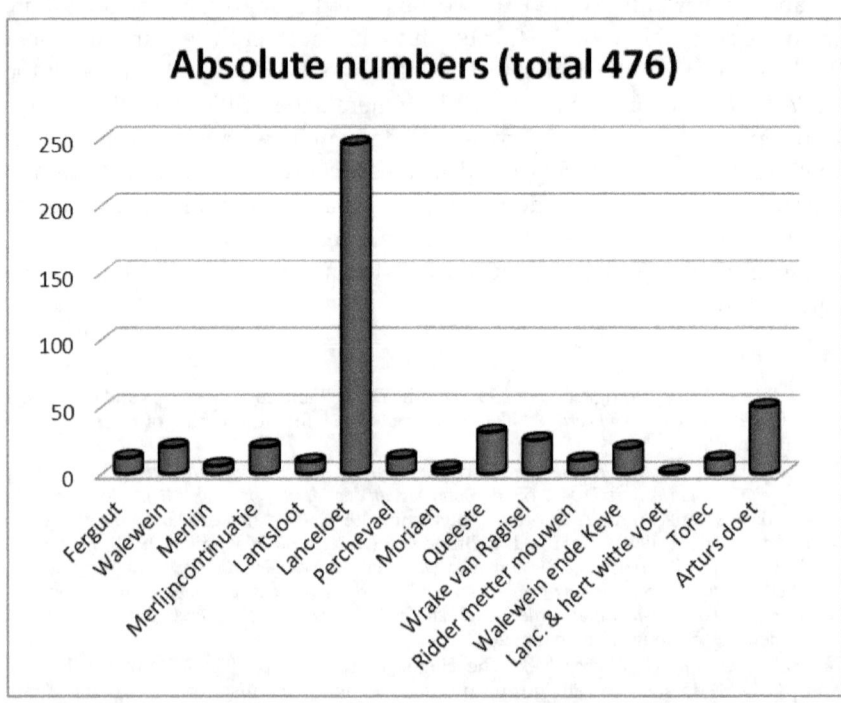

The first question is, of course, do all of these cases represent *ay* and its variants as emotion words? And the simple answer is 'yes'. As will be discussed below, it is not always possible to single out one specific emotion represented by the interjection, but in all cases emotions are at stake. The table does, however, reveal remarkable differences regarding the frequency with which exclamation words were used in the texts.

The almost 37,000 thousand lines of the *Lanceloet* translation of the Prose *Lancelot* contain most examples, over 55 per cent of the total. It has also a very high 'concentration', as the frequency score shows, yet in relation to the number of lines, the difference is not as extreme as the first diagram seems to indicate. A smaller text, the *Wrake van Ragisel*, in fact uses exclamations more frequently. This second diagram gives the number of cases in relation to the total number of lines in the text.

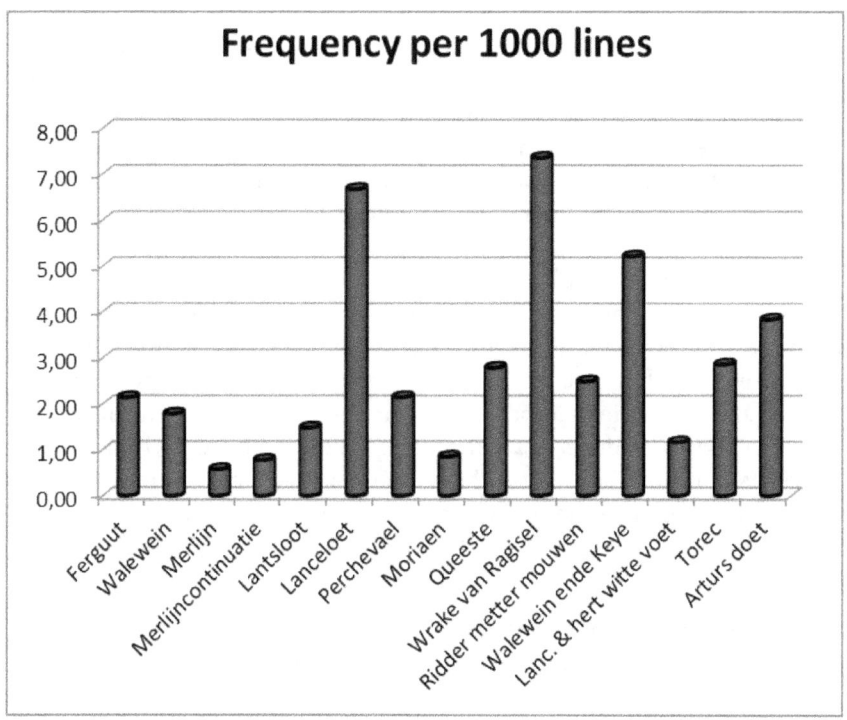

Even though this diagram shows the frequency more adequately, in more detailed analyses of the use of the exclamations the sheer number of *Lanceloet* cases, and to a lesser extent *Arturs doet* cases, carries the risk of dominating the results and rendering the other texts invisible. In the analysis, I have therefore corrected this numeric bias: for *Lanceloet*, only a representative sample of 31 units was taken into account, and for *Arturs*

doet 32 units were used.[24] The intention is to preclude any idiosyncratic tendencies in one or both of these texts from dominating the results. The total number of cases analysed from this point onwards thus becomes 243, a little more than half of the original set of 476.

Monologue and Dialogue, Character Emotions

The queen's speech from the *Lancelot Compilation*, given above, represents a narrative situation in which the experienced reader of medieval texts would expect a word like *ay*. The queen voices a complaint to herself, in what is essentially a monologue, although it later turns out that a lady-in-waiting has overheard her. Exclamations, one expects, belong to monologues, to sad complaints by imprisoned knights or damsels in distress.

Chrétien's *Le Chevalier de la Charrette* confirms this impression when it comes to the use of *ha*. Using the critical edition in the Figura version of the Princeton Charrette Project, I found 18 instances: 13 of those occurred in monologues and expressions of grief.[25] The queen's complaint after cold-shouldering her rescuer has two *ha*'s, and several more are found in the diverse complaints in which Lancelot gives vent to his frustration and sorrow. The main characters express their sadness, speaking to themselves and at the same time to the audience.

Chrétien's text also contains examples – five in all – of *ha* used in a non-soliloquy, or in a full-blown dialogue. These examples also express sadness and fear, and in one case a kind of anxious curiosity. In this example (l. 3708 in the Princeton text), a minor character plays the role of mirror character, voicing a feeling shared with the audience. It occurs in the famous central episode when the name of the queen's rescuer is revealed to the audience. A damsel has asked the queen who the brave knight is and has shouted out his name. To her distress and that of the other spectators, she then sees that the hero now only has eyes for the queen and almost forgets to fight Meleagant. She cries (ll. 3708–9):[26]

> 'Ha! Lancelot! Ce que puet estre
> Que si folemant te contiens?'

> ('Ah! Lancelot! What could make you behave so foolishly?')

---

[24] The samples were intended to number thirty cases, which would give the two texts a quantity of examples more in proportion to the other texts, but in both texts the sample turned out to end in the middle of a character's words. Analysing the whole speech resulted in having one (for *Lanceloet*) and two (for *Arturs doet*) more cases included in the analysis.

[25] Chrétien de Troyes, *Le Chevalier de la Charrette*, digital edition: http://www.princeton.edu/~lancelot/ss/ (consulted January 2014); http://gravitas.princeton.edu/charrette/figura/ (consulted January 2014).

[26] Cf. also Chrétien de Troyes, *Le Chevalier de la Charrette*, in *Romans*, ed. C. Méla (Paris, 1994), ll. 3692–3, and the translation by Kibler in Chrétien de Troyes, *Arthurian Romances*, p. 253.

Her speech goes on to describe her astonishment at seeing such a brave knight fight with one hand behind his back. Lancelot hears her words, feels ashamed, and resumes the fight properly. As the fact that the other spectators and their distress are mentioned just before the damsel's words indicates, she expresses a feeling that is shared by the audience within the text, and thus may also have been shared by the contemporary listeners. Her 'Ha' expresses alarm, curiosity, and also anxiety, so once more we find multiple emotions conveyed by just one word. I will return to the 'mirror function' at the end of this section.

In the Middle Dutch texts, the monologue-dialogue data are simple, yet surprising in comparison to what we see in Chrétien's text.[27] In the Middle Dutch romances, the expected predominance of the monologue is completely reversed: in more than 80 per cent of the cases, the exclamations are used in dialogues, as this diagram shows.

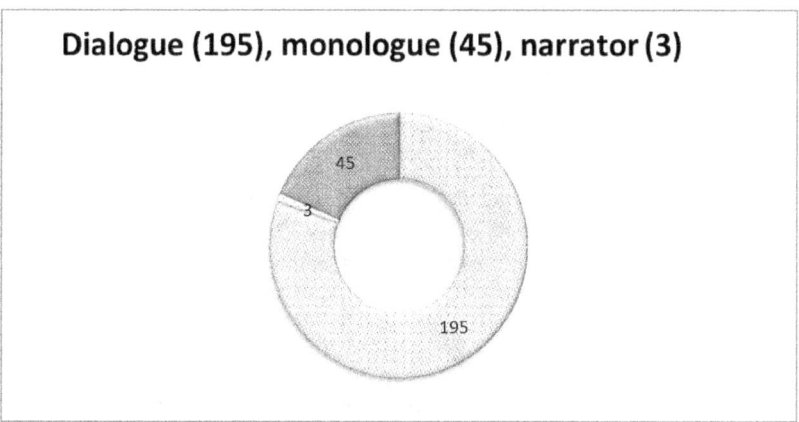

There is little difference between the texts in terms of the proportions of monologue/dialogue per text, with the exception of the *Queeste* and *Merlijn*, which contain interjections only in dialogues.

This example is from *Arturs doet* and combines an interjection in a dialogue with one in a monologue. It concerns the famous scene of throwing Excalibur into the lake:

> 'Wat sagestu daer?' sprac die coninc.
> 'In sach daer,' sprac hi, 'gene dinc
> Anders dan ic sculdich te siene was.'

---

[27] The scores per text are (first the total number, then the number of cases in dialogue (D) and monologue (M): *Ferguut*: 12, D8, M4; *Walewein*: 20, D13, M7; *Merlijn*: 6, D5, 1 exclamation belongs to the narrator's text; *Merlijncontinuatie*: 20, D14, M5, 1 exclamation belongs to the narrator's text; *Lantsloot vander Haghedochte*: 9, D8, M1; *Lanceloet*: 31, D24, M7; *Perchevael*: 12, D11, M1; *Moriaen*: 4, D3, M1; *Queeste*: 31, D31; *Wrake van Ragisel*: 25, D23, M2; *Riddere metter mouwen*: 10, D8, M2; *Walewein ende Keye*: 19, D17, M2; *Lanceloet en het hert met de witte voet*: 1, this single exclamation belongs to the narrator's text; *Torec*: 11, D9, M2; *Arturs doet*: 32, D21, M11. Total: 243 cases: D195, M45, narrator (to be discussed later), 3.

> Die coninc was tonpaise das,
> Ende seide: '*Acharme*, Griflet, twi
> Moestu aldus sere nu mi
> Dune heves dat swaerd gewarpen niet
> Daer ic di beval ende hiet.
> Ganc, werpt daer, dat ic moge al
> Weten watter af gescien sal;
> Want en sal niet, wes seker van desen,
> Sonder groet wonder verloren wesen.'
> Tirst dat Griflet heeft verstaen
> Dat ember moet wesen gedaen,
> Hi kerde weder ten swaerde mettien.
> Hi naemt ende begonst besien,
> Ende hi claget sere embertoe,
> Ende hi sprac wenende doe:
> '*Ay* goet swaerd, rike ende scone,
> En geen es beter onder den trone.
> Hoe grote scade saelt sijn van u,
> Dat gi niet en sult vallen nu
> In enich goets mans hant.'
> Doe warp hi dat swaerd te hant
> Alse verre als hijt werpen mochte.[28]

('What did you see?' the king asked. 'I only saw,' he (Griflet) answered, 'what I was supposed to see.' This made the king unhappy, and he said: 'Oh dear, Griflet, why do you exhaust me like this? You did not throw the sword where I ordered you to throw it. Go back, throw it in, so that I may know what happens; because, rest assured, it will not disappear without a great miracle.'

When Griflet realised it had to be done, he returned to the sword. He took it and looked at it, and bemoaned it greatly, and, in tears, he said: 'Ah, good sword, precious and beautiful, there is no better sword on earth. What a loss it is that you will not come into some good man's hand.' Then he threw the sword as far (into the lake) as he could.)

Arthur's disappointment with Griflet is evident in his 'Acharme', whereas Griflet's 'Ay goet swaerd' again represents more than one emotion: admiration and sadness, since he is sad to throw the sword he admires so much into the water.

In the dialogues and monologues, the characters speak, using interjections to give voice to their emotions. Words like *ay* thus provide the audience with direct access to the characters' minds. In monologues characters express what they feel and the audience listens in, whereas in dialogues the extradiegetic listeners are almost an inconspicuous part of the conversation: as we listen to, or read, a dialogue, we are listeners to each of the

---

[28] *Arturs doet*, in *Roman van Lancelot (XIIIe eeuw). Naar het (eenig-bekende) handschrift der Koninklijke Bibliotheek, op gezag van het Gouvernement*, ed. W. J. A. Jonckbloet ('s-Gravenhage, 1846–9), ll. 12123–47.

speakers, just like the characters themselves. The fact that we are able to complete other people's sentences seems to indicate that, while listening to others, we form their sentences in our minds. We are also invited to formulate answers internally. Much remains unclear concerning these processes in our brains, so I will not speculate further on how this works and may have worked in medieval texts. The authors of the stories, however, do invite the listeners to 'think along' with the characters as they keep placing their protagonists in problematic situations.[29]

Here is a perfect example of such a situation. Lancelot has been poisoned and can only be saved by a damsel who has fallen in love with him and cannot do anything for him, until he has promised to become her lover, which of course he finds impossible to do:

>   Hi seide tot Lyonele doe,
>   Ende hi weende emmertoe:
>   'Lieve hertelike vrient, wat radi
>   Wat ic hier af doe?' Doe seide hi:
>   'Die raet es genomen van desen,
>   Gi moet ter joncfrouwen wille wesen
>   Ocht gi sijt doet, dits waerheit fijn.'
> .   Hi seide: '*Ay God*, hoe mach dat sijn
>   Dat ic plegen sal ongetrouwen
>   Van minnen jegen mire vrouwen?''
> ende Lyoneel antworde hem daer nare:
> .   'Hoe mach dat sijn, dat gi hare
>   Sult doen sterven, die niet en heeft mesdaen,
>   Ende die joncfrouwe, die gi in staeden staen
>   Met rechte sout telker stede,
>   Wilt oec doen sterven mede?
>   Wildi dus doen, die lieden souden
>   U daer bi over verradere houden.'[30]

(He then spoke to Lionel, crying all the time: 'Dear friend of my heart, what do you think I should do?'
He answered: 'The decision has been made, you have to do what the damsel wants or you die, that's the truth of it.'
He said: 'Oh God, how can it be that I would be unfaithful to my lady?'
Lionel answered: 'How can it be that you would cause her, who has done nothing wrong, to die, and make the damsel, whom you should help and assist in all circumstances, die as well? If you would do that, people would consider you to be a traitor.')

---

[29] Douglas Kelly characterized Chrétien's texts as 'problem romances', in the same vein as Per Nykrog, who called the author a 'romancier discutable', cf. D. Kelly, 'Chrétien de Troyes', in *The Arthur of the French: The Arthurian Legend in Medieval French and Occitan Literature*, ed. G. Burgess and K. Pratt (Cardiff, 2006), p. 144; P. Nykrog, *Chrétien de Troyes, romancier discutable* (Geneva, 1995).

[30] *Lanceloet: de Middelnederlandse vertaling, Pars 3*, ed. Brandsma, ll. 12731–46; the corrector has added 'ende' in the margin, as well as two dots, indicating new sentences.

Lancelot's despair is clearly indicated – he is crying all the time he is speaking – but even more forcefully expressed is how strongly he abhors the idea of being unfaithful to the queen. For the audience, this translates into curiosity, suspense, and perhaps even anxiety: will such an inconceivable thing come to pass? Lancelot's emotions and indeed the whole situation draw the audience into the tale. They share his feelings and become eager to know what will happen next. Lionel's final words about 'die lieden' even refer to the people's, and thus quite likely the audience's, opinions of Lancelot.

This example demonstrates the 'mirror function', as did the *Charrette* episode discussed above, and one of the contributing elements in the emotional impact is the exclamation. Since I am interested in this kind of 'automatic' transfer of represented emotions to the audience, my hidden agenda in this survey was the hope that words like *ay* would be good and consistent indicators that the emotional mirror function was at work. In a very elementary way, this turns out to be the case: when a character expresses his or her sadness, fear, or joy, these feelings are understood by means of neurological connections to the listener's or reader's own corresponding feelings. Yet, what I was hoping to find – not unlike the naïve Perceval who thought all knights were angels – was a consistent and deliberate correlation of *ay*-like words with the mirror function, indicating that only mirror characters would use this word. The word would then become an easy to use and digitally detectable guide to relevant emotional passages. This idea was far too simple, of course, and my analysis of the Middle Dutch romances yielded no straightforward correlations between *ay* and mirror characters or the mirror function. Even in the texts that use this narrative technique most often (*Lanceloet* and *Arturs doet*), it was discernible in fewer than half of the cases. In the discussion in the next and final section of the kinds of emotions represented by the exclamations, I will indicate for each text how many cases did reveal the mirror effect.

As for the narrative situation, a tiny number of interesting cases, three in all, remains to be discussed. These fit neither in the monologue nor the dialogue category, since they occur in the narrator's text, rather than in the characters' direct discourse. In these cases, the narrator appeals to the feelings of the audience regarding the present situation in the story.

This example from Jacob van Maerlant's *Merlijn* shows this in its most concise form:

> *O wi*, hoe gram was die baliu![31]
>
> (Oh my, the bailiff was so angry!)

---

[31] Van Maerlant, *Merlijn*, ed. van Vloten, l. 4197.

The remark refers to the bailiff's feelings when the infant Merlin charges him with being a bastard and creates curiosity and suspense in the audience: how does the infant Merlin know that the bailiff, who has arrested Merlin's mother for giving birth to a bastard, is himself conceived out of wedlock? And what will happen next? The narrator distances himself from the character he describes, and most probably the audience's sentiments do not correspond with the bailiff's anger, but with the narrator's *Schadenfreude*.[32]

In the other two cases, the narrator also invites the audience to share his emotional estimation of the situation. In the short romance of *Lanceloet en het hert met de witte voet* (Lancelot and the white-footed stag), to give only one of the cases as an example, a traitor has taken the white foot from the wounded Lancelot and brought it to the queen, whose hand in marriage is to go to whoever brings her this object. The narrator exclaims: 'Ay, hoe serech stont die coninginne' ('Ah, how sadly the queen just stood there'), after describing her tears and distress. The audience, which has been informed by the narrator's words and the character's deeds that this would-be husband is no good, will have shared the queen's and the narrator's apprehension.[33]

The Kinds of Emotions Voiced through 'ay'

Most of the examples discussed so far have shown that the exclamations give voice to more than one emotion, since in most situations complicated emotional issues are at stake. Still, it is possible to indicate in almost all cases the most important emotion in the 243 cases analysed. For this analysis, very general labels were used: 'sadness' was used to cover all levels of sadness, ranging from melancholy to grief and despair; 'joy' represents pleasure and amusement as well as ecstasy.[34] This somewhat rough analysis yields the following distribution of emotions, with the already stated caveat that only one emotion could be captured in the label for each instance. Again, for *Lanceloet* and *Arturs doet* the representative samples were taken into account.

---

[32] In situations like this, quite often dramatic irony plays an important role: the distribution of information in the tale has resulted in the audience knowing more than (some of) the characters; cf. also Larrington's chapter in this volume.

[33] *Lanceloet en het hert met de witte voet*, ed. M. Draak (Culemborg, 1976), l. 434. The other case is from the *Merlin* continuation by Lodewijk van Velthem (ed. van Vloten, l. 24761): the narrator complains in general terms about people who try to disturb marriages, like that of Arthur and Guinevere.

[34] The labels will only be used to discern some general patterns, since I fully agree with Reynolds's warning: 'Labels do not encourage analysis'; cf. S. Reynolds, *Fiefs and Vassals: The Medieval Evidence Reinterpreted* (Oxford, 1994), p. 31.

Text	Out of x	Sadness	Joy	Fear	Admiration	Curiosity	Other	Mirror
Ferguut	12	7	2		2		1	2
Walewein	20	12	1	4	1	1	1	4
Merlijn	6	1	1	1		1	2	1
Merlijn contin.	20	5	4	1	2	2	6	3
Lantsloot	9		1	5		2	1	4
Lanceloet	31	10	2	4	2	6	7	14
Perchevael	12	1	1	2	1	5	2	6
Moriaen	4	1		3				2
Queeste	31	15		4	1	5	6	6
Wrake	25	4	1	7	5	3	5	4
Riddere mM	10	2	1	3	1	2	1	3
Walewein & K.	19	5	2	6	2	1	3	5
Witte voet	1	1						1
Torec	11	4	1	2	2	2		3
Arturs doet	32	18		5	1	4	4	16
Totals	243	86	17	47	20	34	39	74

As expected, sadness prevails (especially in texts like *Arturs doet*), with fear coming second. Anger was the most common emotion in the category 'Other'. Joy was represented by *ay* in almost every text, but it did not occur very often. In connection to the mirror function, the scores for admiration and curiosity are interesting, since a deeper analysis showed that it was in these cases that mirror characters and the ensuing transfer of emotions seemed most often to occur. As for curiosity, this was demonstrated above by the Lancelot example.

Further research is required here, especially with regard to fine-tuning the analysis of the often complex emotions represented by the exclamations. So far, the rough analysis has yielded no specific patterns with regard to, for instance, the exclamations used for sadness or fear by male or female characters. As Anatole Fuksas has shown in this volume, however, Chrétien does differentiate the presentation of emotions by gender. A deeper analysis – beyond the scope of this exploration – may reveal a similar distinction between men and women in the use of *ay* and *o wi*, in general, or in specific situations.

Conclusion

As amusing as it was to come up with the briefest possible title and subject for a paper in the Bristol conference of the Arthurian Society ('Ay'), it led to a certain anxiety with regard to the possibly minimal and disappointing results, yet curiosity overcame fear and led to joyful admiration for the medieval authors' ability to pack these mini-words with so much emotion. *Ay* turned out to be not the answer to all my emotional questions, of course, yet this versatile little word is a very good indication of the diversity and intensity of the emotions described and transferred, especially by means of dialogues. It signposts moments with an exceptional emotional impact, for the medieval performer who may have made the most of the theatrical potential of these situations, and for his listeners. *Ay* is used especially by the main characters in the text, but also by the spectators (often mirror characters), the narrator, and the corrector, and perhaps even by the medieval audience as it listened to, and was emotionally drawn into, the Middle Dutch Arthurian romances.

9

Translating Emotion: Vocalisation and Embodiment in Yvain *and* Ívens saga*

SIF RIKHARDSDOTTIR

In Chrétien's *Yvain*, Laudine, the mourning widow, cries out, faints, claws at herself and tears out her hair at the death of her husband, Esclados the Red.[1] In *Laxdœla saga*, one of the Icelandic sagas, on the other hand, the heroine, Guðrún Ósvífrsdóttir, smiles as one of her husband's killers uses her shawl to wipe the blood off the weapon that killed her husband. We in fact see no evidence of grief on her part until twelve years later, when she goads her sons to avenge the killing of their father by taunting them with their father's bloody clothes. There is not a single exclamation of grief: no tears, no fainting, nor any other visible signs of sorrow.[2] In *Brennu-Njáls saga*, one of the better-known sagas, another heroine, Hallgerðr Höskuldsdóttir, similarly laughs at the news of her husband's slaying before sending the perpetrator to her father, where he will be killed himself.[3] How does one reconcile such different demonstrations of emotional behaviour when comparing one cultural realm to the other – or are these two scenes as different as one might believe?

Some might argue here that I am comparing apples and oranges by juxtaposing scenes from a French romance with examples from the Icelandic sagas. Yet it is precisely in the comparison between the two that the cultural premise of emotional representation can be most fruitfully explored. If the saga examples represent a particular (cultural or literary) mode of feminine bereavement behaviour, how would the distinctly different performance of the French heroine be transmitted

---

* The initial research for this chapter was completed while the author was a Visiting Fellow at Clare Hall, Cambridge, and was funded by a research project grant from the Icelandic Research Fund.
[1] *Le Chevalier au Lion ou Le Roman d'Yvain*, ed. D. F. Hult (Paris, 1994), ll. 1150–61. Quotations from the French text will be cited with the relevant line numbers following the quotation in the text.
[2] *Laxdœla saga*, ed. E. Ó. Sveinsson, Íslenzk fornrit 5 (Reykjavík, 1934), p. 168 and pp. 179–81.
[3] *Brennu-Njáls saga*, ed. E. Ó. Sveinsson, Íslenzk fornrit 12 (Reykjavík, 1954), pp. 50–51.

and received?[4] While the saga material by no means comprises the only literature read or enjoyed by Icelandic medieval audiences, the examples cited are nevertheless representative of the type of literary material that was being written and copied alongside the translated romance material and later indigenous romances.

The topic of this chapter is the translatability of literary representation of emotion across linguistic and cultural boundaries. The central premise is that of the stability of emotional representation and categorisation across cultures. If emotions are to a great extent culturally defined, and therefore unstable and shifting, how does one translate emotional behaviour for an audience that conceives those emotions (or the literary representation of a particular emotion) differently? Furthermore, if emotional representation is dependent on linguistic structures, how does the translator convey the emotive undercurrents of his material within the new signifying system? This chapter considers Chrétien de Troyes' *Yvain* and its Norse translation, *Ívens saga*, and the complexities of translingual and transcultural emotion and emotion research.

The Cultural Contingency of Emotion

Yvain was most likely translated around the mid-thirteenth century in Norway as part of a large importation of French materials at the court of King Hákon Hákonarson (r. 1217–1263).[5] We do not know precisely what sort of literary materials the original audience might have been familiar with, although these most likely consisted of religious texts, sagas of kings, heroic legends and even possibly some Icelandic saga material. The Norse translation has, however, only been preserved in Iceland, where it was copied well into the nineteenth century. The three extant primary manuscripts stem from the fifteenth and seventeenth centuries.[6] One can assume, based on the close connections between the two countries and evidence of familiarity with the material early on in Iceland, that the story

---

[4] It should be noted here that the two examples cited at the beginning of the chapter do not represent the entire spectrum of female mourning in the sagas, which ranges from the aloof reaction of Hallgerðr Höskuldsdóttir, to crying, and finally to whetting (urging family members to vengeance) in the manner of Guðrún Ósvífsdóttir. Yet they are representative in the sense that their reactions highlight a comportment that was presumably recognised by its audience as particularly meaningful within the matrix of the saga material.

[5] For a general discussion of the transmission of French material into Norse see S. Rikhardsdottir, *Medieval Translations and Cultural Discourse: The Movement of Texts in England, France and Scandinavia* (Cambridge, 2012), and *Rittersagas: Übersetzung, Überlieferung, Transmission*, ed. J. Glauser and S. Kramarz-Bein (Tübingen, 2014), as well as C. Larrington, 'The Translated *Lais*', and other essays in *The Arthur of the North: The Arthurian Legend in the Norse and Rus' Realms*, ed. M. Kalinke (Cardiff, 2011).

[6] For information on the manuscripts see *Ívens saga*, ed. F. W. Blaisdell, Editiones Arnamagnæanæ Series B, vol. 18 (Copenhagen, 1979), pp. xi–clv.

passed to Iceland relatively shortly after being translated in Norway. Furthermore, both translated and native romances co-existed alongside saga material (frequently in the same manuscript collections) and presumably shared reading communities. Amendments to the emotional representation in the translation process can therefore provide significant insight into how cultural and linguistic communities embody emotions, about the available emotive vocabulary and about the influence of literary conventions in emotional demonstration.

While it should be noted that medieval Icelandic writers were probably more familiar with and more immersed in continental tradition than has previously been assumed – as both Torfi Tulinius and Margaret Clunies Ross have pointed out – the Norse translation of *Yvain* nevertheless forms part of the earliest known French material translated into Norse.[7] Moreover, just as cultures are not monolithic stable entities but multi-faceted, complex and evolving, so are literary traditions. While Icelandic literary production formed part of a larger pan-European tradition, it nevertheless had its own unique characteristics, neither stable nor uniform, but distinct nevertheless. These characteristics would, like any cultural artefact, be influenced and shaped by multiple factors, ranging from language to gender relations. Any literature produced would thus contain elements that reflected its authorial background, although this does not mean that they might not transcend these originating boundaries. Any new input, whether through translation or exposure to other linguistic or literary traditions, would thus complement the existing material, thereby reshaping and reconstructing the tradition. The new object – that is, the translated text – would by the same token reveal the impressions of being moulded by existing linguistic and literary structures and conventions.

The thirteenth-century Norse translator and later Icelandic redactors of Chrétien's *Yvain* therefore had to convey their material in a manner that would have been comprehensible to their Nordic audiences; audiences whose emotional perceptions and habits – and more importantly, conventions of literary representation of emotional behaviour – might have differed substantially from those of Chrétien's original twelfth-century aristocratic audience. Yet there is no evidence of a brazen Nordic version of Laudine, laughing in the face of her husband's killer in the manner of the saga heroines. The Norse text is in fact quite similar to the French one. There are, nevertheless, certain distinct modifications in the way in which the translator conveys the emotive content of his original that reveal the process of adaptation to different conventions. There is a

---

[7] T. Tulinius, 'The Self as Other: Iceland and Christian Europe in the Middle Ages', *Gripla* 20 (2009), 199–215, and M. Clunies Ross, 'Medieval Iceland and the European Middle Ages', in *International Scandinavian and Medieval Studies in Memory of Gerard Wolfgang Weber*, ed. M. Dallapiazza, O. Hansen, P. M. Sørensen and Y. S. Bonnetain (Trieste, 2000), pp. 111–20.

general and overall reduction in emotional vocabulary in the Norse translation when compared with the French text.[8] By 'emotional vocabulary' I mean words that indicate emotional content, such as 'anger' or 'angry', 'joy' or 'joyous'. The definition of such vocabulary is, however, likely to be a matter of contention.[9] How does one define emotion words, and where does one draw the boundaries? This may again be a question of cultural prerogative. The choices here do not necessarily reflect a firm conclusion as to what should in fact be considered emotional vocabulary. A consensus is needed on how broadly one can extend the concept, but for the sake of the argument here, the definition will be non-discriminatory and refer generally to words that indicate a presumed feeling.[10]

In the Norse text there is a reduction both in the quantity of emotion words used and the variety of such words. The French text ascribes emotion frequently (when compared with the Norse text) and assigns an array of both positive and negative emotions to its characters. These range from pleasure, delight, joy, happiness and love, to fear, distress, shame, hate, sorrow, grief, anguish, anger and so forth.[11] A short example from the initial scene should suffice to reveal the extent of the author's (or scribes') attribution of emotion to his characters. The queen has retold Calogrenant's story to the king, who has promptly decided that his court

---

[8] For an analysis of the emotive vocabulary of Old Norse see C. Larrington, 'Learning to Feel in the Old Norse Camelot?' *Scandinavian Studies*, special issue on 'Arthur of the North: Histories, Emotions, and Imaginations', ed. B. Bandlien, S. G. Eriksen and S. Rikhardsdottir, 87.1 (2015), 74–94.

[9] Within the 'natural school', emotions have been quantified as a limited number of basic emotions that have a biochemical and neurological origin, generally defined as happiness, anger, sadness, surprise, fear and disgust (see, for instance, P. Ekman and W. V. Friesen, 'Constants across Cultures in the Face and Emotion', *Journal of Personality and Social Psychology* 17.2 (1971), 124–9). The list is extended in P. Ekman, 'All Emotions Are Basic', in *The Nature of Emotion: Fundamental Questions*, ed. P. Ekman and R. J. Davidson (Oxford, 1994), pp. 15–19, and 'Basic Emotions', in *Handbook of Cognition and Emotion*, ed. T. Dalgleish and M. Power (Chichester, 1999), pp. 45–60. While the categories of basic emotions are useful in terms of defining generalised cross-cultural behaviour traits, the limited range excludes the complex landscape of emotional behaviour, particularly as it is expressed in literature.

[10] Barbara Rosenwein's approach of examining emotion words used by medieval scholars as means of accessing the vocabulary of emotion that was available to medieval writers is duly noted ('Emotion Words', in *Le sujet des émotions au Moyen Âge*, ed. D. Boquet and P. Nagy (Paris, 2009), pp. 93–106). While this approach would provide a more concrete notion of words with a definite emotive association for medieval scholars, it is unlikely that such a list could encompass the entirety of words that might have had an emotional attachment or generated feelings (nor does Rosenwein suggest it would). In the absence of such a pre-established list of emotion words, I have therefore opted for a non-discriminatory approach despite the inherent risk of superimposing modern assumptions onto these terms.

[11] Some of the frequently cited emotion words appearing in the French text are: 'amours' (love), 'angoisse' (anguish), 'dolour' (suffering, pain), 'joie' (joy), 'ire' (anger), 'anui' (distress, sadness, sorrow), 'paour' (fear), 'duel' (affliction, sorrow), 'mescheoir' (to fall into depression, sorrow), 'rage' (madness, furor, pain), 'melancolie' (melancholy, sadness), 'esbahir' (feel bewildered), 'mautelent' (resentment, angry), 'aimer' (to love), 'a bele chiere' (cheerful, with a radiant face),' lié' (joyeous), 'esjoier' (to be joyeous), 'tenir chiers' (cherish, hold dearly). Cf. also Anatole Fuksas's chapter in this book.

will proceed to the fountain to observe the marvels and to do battle with the knight:

> De che que li rois devisa,
> Toute la cours miex l'em prisa,
> Car mout y voloient aler
> Li baron et li bacheler.
> Mais qui qu'en soit liés et joians,
> Mesire Yvains en fu dolans,
> Qu'il en quidoit aler tous seus,
> S'en fu dolans et angousseus
> Du roi qui aler y devoit. (ll. 671–9)[12]

> (And everything the king had decided
> Delighted the entire court,
> For every knight and every
> Squire was desperate to go.
> But in spite of their joy and their pleasure
> My lord Yvain was miserable,
> For he'd meant to go alone,
> And so he was sad and upset
> At the king for planning his visit.)[13]

The emotion words here ascribe emotion states or feelings to both the courtiers, who are 'liés et joians' (joyous and happy), and to Yvain, who is, on the contrary, 'angousseus' (upset) and 's'en fu dolans' (felt sad).[14] The contrast between Yvain's state of mind and that of the court foregrounds the emotional incentive that underlies Yvain's decision to depart ahead of the king. Emotional states are made explicit through emotive words, rather than being inferred from characters' actions, underscoring their function as interpretative signals within the narrative fabric.

The Norse translation reveals less of the emotional life of the characters, and the range of the emotions expressed is more limited. Happiness and love are the predominant positive markers, and fear, anger and

---

[12] For information on the manuscripts used, see Hult's edition.

[13] Chrétien de Troyes, *Yvain: The Knight of the Lion*, trans. B. Raffel (New Haven, 1987), ll. 673–81. Further quotations will be cited with line numbers following the quotation in the text.

[14] The difficulty in conveying medieval emotion to the modern reader becomes apparent in the English translation of the Old French verse. The translator must convey an approximate equivalence for the perceived emotion being described in the original and decide whether or not to indicate emotion where one is either hinted at or nascent in the original. The first two lines in the French example, for instance, would translate roughly as the court much appreciating (or esteeming) that which the king had decided or declared. Raffel has chosen 'delighted' to convey this, which has a stronger emotive impression than 'esteem', which conveys a sense of ethical judgement of the act. Then again, the act of appreciating a gesture by the king may well have contained feelings of delight, which would then be aptly conveyed in the translation. The necessity of making such translational choices (apparent in Raffel's excellent translation) foregrounds the instability of emotional content and its expression through language.

sorrow the main negative ones.¹⁵ The passage quoted above is shortened, and its emotive content is eliminated in the Norse translation. The narration moves directly on from the king's decision to take his court to the fountain to Yvain's departure without any comment on the court's reactions or on Yvain's feelings about the king's decision:

> ok er kongr heyrdí þetta. þa sor hann ath Jnnan halfsmanadar skyldí hann heimann fara med allrí sinní hírd ok koma ath keldunní hitt seinazsta ath Jons messu. ok nu hugsadí Ivent sítt mal ok ef hann færi med kongi þa mundí Kæi spotta hans mal sem fyr ok eigi væri vist ath honum mundí þessa eínvigís audít verda ok hugsadí ath hann skyldí einn samann brott fara.¹⁶

> (When the king heard this, then he swore that within a half month he would leave home with all his court and come to the spring at the latest at the eve of St. John. Now Iven thought about his cause and that if he went with the king, then Kæi would mock his cause as before, and it would not be certain that this duel would be granted to him, and thought that he should go away alone.)¹⁷

The emotive words and reactions of both the court and Yvain have been eliminated in the translation (or subsequent scribal copying), yet the underlying emotional reality is nevertheless present in the scene. Yvain's concern with Kay's mockery comprises an emotive valuation. His decision to depart is thus (as before) based on a judgement that has, as its basis of reference, an emotional motivation. The underlying emotional motivation might involve desire for honour, fear of mockery and possible anger at previous derision and displeasure with the current state of affairs. Rather than being expressed, however, these emotions have to be inferred from the text. There is therefore a distinct curtailing of emotive representation.

Many of the Norse translations of French material reveal similar signs of cultural adaptation in the behaviour of the characters.¹⁸ Furthermore, such emotive behaviour is generally attributed to physiological causes:

---

[15] The corresponding Norse words would be 'gleði' (glaðazst, glöddumst, fagnaður), 'ást' (elskaði), 'hræðsla' (ógn, hræðsla, óttadiz), 'reiði' (reiðr), 'hryggleiki' (harmr, harmfullr, hugarangr, sorg). As with the French version, the English words used to convey the meaning of the original are given with the qualification that they do not capture the entirety or the multiplicity of the meanings of the original words in their textual context. They nevertheless provide the closest equivalence and the common usage of those words.

[16] *Ívens saga*, pp. 23–4. The quotation is taken from MS A, but the other versions agree generally in the textual representation of this passage. Further quotations from *Ívens saga* will be cited by page numbers in the text.

[17] Ibid., p. 161. Foster's translation, which follows the Norse text in the edition, is used throughout. I have eliminated variant readings of the passage in the cited quotation for ease of reading. Further English translations of the Norse text will be based on Foster's translation and will be cited by page numbers following quotations.

[18] See S. Rikhardsdottir, 'Bound by Culture: A Comparative Study of the Old French and Old Norse Versions of *La Chanson de Roland*', *Mediaevalia* 26.2 (2005), 243–65, and *Medieval Translations and Cultural Discourse*, particularly pp. 66–70.

that is, internal and involuntary impulses, as opposed to external and symbolic representation. This shift in the representational function of emotive behaviour calls attention to a presumed cultural preference for emotional suppression or concealment (as opposed to demonstration). At the same time it acknowledges the existence of such emotions and the self-command needed to 'overcome' them. This model of emotions is based on the medieval medical understanding of the body as 'affective' and Hippocrates' theory of the humours.[19] Emotions are thus perceived to arise within the body, at times resulting in somatic reactions beyond the character's control. As Barbara Rosenwein has noted, this model has been surprisingly enduring, surviving well into the twentieth century and beyond.[20]

The Emotive Interior and Public Masking

This apparent tendency to reduce emotional exuberance in the Norse translations evokes questions of literary precedence and cultural conventions and shifts the focus back to the saga examples. Saga literature is, of course, notorious for its lack of emotional display. The same can be said to apply to many medieval Icelandic genres, such as *konungasögur* (sagas of kings) and *fornaldarsögur* (legendary sagas). This does not imply that the sagas are devoid of feelings – quite the opposite, in fact, as they often describe dramatic events and the efforts of characters to come to terms with those events. Rather, internal emotions are frequently translated into actions, exhibited through involuntary physical reactions (reddening, swelling or sweating) or conveyed through verbal retorts that are intended to hide the emotional turmoil that evoked them. While somatic description is fairly rare in the sagas, it is nevertheless used efficiently to convey underlying emotions that the character is unable to contain or suppress.

William Ian Miller notes that emotions in the sagas must be inferred.[21] Furthermore he considers dialogue and action to be the most frequent indicators of the emotive life of saga characters.[22] While I agree with Miller's

---

[19] For a discussion of the 'affective' body in medieval literature see, for instance, C. Saunders, 'The Affective Body: Love, Virtue and Vision in English Medieval Literature', in *The Body and the Arts*, ed. C. J. Saunders, U. Maude and J. Macnaughton (Basingstoke, 2009), pp. 87–102.

[20] Rosenwein terms this perception of emotions the 'hydraulic model' and points out that it is in fact a direct inheritance of the medieval notions of the humours. She furthermore states that it was not until the 1960s, with developments in cognitive sciences, that it was replaced (at least within scientific circles) by a conception of emotions as 'part of a process of perception and appraisal, not forces striving for release'. See 'Worrying about Emotions in History', *American Historical Review* 107.3 (2002), 821–45, at pp. 834 and 837.

[21] W. I. Miller, *Humiliation and Other Essays on Honor, Social Discomfort, and Violence* (Ithaca, NY, 1993), p. 111.

[22] W. I. Miller, 'Emotions and the Sagas', in *From Sagas to Society: Comparative Approaches to Early Iceland*, ed. G. Pálsson (Enfield Lock, 1992), pp. 89–109, at p. 107.

observation that dialogue is a rich source for accessing the emotional life of saga characters, there is a difference in the manner in which dialogue is used to convey emotions in the French versus the Norse texts. Dialogue is, in fact, frequently used to *obscure* internal emotive life in the sagas, rather than *expressing* it as in the French romance. While the emphasis is thus on vocalisation of emotion in *Yvain*, verbal utterance is by contrast used to mask emotion in the saga examples.

The example cited at the outset of this chapter of Hallgerðr's reaction to the news of her husband's killing reveals an exchange that is designed to suppress or conceal internal emotions. Glúmr, Hallgerðr's husband, is killed after a quarrel with Hallgerðr's servant, Þjóstólfr. Þjóstólfr has made a snide remark regarding Glúmr's lack of skills and strength to do anything other than 'brölta á maga Hallgerði' ('bounc[e] around on Hallgerd's belly').[23] Glúmr retaliates in anger, resulting in Þjóstólfr sinking his axe into Glúmr's shoulder. After Glúmr's death, Þjóstólfr removes a golden bracelet from Glúmr's body, covers it with rocks and returns to Hallgerðr:

> Hallgerðr var úti ok sá, at blóðug var øxin. Hann kastaði til hennar gullhringinum. Hon mælti: 'Hvat segir þú tíðenda? eða hví er øx þín blóðug?' Hann svaraði: 'Eigi veit ek, hversu þér mun þykkja: ek segi þér víg Glúms.' 'Þú munt því valda,' segir hon. 'Svá er,' segir hann. Hon hló at ok mælti: 'Eigi ert þú engi í leiknum.'[24]
>
> (Hallgerd was outside and saw that his axe was bloody. He threw the gold bracelet to her.
> She spoke: 'What news do you bring? Why is your axe bloody?'
> He answered, 'I don't know how you'll take this, but I must tell you of the slaying of Glum.'
> 'You must have done it', she said.
> 'That's true', he said.
> She laughed and said, 'You didn't sit this game out.')[25]

The passage is devoid of emotive words and is deceptively laconic and matter-of-fact. Any emotions on behalf of the participants must be inferred through contextualisation and interpretation of their acts and the implications of their words. Hallgerðr's decision to send Þjóstólfr to her uncle Hrútr signals an underlying emotion that is hidden beneath the seemingly dispassionate discourse. Hrútr's immediate reaction of slaying Glúmr's killer reveals that he has read her action accordingly and that, even if it is not made explicit, the emotive framework for her behaviour (the desire for revenge) is legible to the saga's audience.

Hallgerðr's perplexing laughter thus becomes a pregnant symbol of an emotional interior and its public masking. The disparity between emotional

---

[23] *Brennu-Njáls saga*, p. 49, and *Njal's saga*, trans. R. Cook (London, 1997), p. 32.
[24] *Brennu-Njáls saga*, p. 50.
[25] *Njal's saga*, trans. R. Cook, p. 32.

representation in the saga context and in romance is thus located in the *function* of emotional representation. Whereas the object of the emotive discourse in the French text is to express presumed internal emotions, the retorts in saga literature seem conversely to have been intended to conceal those emotions. Once the intent is to deflect emotional communication, the discourse can no longer be considered emotive – although it can, of course, be emotional and may very well have been understood as such by its medieval audience.

This method of emotional suppression, or concealment, can be said to apply equally to the example cited at the outset of Guðrún's reaction to her husband's killing. In *Laxdæla saga*, Guðrún's husband, Bolli Þorleiksson, is killed outside their house in a retaliatory attack. After the attack, one of the killers, Helgi Harðbeinsson, walks toward Guðrún and wipes the blood of the spear with which he has just run Bolli through on the end of her shawl: 'Guðrún leit til hans ok brosti við' (Gudrun looked at him and smiled).[26] Rather than expressing a feeling of joy or friendliness – the cognitive function of a smile in human communication – the heroine's smile masks the presumed emotion beneath. In fact, Helgi's reaction to his companion's criticism of his cruelty reveals that he has read her smile accurately: 'Helgi bað hann eigi þat harma, – "því at ek hygg þat," segir hann, "at undir þessu blæjuhorni búi minn höfuðsbani."' (Helgi told him to spare his sympathy, 'as something tells me that my own death lies under the end of that shawl').[27]

Miller notes that smiles in the saga realm are 'markers more often of hostility than of amiability', which suggests that literary representation of emotional signs may indeed be governed by generic conventions as well as being culturally determined.[28] These generic codes would thus alert the audience to the value system and emotional framework of the text in question. The use of the smile here may indeed be a literary device intended to forewarn the reader of the impending doom of the recipient, a narrative device intended to build up anticipation.[29] The smile may also be seen as emblematic of the suppression of emotion, a means of

---

[26] *Laxdæla saga*, ed. E. Ó. Sveinsson, p. 168, and *The Saga of the People of Laxardal*, trans. K. Kunz, in *The Sagas of Icelanders: A Selection* (New York, 2001), pp. 270–421, at p. 381. The English translation has been adjusted slightly to better reflect the emotional undercurrent.

[27] Ibid.

[28] Miller, *Humiliation*, p. 96.

[29] Miller discusses both Hallgerðr's and Guðrún's responses to their husbands' slayings in 'Emotions and the Sagas', pp. 91–2, and later in his book *Humiliation*: see particularly pp. 94–7. For a discussion of smiles or laughter generally in the sagas see also L. S. Ai, 'The Mirthless Content of Skarphedinn's Grin', *Medium Ævum* 65.1 (1996), 101–8, and J. Le Goff, 'Laughter in *Brennu-Njáls saga*', in *From Sagas to Society: Comparative Approaches to Early Iceland*, ed. G. Pálsson (Enfield Lock, 1992), pp. 161–5. For information on the use of smiles as signals for dramatic irony see, for instance, P. Ménard, *Le rire et la sourire dans le roman courtois en France au moyen âge (1150–1250)* (Geneva, 1969), and J. A. Burrow, *Gestures and Looks in Medieval Narrative* (Cambridge, 2002).

preparing for the whetting or the vengeance to come. Yet it also conveys the complex orchestra of emotions that are present, all of which are, however, hidden beneath the smile. With the smile the emotive subject has displaced the emotion of sorrow currently experienced into a future in which the sorrow will generate a successful *hvöt* (goading). The expression thus acts as a victorious declaration of exercised control, successful transference and certainty of the recipient's doom.

Kathryn Starkey comments on the function of smiles in the German epic *Das Nibelungenlied*. She argues that the smile serves as a 'political and performative gesture' within the epic, thereby clearly defying the presumption that it is a spontaneous somatic or affective response.[30] At the outset of the epic, while the Burgundians prepare to woo Brunhild with a show of strength, Gunther's men grumble about the removal of their weapons and declare that they would kill the queen if they had their swords and armour. Brunhild, who overhears their words, smiles at Hagen and Gunther before offering to return the Burgundians their previously confiscated weapons:

> Wol hort diu kuniginne, waz der degen sprach
> mit smielendem munde si uber ahsel sach:
> 'nu er dunche sich so biderbe, so tragt in ir gewant,
> und ir vil scharpfen waffen gebt den recken an die hant'[31]
>
> (Noble Brunhild had no trouble hearing their words.
> Smiling over her shoulder, she spoke to her men: 'Return their
> armor, let these men, who think themselves such warriors,
> have their shields, and also give them back their good sharp
> swords.')[32]

The smile is, as Starkey notes, apparently out of context, as Gunther's men have just intimated that if they had their weapons they would kill her. Starkey considers the smile to serve here as 'assessment of the power dynamics and an assertion of her superiority over her guests', revealing the appropriation of a somatic signal of friendliness to convey an undertone of menace.[33] This conscious manipulation of the smile within the narrative framework of the epic is similar to the way in which the smile is used in the saga, hinting at some tantalising implications of the generic functions of somatic indicators. The smile and laughter of the saga heroines discussed above can therefore be considered as fairly powerful evidence of the manipulation of physiological indicators of internal feel-

---

[30] K. Starkey, 'Performative Emotion and the Politics of Gender in the *Nibelungenlied*', in *Women and Medieval Epic: Gender, Genre, and the Limits of Epic Masculinity*, ed. S. S. Poor and J. K. Schulman (New York, 2007), pp. 253–71, at p. 255.

[31] *Das Nibelungenlied: Nach der Handschrift C der Badischen Landesbibliothek Karlsruhe*, ed. and trans. U. Schulze (Düsseldorf, 2005), p. 150 (v. 457).

[32] *Das Nibelungenlied: Song of the Nibelungs*, trans. B. Raffel (New Haven, 2006), p. 63 (v. 447).

[33] 'Performative Emotion', p. 255.

ings, possibly to conceal an emotion, or perhaps as a disquieting signal of impending doom for the recipients of those smiles.

Emotive Vocalisation and Embodiment

In the scene of Laudine's mourning in Chrétien's *Yvain*, the reader witnesses Laudine's reaction to the loss of her husband, Esclados the Red, who has been killed by Yvain. The focal point remains with Yvain and the reader therefore visualises her through his eyes:

> ... da duel faire estoit si fole
> C'a poi que'ele ne s'ochioit.
> A la feÿe s'escrioit
> Si haut qu'ele ne pooit plus,
> Si recheoit pasmee jus.
> Et quant ele estoit relevee,
> Aussi comme femme desvee
> S'i commenchoit a deschirer,
> Et ses chaveus a detirer.
> Ses chaveus tire et ront ses dras,
> Et se repasme a chascun pas,
> Ne riens ne le puet conforter. (ll. 1150–61)

> (Her grief was so intense
> She seemed ready to take her own life.
> And then she cried out so loudly
> That she seemed to have exhausted herself
> And dropped to the ground, unconscious.
> And when they lifted her up
> She began to tear at her clothes
> Like a woman gone mad, and she pulled
> At her hair, and ripped it out,
> And she tore at her dress, and at every
> Step fell in a faint,
> And nothing could relieve her pain.)

What stands out from this passage is the dual representation of Laudine's sorrow through voice and body. She vocalises her grief by crying out repeatedly and later by lamenting her husband's death. The presumed internal sorrow is embodied by quite literally displaying it on the body, through the torn hair, scratched face and rent clothes, all standard representations of female grieving in the romance tradition. While the text refers to her 'duel' (grief), a presumably internal condition, this interiority is nevertheless only made available through external exhibitors: that is, through vocalisation and embodiment.

The reference here to the exhibited embodiment of her grief does not denote somatic response in the proper sense. Such somatic responses would include swelling or reddening and even possibly fainting, related to physiological processes, such as fluctuations in blood pressure (which would have been construed as humoral instability). What I intend here is to identify a *demonstrated* grief, one that is deliberately performed on the body. Such a representational enactment of emotion differs fundamentally from automatic or involuntary emotional responses that result in (or are the result of) neurological reactions that are evidenced on the body as somatic reflexes. Moreover, the mourning is a public scene that takes place amidst her people in a communal burial procession. Even later, as she remains behind 'qui souvent se prent par la gole,/ et tort ses poins, et bat ses paumes' (ll. 1416–17) ('clutching at her throat, wringing/ her hands, beating her palms') (ll. 1412–13), she still occupies her public role as the mourning widow and, in fact, continues to be observed in this role by Yvain, who is watching her through the window. Given the intimate connection between social performance and social identity, Laudine can be perceived as performing her prescribed role, which confirms and asserts her feudal status and identity. Susan Crane in fact notes that 'public appearance and behavior are thought not to falsify personal identity but, on the contrary, to establish and maintain it', calling attention to the function of public performance of medieval elites as a means of confirming and sustaining a personal identity.[34]

It is not until she has retired to her rooms and is alone that we see a different Laudine altogether. Lunete, her maid, has scolded her for her excessive grief and suggested a better lord can be found, at which Laudine dismisses her in anger; but once in private she sets to calmly evaluate her options:

> Et le dame se rapensa
> Qu'ele avoit mout grant tort eü;
> Mout vausist bien avoir seü
> Comment ele porroit prouver
> C'on porroit chevalier trouver
> Melleur c'ongques ne fu ses sire,
> Mout volentiers li orroit dire. (ll. 1654–60)

> (And when the lady reflected
> She knew she'd been very wrong;
> And all her desire was to know
> How the girl could have proven
> That a better knight could be found
> Than her lord had ever been.
> And she wished she could hear her explain.)[35]

---

[34] S. Crane, *The Performance of Self: Ritual, Clothing, and Identity during the Hundred Years War* (Philadelphia, 2002), p. 4.

[35] I have made minor amendments to the first line of Raffel's translation better to capture the pensive nature of the sentence in French.

There is a discernible shift in emotional register that occurs as we move from her public role, as the grieving widow, to the private sphere, where we witness the apparently dispassionate deliberation of her current state and the means of remedying her situation. The move from the exuberant display of emotions to internal reflection, quite dramatically different from the apparent state of mental disarray that came before it, indicates that the crying and tearing of her clothes may simply reflect a socially prescribed behaviour pattern for a grieving widow, rather than a deeply felt sorrow.

Female lamentation is commonly indicated (or represented) by dishevelled hair, torn clothes and wailing.[36] The existence of a prescribed behaviour pattern certainly does not negate the possibility of authentic feelings behind those actions. One can only assume that such socially coded behaviour patterns in many ways exist as an outlet for existent emotions, as a socially appropriate and approved means of expressing them. Then again, such coded performances might also be devoid of emotions; they may be initiated without underlying emotion in order to fulfil a political or social function. Emotive performances may indeed incite certain emotions through the coded verbal or physical act; in effect, the prescribed act may unleash the emotion itself. Richard Huntington and Peter Metcalf observe that in ritualised performances of mourning the act of weeping is not necessarily brought on by the sentiments, but that 'wailing at the prescribed moment and in the prescribed manner creates within the wailer the proper sentiment'.[37] The prescribed pattern of emotive behaviour calls attention to the artificiality of the literary scene, as opposed to the authenticity of the emotive experience. This artificiality need not diminish the emotive value of the scene, but it does foreground the function of its components as literary signifiers.

The fact that Laudine's sorrow is externalised and embodied intimates a ritualised aspect. Jutta Eming observes that 'ritualized expres-

---

[36] See, for instance, A. E. Bailey, 'Lamentation Motifs in Medieval Hagiography', *Gender & History* 25.3 (2013), 529–44. The existence of communal patterns of public behaviour for bereavement has been demonstrated in various ethnographic studies, see, for instance, G. Urban, 'Ritual Wailing in Amerindian Brazil', *American Anthropologist* 90.2 (1988), 385–400, and B. Grima, *The Performance of Emotion among Paxtun Women* (Austin, TX, 1992).

[37] P. Metcalf and R. Huntington, *Celebrations of Death: The Anthropology of Mortuary Ritual* (Cambridge, 1980), p. 26. Metcalf's and Huntington's statement refers specifically to Andamanese culture. Yet the socialising function of mourning rites is nevertheless more widely applicable, since most societies have certain conventions or standards of acceptable grieving behaviour. Bade Ajumon's discussion of professional mourners and dirge performances similarly reveals 'a Western cultural bias [that] regards lamentation for the dead as representing an outburst of emotions caused by feeling of sorrow for the departed fellow'. See B. Ajumon, 'Lament for the Dead as a Universal Folk Tradition', *Fabula* 22.3/4 (1981), 272–80, at p. 275. For information on the lament tradition in medieval literature, see J. Tolmie and M. J. Toswell, *Laments for the Lost in Medieval Literature* (Turnhout, 2010), and V. B. Richmond, *Laments for the Dead in Medieval Narrative* (Pittsburgh, 1966).

sion communicates and authenticates emotions through an ostentatious styling of the body, through facial expression, gesture, movement, voice and speech'.[38] These expressions are therefore based on aesthetics rather than on presumed interiority. Laudine's calm reflections once in private suggest that the external display of emotion need not necessarily reflect an internal state. This disjunction between external and internal would explain the rapid move from apparent despair to stoic internal reflection, to a projected future state of contentment (if she were to find a better knight to replace the one who recently passed away). It is also quite possible that public grieving was considered to be cathartic by its audience. The performative mourning might thus have been perceived as an outlet for Laudine's emotions. Once the emotions had been exhibited, further grieving might have been judged inappropriate and might have been suppressed in favour of a calm exterior. Lunete's criticism of Laudine's excessive grieving lends some credibility to the idea of a preconceived period of mourning:

> 'Pour Dieu, car vous en chastïés?
> Si laissiés seviax non pour honte:
> A si haute femme ne monte
> Que duel si longuement maintiengne'. (ll. 1668–71)

> ('By God! Get control of yourself,
> Stop it, if only for shame.
> No highborn lady ought
> To keep up her mourning so long.')

It should nevertheless be kept in mind that Lunete's words are intended to facilitate the reconciliation of her lady with her husband's killer. It is therefore vital to reconfigure her emotional state from sorrow to concern for her status as the latter is more likely to result in a successful wooing. If one assumes the original audience would have been aware of (or even expected) such a disjunction between internal state and external presentation, then Laudine's acceptance of the killer of her husband as her new lord – often illogical to modern readers conditioned by romanticised ideas of love – makes perfect sense within the narrative framework of the story.

---

[38] J. Eming, 'On Stage: Ritualized Emotions and Theatricality in Isolde's Trial', *Modern Language Notes* 124 (2009), 555–71, at p. 556. While her argument relates to Middle High German courtly literature, more particularly to Gottfried von Straßburg's story of Tristan and Isolde, the reference to ritualised or conventionalised expressions of emotion 'like crying, audible mourning, tearing out of hair, and beating one's breast' (p. 562) could just as well apply to the romance of Yvain. In fact, given that French courtly romance (including Chrétien's material) was translated relatively promptly into German it is not unlikely that such ritualised (and possibly generic) sequences of emotional behaviour may have been transmitted along with the material to its new audience and established new conventions for the literary depiction of emotion.

Lunete's behaviour becomes more logical in this context too. Her apparent nonchalance with respect to the death of her lord appears in stark contrast to the other townspeople, who are described as enraged, storming, screaming and ranting as a result of their anguish (ll. 1109–10, 1189–95). Her own words provide some insight into the apparent breach between internal emotion and external behaviour as she tells Yvain:

> ... je n'os chi plus arrester.
> Je porroie tant demourer,
> Espoir, qu'ele me meskerroit
> Pour che qu'ele ne me verroit
> Avec les autres en la presse. (ll. 1337–41)
>
> (... 'I dare not stay here longer,
> If I stay on here with you
> Perhaps they'll begin to suspect me,
> Not seeing me there with the others,
> Milling in that crowd down there.')

One would assume that upon joining the crowd she would display the same symptoms of grief as the others, suggesting that they too may be performing a ritualised public enactment of grief. This would further explain how Chrétien can state, perhaps with some irony, when Yvain marries Laudine and becomes lord, that:

> Et li morz est tost obliés:
> Cil qui l'ocist est maries
> En sa fame, et esamble gisent.
> Et les genz aiment plus et present
> Le vif c'onque le mort ne firent. (ll. 2167–71)
>
> (... and the dead man forgotten
> And the man who killed him married
> To his wife, and sharing her bed,
> And his people are happier with their living
> Lord than they were with the dead one.) (ll. 2165–9)

Fredric Cheyette and Howell Chickering point out that within twelfth-century aristocratic society love signified not only personal feelings (or devotion), but also political loyalty: the fidelity between a lord and his (or her) follower.[39] The emotions displayed by Laudine and her people can be understood in relation to this convention as a sign of feudal tribute rather than a demonstration of personal (or internal) sorrow. While the sorrow may be perceived as authentic, it would nevertheless be intended and understood as an act of homage, a socially prescribed gesture of feudal fidelity. Such an interpretation of the scene would explain the rapid

---

[39] F. L. Cheyette and H. Chickering, 'Love, Anger, and Peace: Social Practice and Poetic Play in the Ending of *Yvain*', *Speculum* 80.1 (2005), 75–117.

recuperation of both Laudine and her people once a new lordship has been established and new feudal allegiance guaranteed. The fact that the grief exhibited is born out of fidelity or loyalty to a lord does not negate the existence of personal feelings or, for that matter, the argument that such publicly professed fidelity may in effect engender emotions. In fact, Laudine's anger seems more severe and harder to quell at Yvain's later breach of his promise to return than previously at the loss of Esclados the Red. This is so because Yvain has in fact failed to fulfil his duty to love, as an act of homage, and to honour her (to keep his word). These are acts born not (or not solely) out of emotion, but out of social obligation.

According to Cheyette and Chickering, 'offense to fidelity was also an offense to love':

> In its routine use in political contexts, 'love' signified political and personal loyalty, a layer of meaning that the troubadours continually drew upon when they used 'love' in an erotic sense. In their poetry, and here in *Yvain*, one meaning did not cancel out the other, a medieval balancing act that a modern reader must constantly remember.[40]

Yvain has transgressed social codes that form the foundation of aristocratic society. Laudine's anger, Yvain's subsequent madness and the eventual reconciliation are political situations encoded through emotional signifiers that were comprehensible and meaningful to their twelfth-century aristocratic audience. In fact, the emotional displays of shame and guilt are critical for the successful re-integration of Yvain into the social fabric. Yvain's madness, a symptom of the shame and guilt felt at his breaching of the social code and the implicit social ostracism, is necessary to rehabilitate him. Richard A. Dienstbier points out that emotions play a fundamental role in the socialising process of moral behaviour.[41] The emotional experience of fear, shame and guilt underlies the process of moral decision-making and hence the successful integration of an individual into society. Yvain's subsequent adventures thus bespeak his internalisation of the proper moral behavioural codes.

If the scene of Laudine's mourning does not reveal an internal emotion, but rather (or also) a politicised social action, how would one translate it for a reading community that has different social or political structures?[42]

---

[40] Ibid., 84.

[41] R. A. Dienstbier, 'The Role of Emotion in Moral Socialization', in *Emotions, Cognition, and Behavior*, ed. C. E. Izard, J. Kagan and R. B. Zajonc (Cambridge, 1984), pp. 494–514.

[42] As we do not have access to the Norse translation of *Yvain* in its thirteenth-century form, one must deduce from existing later Icelandic copies the sort of changes that the text might have undergone. The slight variations between the three primary manuscripts indicate that the later versions are likely to have been modified to some extent from the original translation, mostly through abridgement. The texts as we have them today therefore reveal more about their Icelandic reading communities, particularly in terms of audience predilection and perception of the texts, than about thirteenth-century Norwegian audiences. Yet the texts contain varying layers of cultural influence of the original translative effort and possible adjustments by later scribes.

If one assumes, as suggested above, a feudal act of homage as the underlying motivation behind the emotional display in the French original, the translator would have had to reconstruct not only a recognisable literary demonstration of an emotion, but moreover a *politicised* emotion. In the Norse text Laudine's mourning is related as follows: 'hun syrgdi ok æpti sínn harm stundum fell hun j ouít' (pp. 35–6) ('she mourned and cried out her sorrow. At times she fell in a faint') (p. 168).[43] The text contains the essential semantic elements of the episode as described in the French text (mourning, crying and fainting). Yet the passage has been both subdued and shortened. The elaborate depiction of the sorrow, the multiple swoons and the inconsolable grief, has been reduced to two sentences stating the bare facts: namely, that she mourned and cried and sometimes fainted. More significantly, however, the entire elaborate demonstration of the grief – that is the tearing of her hair and the clawing at her face and her clothes – is entirely missing.[44] The ritualised depiction of the mourning widow – the embodied gestures of the presumed internal grief – has been eliminated. If one hypothesises, as suggested above, that the scene presents a socially prescribed performance in a political role, assumed here by Laudine and understood as such by its French audience, this elaborate embodiment of the grief becomes redundant once the political context no longer applies.

Conclusion

Medieval Icelandic authors and audiences seem to have preferred to deduce the internal emotional life of their fictive characters through acts (but not through gestures), through somatic indicators (but not through bodily behaviour) and through verbalisation (but not through verbal expression). What is noticeable in the comparison of the Norse translation of *Yvain* and the two examples from the sagas is the absence of either vocalisation or embodiment from both saga passages. What we have instead is what I would term 'transference'. The somatic marker of happiness – i.e., a smile or laughter – is used either to hide actual emotions or to contain those emotions. In the French text, there is no need to hide or contain the sorrow as it is a necessary part of the process of re-establishing social balance. As Carol Clover points out, the lament in Old Norse literature is intimately linked to the concept of 'hvöt' (whetting) as 'whetting and

---

[43] The quotation is drawn from MS B as MS A has a lacuna here. MS C differs from B here. In MS C the entire episode of the procession is missing and Íven only sees her later as she is sitting down, presumably after the funeral.

[44] While it is of course quite possible that this reflects later amendments by Icelandic scribes, the passage nevertheless reveals the adaptation to a reading community whose habits of mourning may have differed from the original context of Chrétien's text and whose literary tradition of emotional representation did indeed differ.

lamenting are equivalent and interchangeable elements' that the audience would have appreciated and understood.[45] This intimate link between lamenting a loss and the incitement for revenge again shifts the representational function of emotive behaviour. In the previously cited example of Guðrún Ósvífrsdóttir, the presumed grief is veiled by her smile, only to be unleashed twelve years later in the goading of her sons to revenge – an act that will ensure that the memory of the dead will be properly honoured. The delay of twelve years intimates that this is not a spontaneous outburst of grief, but a social gesture of remembrance and respect.

In the case of the translated romances, there is of course no need for whetting as the social conditions depicted are radically different. Once the correlation between the literary topos of whetting and lamenting is broken, the signifying potential of emotive behaviour is inevitably shifted. There is no need for the Norse Laudine's grief to be contained or transferred as there is no familial obligation which could correspond with the saga convention of blood-revenge. The disassociation of the social obligations of the blood-feud society from the lament leaves the Norse audience to interpret the emotion itself, detached from both the feudal concern in the French text and the whetting obligations of the saga material. Whereas the lament is directly associated with feudal honour in the French original, here it is extricated from any such political subtext. What remains is an emphasis on the emotion itself, the presumed sorrow. The passage therefore depicts an effort to adjust an emotive behaviour to new cultural conventions of emotional representation.

The examples listed at the outset of this chapter reveal that emotional representation is not only culturally contingent and socially determined, but moreover reflects generic dispositions that one must assume audiences would have recognised and to which they would have responded. Admittedly generic distinctions are to some extent modern categorisations and serve a modern desire for demarcations of the medieval past. Fixed modern notions may contain and stabilise the shifting concept of the Middle Ages, rather than illuminate medieval perceptions of literary traditions. Nevertheless, such differences suggest that audiences are likely to have been able to decode the varying representations of emotion accurately and to situate them within a political, cultural and, significantly, generic context, thereby providing those codes with signifying potential. Since love signalled political as well as personal loyalty, the feudal subtext of political manoeuvres, negotiations and resolutions is intricately interwoven with Chrétien's apparent narrative concern with love. In the Norse text this subtext – while not eradicated – is redirected towards notions of honour. The concept of honour is here again intimately interlinked with

---

[45] C. Clover, 'Hildigunnur's Lament', in *Cold Counsel: Women in Old Norse Literature and Mythology*, ed. S. M. Anderson and K. Swenson (New York, 2002), pp. 15–54, at p. 23.

the social circumstances of medieval Iceland and reflects a personal and family-oriented responsibility, rather than a feudal or class-based concern.

The emotive potency of expression and gestures lies ultimately in the linguistic and literary conventions for embodying emotion, and the audience's engagement with this emotive content. The demonstrative public mourning of Laudine, representative of the feudal context of political allegiance and social obligations, conveys a social meaning as well as an emotive one. Similarly the substitution of a somatic marker of happiness, such as a smile, for an expression of sorrow in the sagas may well have signalled to its audience underlying conflicting emotions. These may have been perceived as a prelude to vengeance, an evocative gesture within the blood-feud society depicted in the sagas. The Norse translation of the grieving widow from the French text has, however, been divested of these feudal implications. Yet it has maintained the romance's generic conventions for representing emotional behaviour. The subtle tempering of Laudine's grief in the Norse translation internalises the grief and depoliticises it. Rather than serving as a social gesture, her behaviour signals instead a perceived emotive interiority. The expression of that presumed interiority alerts the audience that they are no longer in the world of feuds, where such interiority must be masked and projected into action, but in the world of romance, where emotionality in fact propels the action.

10

Afterword: Malory's Enigmatic Smiles

HELEN COOPER

What happens when an emotion is unreadable? This book gives a full account of how emotions work in the mind and the body, according to both medieval and modern theories (Introduction, Saunders); how they function within a society or a group, notably that of the Round Table, or of the audience and readers of Arthurian literature (Gilbert, Lynch, Radulescu); the disjunction between emotion and effective action (Lynch); the mechanisms by which the emotions of a fictional character can be mirrored in a reader (Larrington); the capacity of sounds – even sounds with no semantic content – to convey feeling (Brandsma); and whether (or how far) emotions can be transferred across cultures (Rikhardsdottir). Their overlap and intersection with other schemata, of the passions or the vices, are discussed, along with the specific terms used to describe fear or anger or shame (Fuksas). The bodily expressions most commonly attached to specific emotions are explored, of going pale or red, changing expression, flinching or weeping. Medieval authors will typically portray emotions so as to suggest some kind of social function for their readers: how a king, or a knight, should act as well as feel. The model underlying all of these is the assumption that emotions are communicated socially. Even if the character feeling the emotion keeps it to him- or herself, the reader is granted privileged access to their unexpressed thoughts or feelings. Kings may be under an obligation not to be too open about their emotions (Baden-Daintree), but the readers will be shown what they feel; lovers may blush in public before retreating to their chamber or some other isolated spot to lament their state, as an abundance of Arthurian and other romances demonstrate, but the symptoms will be thoroughly familiar to readers trained to recognize them. But what happens when a bodily sign of emotion carries neither a familiar meaning nor an explanation within the text?

Sir Thomas Malory can be a particularly challenging, or imaginatively engaging, author in this respect. Of all Arthurian writers, Malory is one of the least forthcoming about expressions of emotion, not least in comparison with the abundance found in his French sources. Many of the emotions he does describe, or their outward expressions (kneeling, weeping, drawing a sword), carry their meanings with them in all the ways this book has discussed. Sometimes, however, those outward expressions are much harder to read, or raise those questions of cultural transferability – of whether a modern reader may be misunderstanding them. There is probably not much cultural distance when a man safely enclosed in his castle responds to the fury of the hero he has shut out with, 'As for that thretynge, we woll go to dynere'; and not much that an insider familiarity with the contemporary culture can add to the statement that a messenger damsel and Sir Palomides 'had langage togyder whych pleased neythir of them'.[1] Those convey emotion with minimal explicit statement, and the reader's response is probably one of delight at their very laconicness, not necessarily at all the same emotion as that implied for the characters. On other occasions, emotion words can themselves be hard to interpret. Smiling and laughter can be particularly difficult: by contrast with weeping or mourning, they are somatic signs that do not carry their immediate meanings with them. In themselves and devoid of any context, to both medieval and modern readers they probably suggest conviviality, pleasure or amusement; but as Sif Rikhardsdottir's study shows, that response may be way off the mark. Just by virtue of being more understated as an expression of feeling, a smile may often be more enigmatic than laughter – witness the Mona Lisa – but one would expect laughter, as being expressive of a stronger emotion, to convey its meaning more openly. The quickest glance at the reception history of some of the most famous medieval smiles or laughs, however, shows that things are more problematic, though the problems are not always noticed. Emotional responses on the part of readers tend to happen below the critical radar, so it is easy to take one's own first response as being what the text is out to elicit, and not consider other possibilities. A distinctively modern or post-modern reaction to narrative laughter is that it must represent not pleasure but mockery. So Troilus's laughter from the height of the eighth sphere at 'those who wepten for his death so fast' is almost universally taken to signify scorn; the court's laughter at Gawain's confession at the end of *Sir Gawain and the Green Knight* is likewise commonly taken as scornful, or at least belittling. Both moments, however, carry within themselves a clear contrast with grief – the grief of those mourning Troilus's death, or of Gawain's bitter sense of failure – and the antonym of grief is joy. Troilus is a pagan, and Chaucer cannot quite despatch him to a Christian heaven, but the poem implies something comparable for him: he is at least allowed a glimpse of the 'pleyn felicite/ That is in hevene above' in contrast to 'this wrecched world', to which a response

---

[1] *The Works of Sir Thomas Malory*, ed. E. Vinaver, rev. P. J. C. Field, 3 vols (Oxford, 1991), I:329 (Gareth and Gryngamoure), II:536. References in the text below are to this edition.

of laughter is by no means inappropriate.² Arthur's court had wept when Gawain set out, so their laughter may well be intended as an expression not of scorn, whether at his failure of perfection or at his excessive distress over a slight fault, but simply of joy at his safe return. It might, as it is also often understood, be a sign of their lack of seriousness, their inability to appreciate Gawain's passionate identification with the values by which he lives; but joy is given divine endorsement in Heaven, and the joy of an earthly company, however limited by comparison, need not be dismissed as trivial.

Although Malory will usually give a clear indication as to what emotions make his characters act as they do, not least because of the surrounding narrative action or through speech, he is a master too at suggesting a deep imaginative hinterland behind their actions without any clear explanation of what is going on inside them. Critics as well as creative writers have found it irresistible to fill in these emotional gaps, not least as such silences tend to occur in relation to some of the most important elements in the entire work. Such issues as what Arthur really thinks about Guinevere, the details of her relationship with Lancelot or what motivates Merlin or Morgan le Fay have been the inspiration of the whole Arthurian industry deriving from the *Morte Darthur*. It is indeed remarkably difficult to say anything about Malory's narrative without supplying explanations that he avoids. Explanation is unavoidable in places where the emotions are both strong and undefined, as is evident in Raluca Radulescu's close analysis of the confrontation between Lancelot, Arthur and Gawain towards the end of the work; and she herself, after spelling out how Mordred and Aggravayne are driven to their disclosure of Guinevere's adultery by a sense of family honour, finally notes that an alternative explanation could be envy – an alternative that would make a big difference to the whole ethical balance of the fall of the Round Table. The brothers themselves cite wounded honour as their motive (but they would, wouldn't they?); but what in the modern age would be a cover-up, and therefore to be deplored, could in the Middle Ages be rather an avoidance of 'noise', scandal. Honour, after all, is scarcely enhanced by naming a man a cuckold. So even when Malory seems to provide answers, they are not necessarily trustworthy; and sometimes he does not even do that. Arthur responds to Lancelot's return of Guinevere to him and their kneeling before him by sitting still and saying nothing; 'and whan sir Launcelot saw hys countenaunce he arose up and pulled up the quene with hym' (II:1197). Here, the emotion is the magical kind described by Jane Gilbert, associated with 'the shocking face-to-face encounter with another consciousness' (p. 16), though no actual emotions are identified. Arthur's silence, or his expression, or the very sight of the king, none

---

² Geoffrey Chaucer, *Troilus and Criseyde*, V.1816–22, in *The Riverside Chaucer*, ed. L. D. Benson (Boston, 1987; Oxford, 1988).

the less prompts Lancelot to embark on his longest speech in the whole work, and one that is entirely Malory's invention. In the same scene, emotion is implied even by the spatial arrangement of the characters, in the placing of the implacable Gawain between Lancelot and the king: 'And Sir Gawayne sate afore [king Arthur], and many other grete lordes' (II:1196). It is at once a personal moment, reflecting how the king and his leading knight have been forced apart beyond any hope of reconciliation; and a deeply political one, suggesting the magnates' determination not to let Arthur make peace whatever his private feelings might be.

Arthurian literature tends to take itself seriously, and Malory is no exception. He is generally explicit about the expression of joy and grief, but sorrow dominates. There are some five times as many occasions for weeping as there are for laughter in the *Morte*: a mere twenty-six against several score.[3] Weeping most commonly expresses compassion or pity (in best mirror neuron fashion), but weeping for joy is not unusual – a reaction that makes it oddly double-edged; and these responses are usually communal, almost choric, as if to invite the readers to share the emotion. Sometimes, however, it is impossible to tell what impels the weeping, as when Lancelot 'wepte as he had bene a chylde that had bene beatyn' after he has succeeded in healing Sir Urry (III:1152). One would expect the simile to provide the underlying motive, but it describes the quality of the weeping, not its cause, and no one else in the scene shares that response.

Laughter is comparably variable. Laughter 'at' someone is usually scornful or mocking, though it may be a response to comedy too. The majority of the references to laughing cluster around Dinadan, who regularly plays up to his audience in ways that make them laugh: Guinevere on one occasion so hard that she can't stand up (II.670), Arthur and Lancelot to the point where they can't stay on their seats (II.758). The laughter when King Mark is pursued by Dagonet, whom he believes to be Lancelot, is likewise comic but less kind (II:588). Laughter can be coupled with 'good cheer', to indicate joy (on which see Lynch, pp. 62–3 above), as it does when the anxiety over Tristram that causes Isode to weep is followed by laughter when she sees he is safe (II.737). It may also, however, carry a foreboding undertone of its antonym weeping, as when Tristram and Isode laugh after drinking the love-potion (I:412). Malory does no more than start the next sentence with 'but', and note that their love never failed 'for well nother for woo'; but that is enough to alert the readers to the tragic irony of what is happening, even though such a response is unavailable at this point to the characters. Laughter for them has more in common with its use as a signifier for joy contingent on a discovery, as with the 'lawghyng and smylyng' that greet the revelation

---

[3] K. Mizobata, ed., *A Concordance to Caxton's 'Morte Darthur'* (Osaka, 2009); for laughter, s.v. laugh-, lough-.

that Lancelot has been fighting in Kay's armour (I.286). For Tristram and Isode, laughter depends on their ignorance of the future; elsewhere it is more likely to indicate privileged knowledge, as when Merlin laughs as he prophesies what will happen to Balyn's sword (I.91). There is just one usage of the noun 'laughter' in the whole work. At the very end, Lancelot's companions have gone to bed weeping after he has been given the last rites; but then they are awakened by the bishop of Canterbury falling 'upon a grete laughter' (III:1258), the laughter of pure joy of a man who has seen Lancelot being heaved up into heaven by the angels.

Laughter in Malory, as these instances show, is open. Its emotional causes are spelled out, and it is most often a collective experience, shared both by characters within the work and by extension the readers. Smiling is even less common than laughter, occurring on a mere eleven occasions. Two of those occasions, moreover, relate to characters who are dead.

Authors can give a good idea of why their living characters feel particular emotions, if not by direct description of their feelings (something Malory does rather rarely), then by their outward actions or speeches. The dead do not have feelings, nor do they speak, so the normal means of implying inner life or subjectivity are ruled out. Even in the case of living smiles in Malory, it is not always easy to be sure what it signifies. Just occasionally, as with the 'lawghyng and smylyng' mentioned above, the context, what Fuksas calls the 'environmental circumstances', will provide the explanation. The same happens when Lancelot smiles as he cites a proverb after hearing of the adventures of Kay and Gaheris, 'Harde hit ys to take oute off the fleysshe that ys bredde in the boone', at which they all 'made hem myrry togydirs' (II.550): it is an occasion for the reunion of fellows and some gentle wit, and the smiling expresses pleasure. The narrative, however, is not always sufficient: as in the cases of Troilus and Gawain discussed above, it may have the wrong implications for a modern reader. Malory may be assuming a different ideological context – a set of environmental circumstances located not in the work but in the mental and emotional experience of the audience.

Smiling is especially hard to analyse since so many of the instances in the *Morte* are private: they are not part of a collective response, and the instances of the dead smiling take that to an extreme (the response of the other knights to the finding of Lancelot's smiling corpse is 'wepyng and wryngyng of handes'). Moreover, four of the occasions that elicit smiles are tied to the fact that the character is in possession of knowledge that their interlocutor is not, as if the smile is a code for secret or privileged knowledge. It expresses a one-sided recognition, an inward thought, rather than being in the first instance (or at all) a social or shared expression of pleasure, though the smile may be visible to others as something that requires explanation. Ulphuns and Brastias smile when they recognize the disguised Merlin in Sherwood Forest when Arthur does not, though they tell Arthur right away (I:38); Tristram smiles when he recognizes Lamerok but Lamerok does not recognize him, an exchange that is the preface to something close to a quarrel (I:443); Bors smiles when Perceval fails to recognize him in his helmet and thinks perhaps his appearance is miraculous, a preface to the 'grete joy' they feel when the recognition is completed (II:975); and Arthur smiles when he recognizes the disguised Lancelot on his way to the great tournament at Camelot, but refuses to identify him to anyone else (II:1067). Lancelot himself smiles at a different kind of privileged knowledge, the very point of which is that it should remain secret to himself: the fact that he has an exceptionally good spear (I:278).

Two other occasions involve Tristram and Dinadan. Dinadan, as noted above, is the dominant single cause of laughter in the *Morte*, and he elicits it deliberately. One of Tristram's smiles results from a shared joke: at the tournament at Lonazep, Dinadan is complaining that Tristram is even 'wyldar' than he had been on the first day, and Tristram responds with a smiling invitation to him to stay close behind so that if he sees him 'ovirmacched', Dinadan can take over (II:750). The other occasion is more complex – it is indeed the most enigmatic smile of any living character in the work. Palamides is in pursuit of the desperately wounded Tristram, and Dinadan tells Tristram to retreat to a nearby castle and leave him to deal with Palamides 'and do to hym what I may, and yf I be slayne ye may pray for my soule'. It is the kind of act of reckless courage that Dinadan has made a habit of avoiding, but he makes the offer in the full knowledge of what its cost is likely to be. Then 'Sir Trystram smyled and seyde, "I thanke you, sir Dynadan, [of your good wylle], but ye shall undirstonde that I am able to handyll hym"' (II.532). Is this again a smile of privileged knowledge, that he knows what he is still capable of doing, or of the more public knowledge of the limitations of Dinadan's abilities? Is it private pleasure at Dinadan's display of courage, or of care for his companion? Is it (and it would be unique in the work if this were the case) a smile intended to be shared by Dinadan as part of his expression of thanks? It is an oddly moving moment for the reader, a moment that expresses something crucial about their relationship; but Malory holds back from giving any of the obvious clues about how to interpret it, or to explain why we should be moved.

The smiles of the dead are the most extreme form of privileged knowledge, since all subjectivity is removed from a corpse. Both occasions are unprompted by anything in Malory's sources, the English stanzaic *Morte Arthur* or the French *Mort Artu*. Whatever his motives for the interventions, they are not explained within the text: the narratorial voice no longer has the option of giving or withholding information about a character's inward state, as that state no longer exists. It is that very quality of death, however, that helps to carry the meaning of one of these smiles. When the dead Lancelot is found by his fellows, 'he laye as he had smyled, and the swettest sauour aboute hym that ever they felte' (III:1258). The 'as' separates this off from the normal smile of the living, but together with the sweetness of savour and the bishop's vision of him being heaved into heaven by the angels, it confirms Lancelot's salvation: that he has been granted the bliss of heaven. Malory avoids confirming his destiny in his authorial voice – the work has, after all, made it abundantly clear that he is a sinner; but the smile is none the less the outward sign of a state, or a perhaps a dying vision, beyond what is accessible to anyone left on earth, whether within the fiction or as reader. The happiness with which he is endowed (it seems wrong to speak of it in more subjective terms) is moreover at the opposite extreme from his companions' response of weeping and wringing their hands, and making 'the grettest dole ... that euer made men'.

The same contrast appears between the smile of the dead Elaine of Ascolat and those who find her. She has died of unrequited love, after defending that love forcefully against the confessor who has demanded that she should abandon it; yet when the barge in which her body is floating arrives at Camelot, 'she lay as she had smyled' (III:1096). The response of the onlookers to the sight of the corpse, as with the dead Lancelot, is to weep, and readers are implicitly invited to do the same. The response to the smile is, I suspect, much harder to define. There is certainly the suggestion in that smile that God has not taken as hard a line on her love as her confessor did; and it may be that medieval readers took it the same way, though their religious presuppositions might make them hesitate. It is not so obviously a smile of salvation as Lancelot's is, however, nor one that is so evidently reaching back into the world of the living from the other side of death. It feels – and one can only appeal to feelings, since there is no explanation given of any kind – as if she herself has recognized that she has reached some kind of consummation, the right conclusion for the fullness of her love even though, or because, it cannot have a happy outcome; but Malory tells us nothing. Interpretation in this case is disabled at the source: finally, the emotions of the dead are beyond speculation.

Carolyne Larrington calls attention in her essay to the critical division between the emotions elicited by the artefact, the artistry of the writer, and those inherent in or elicited by the fiction. Malory is something of a test case both for this and for a good many other of the theories of emotions discussed in this book: their dependence on emotional signifiers, cultural differences in the expression and meanings of emotions, their social or collective nature, the reciprocity of emotion in the text and the reader. There are plenty of occasions when he fulfils all those principles, but plenty too where he transgresses them. As the editors write in their Introduction, 'The only available resources for discovering and understanding emotions of the past are the texts (and images) that have come down to us' (p. 2). Arthurian romance is a long way from the psychological novel, Malory more obviously so than many of his sources; yet a committed reading of him, one that responds to the forceful emotions the text contains, has to become a counter-intuitive one, which resists the temptation to write the novel that Malory does not. The *Morte Darthur* demonstrates how even an author who appears to carry his meanings close to the surface can require a minutely detailed attention in order to open up its imaginative hinterland.

Bibliography

PRIMARY SOURCES

Ælred of Rievaulx, *Speculum caritatis*, PL 195: 501–620, ed. A. Hoste and C. H. Talbot, CCCMI (Turnhout, 1971)
Aquinas, Thomas, *Summa Theologiae*, ed. P. Caramello, 4 vols (Turin, 1952–6)
Arthurian Fiction in Medieval Europe: Narratives and Manuscripts, http://www.arthurianfiction.org
L'Atre Périlleux, ed. B. Woledge (Paris, 1936)
L'Atre Périlleux, trans M.-L. Ollier, in *La légende arthurienne; le graal et la Table Ronde*, gen. ed. D. Régnier-Bohler (Paris, 1989)
Avicenna, *Liber de anima seu Sextus de naturalibus*, ed. S. E. van Riet (Leiden, 1968)
Brennu-Njáls Saga, ed. E. Ó. Sveinsson, Íslenzk fornrit XII (Reykjavík, 1954)
La Chanson de Roland, ed. I. Short, 2nd edn (Paris, 1990)
Chaucer, Geoffrey, *Troilus and Criseyde*, in *The Riverside Chaucer*, ed. L. D. Benson (Boston, 1987; Oxford, 1988)
Chrétien de Troyes, *Arthurian Romances*, trans. D. D. R. Owen (London, 1987)
——, *Arthurian Romances*, trans. W. W. Kibler and C. W. Carroll (Harmondsworth, 1991)
——, *Le Chevalier au Lion (Yvain)*, in *Les Romans de Chrétien de Troyes*, Les Classiques français du Moyen Age, ed. M. Roques, 5 vols, vol. IV (Paris, 1982)
——, *Le Chevalier au Lion ou Le Roman d'Yvain*, ed. D. F. Hult (Paris, 1994)
——, *Yvain: The Knight of the Lion*, trans. B. Raffel (New Haven, 1987)
——, 'Der Karrenritter und Das Wilhelmsleben (Guillaume d'Angeleterre) von Christian von Troyes', ed. W. Foerster (Halle, 1899)
——, *Le Chevalier de la Charete*, in *Les Romans de Chrétien de Troyes*, Les Classiques français du Moyen Age, ed. M. Roques, 5 vols, vol. III (Paris, 1972)
——, *Le Chevalier de la Charrette (Lancelot)*, ed. A. Foulet and K. Uitti (Paris, 1989)
——, *Le Chevalier de la Charrette*, in *Romans*, ed. C. Méla (Paris, 1994)
——, *Le Chevalier de la Charrette* (digital edition), The Princeton Charrette Project, http://www.princeton.edu/~lancelot/ss/
——, *Le Conte de Graal*, in *Les Romans de Chrétien de Troyes*, ed. F. Lecoy, 6 vols (Paris, 1972–5)
——, *Le Conte du Graal*, in *Romans*, ed. C. Méla (Paris, 1994)
——, *Erec et Enide*, in *Romans*, ed. J. M. Fritz (Paris, 1994)
——, *Erec and Enide*, in *Arthurian Romances*, trans. W. W. Kibler and C. W. Carroll (Harmondsworth, 1991)

The Continuations of the Perceval of Chrétien de Troyes, ed. W. Roach, 6 vols (Philadelphia, 1949)

The Death of King Arthur, trans. J. Cable (Harmondsworth, 1971)

Descartes, R., *Passions of the Soul*, in *The Philosophical Writings of Descartes*, trans. J. Cottingham, R. Stoothoff and D. Murdoch, 3 vols (Cambridge, 1985), I:325–404

Four English Political Tracts of the Later Middle Ages, ed. J.-P. Genet, Camden 4th series 18 (London, 1977)

French Romance: III: Le Chevalier as deus espees, ed. and trans. P. V. Rockwell, Arthurian Archives XIII (Cambridge, 2006)

Guillaume de Lorris and Jean de Meun, *Le Roman de la Rose*, ed. F. Lecoy, 3 vols, vol. I, CFMA 92, 95, 98 (Paris, 1965–70)

— —, *The Romance of the Rose*, trans. F. Horgan (Oxford, 1994)

Heinrich von dem Türlin, *Diu Crône: Mittelhochdeutsche Leseausgabe mit Erläuterungen*, ed. G. Felder (Berlin and Boston, 2012)

— —, *The Crown*, trans. J. W. Thomas (Lincoln, NE and London, 1989)

Historie of the Arrivall of King Edward IV, in *Three Chronicles of the Reign of Edward IV*, ed. K. Dockray (Gloucester, 1998)

Hoccleve, Thomas, *Thomas Hoccleve's Complaint and Dialogue*, ed. J. A. Burrow, EETS OS 313 (Oxford, 1999)

Homer, *The Iliad*, trans. R. Fagles (New York and London, 1990)

Hume, D., *A Treatise of Human Nature* (1739), ed. L. A. Selby-Bigge (Oxford, 1978)

— —, 'An Enquiry concerning Human Understanding', in *Enquiries concerning Human Understanding and concerning the Principles of Morals* (1777), ed. L. A. Selby-Bigge (Oxford, 1975)

Ipomadon, ed. R. Purdie, EETS OS 316 (Oxford, 2001)

Ívens saga, ed. F. W. Blaisdell, Editiones Arnamagnæanæ series B, vol. 18 (Copenhagen, 1979)

King Arthur's Death, ed. L. D. Benson (Exeter, 1986)

The Knight of the Cart (Lancelot), in *Chrétien de Troyes: Arthurian Romances*, trans. W. W. Kibler and C. W. Carroll (Harmondsworth, 1991), 207–94

The Knight with the Lion, in *Chrétien de Troyes: Arthurian Romances*, trans. W.W. Kibler and C.W. Carroll (Harmondsworth, 1991), 295–380

The Lais of Marie de France, ed. and trans. K. Busby and G. Burgess (Harmondsworth, 1986)

Lanceloet: de Middelnederlandse vertaling van de Lancelot en prose overgeleverd in de Lancelotcompilatie, Pars 1 (vs. 1–5530, vooraf gegaan door de verzen van het Brusselse fragment), ed. B. Besamusca and A. Postma (Hilversum, 1997); *Pars 2*, ed. B. Besamusca (Assen and Maastricht, 1991); *Pars 3*, ed. F. Brandsma (Assen and Maastricht, 1992); *Pars 4*, ed. A. Postma (Hilversum, 1998)

Lanceloet en het hert met de witte voet, ed. M. Draak (Culemborg, 1976)

Lancelot-Grail: The Old French Arthurian Vulgate and Post-Vulgate in Translation, Garland Reference Library of the Humanities 941, trans. N. J. Lacy et al., 5 vols (New York and London, 1992–6)

Lancelot: roman en prose du XIIIe siècle, ed. A. Micha, 9 vols (Geneva, 1978–83)

Lanval, in *Marie de France, Lais*, ed A. Ewert (Oxford, 1969)

Laxdœla saga, ed. E. Ó. Sveinsson, Íslenzk fornrit V (Reykjavík, 1934)
The Saga of the People of Laxardal, trans. K. Kunz, in *The Sagas of Icelanders: A Selection* (New York, 2001), pp. 270–421
Layamon's Arthur: The Arthurian Section of Layamon's 'Brut', ed. W. R. J. Barron and S. C. Weinburg (Exeter, 1991)
La légende arthurienne: le graal et la Table Ronde, ed. D. Régnier-Bohler (Paris, 1989)
Locke, J., *An Essay concerning Human Understanding* (1689), in *The Clarendon Edition of the Works of John Locke*, ed. P. Nidditch (Oxford, 1975)
Lydgate and Burgh's Secrees of old Philisoffres, ed. R. Steele, EETS ES 66 (London, 1894)
van Maerlant, Jacob, *Merlijn, naar het eenig bekende Steinforter handschrift uitgegeven*, ed. J. van Vloten (Leiden, 1880)
Malory, Sir Thomas, *Works*, ed. E. Vinaver, rev. P. J. C. Field, 3 vols (Oxford, 1991)
——, *Le Morte Darthur*, ed. P. J. C. Field, Arthurian Studies LXXX, 2 vols (Cambridge, 2013)
Mandeville's Travels, ed. M. C. Seymour (Oxford, 1967)
Middle English Dictionary, available online at http://quod.lib.umich.edu/m/med/
Middelnederlandsch Woordenboek (The Hague and Antwerp, 1998) [CD-ROM]
De Middelnederlandse 'Perceval'-traditie: inleiding en editie van de bewaarde fragmenten van een Middelnederlandse vertaling van de 'Perceval' of 'Conte du Graal' van Chrétien de Troyes, en de 'Perchevael' in de 'Lancelotcompilatie', ed. S. Oppenhuis de Jong (Hilversum, 2003)
La Mort le Roi Artu: roman du XIIIe siècle, ed. J. Frappier, 3rd edn (Geneva, 1964)
Morte Arthure: A Critical Edition, ed. M. Hamel (New York and London, 1984)
Morte Arthure, ed. J. Finlayson (London, 1967)
Das Nibelungenlied: Nach der Handschrift C der Badischen Landesbibliothek Karlsruhe, ed. and trans. U. Schulze (Düsseldorf, 2005)
Das Nibelungenlied: Song of the Nibelungs, trans. B. Raffel (New Haven, 2006)
Njal's saga, trans. R. Cook (London, 1997; repr. 2001)
Oxford English Dictionary, available online at http://www.oed.com
The Poems of the Pearl Manuscript: 'Pearl', 'Cleanness', 'Patience', 'Sir Gawain and the Green Knight', ed. M. Andrew and R. Waldron, 5th edn (Exeter, 2007)
La Queste del saint Graal, ed. A. Pauphilet (Paris, 1923)
Roman van Lancelot (XIIIe eeuw). Naar het (eenig-bekende) handschrift der Koninklijke Bibliotheek, op gezag van het Gouvernement, ed. W. J. A. Jonckbloet ('s-Gravenhage, 1846–9).
Secretum Secretorum: Nine English Versions, ed. M. A. Manzalaoui, EETS OS 276 (Oxford, 1977)
Sir Gawain and the Green Knight, in *The Poems of the Pearl Manuscript*, ed. Andrew and Waldron, pp. 207–300
Sir Launfal, in *Of Love and Chivalry: An Anthology of Middle English Romance*, ed. J. Fellows (London and Rutland, VT, 1993), pp. 199–229
Sir Launfal, in *The Middle English Breton Lays*, ed. A. Laskaya and E. Salisbury

(Kalamazoo, 1995); http://d.lib.rochester.edu/teams/text/laskaya-and-salisbury-middle-english-breton-lays-sir-launfal

The Song of Roland, trans. G. S. Burgess (London, 1990)

Three Prose Versions of the 'Secreta Secretorum', ed. R. Steele, vol. 1, EETS ES 74 (London, 1898)

Trevisa, J., *The Governance of Kings and Princes: John Trevisa's Middle English Translation of the 'De regimine principum' of Aegidius Romanus*, ed. D. C. Fowler, C. F. Briggs and P. G. Remley (New York, 1997)

The Vulgate Version of the Arthurian Romances, ed. H. O. Sommer, 8 vols (Washington, 1908–16; repr. New York, 1979)

Wace's Roman de Brut: A History of the British, ed. and trans. J. Weiss, rev. edn (Exeter, 2002)

White, T. H., *The Once and Future King* (New York, 1987)

White, T. H., *Arthur, koning voor eens en altijd*, trans. M. Schuchart (Utrecht, 1998)

Ywain and Gawain, in *Ywain and Gawain, Sir Percyvell of Gales, The Anturs of Arther*, ed. M. Mills (London, 1992), pp. 1–102

SECONDARY SOURCES

Abels, R., '"Cowardice" and Duty in Anglo-Saxon England', *Journal of Medieval Military History* 4 (2006), 29–49

Ai, L. S., 'The Mirthless Content of Skarphedinn's Grin', *Medium Aevum* 65.1 (1996), 101–8

Ajumon, B., 'Lament for the Dead as a Universal Folk Tradition', *Fabula* 22.3/4 (1981), 272–80

Allen, V., 'Waxing Red: Shame and the Body, Shame and the Soul', in *The Representation of Women's Emotions in Medieval and Early Modern Culture*, ed. L. J. Perfetti (Gainesville, 2005), pp. 191–210

Atanassov, S., *L'idole inconnu: le personnage de Gauvain dans quelques romans du XIIIe siècle* (Orléans, 2000)

Atkin, A., 'Peirce's Theory of Signs', in *The Stanford Encyclopedia of Philosophy*, ed. E. N. Zalta (Stanford, CA, 2013)

Aurner, N. S., 'Sir Thomas Malory – Historian', *PMLA* 48.2 (1933), 362–91

Baden-Daintree, A., 'Blood, Tears, and Masculine Identity in the Alliterative *Morte Arthure*', unpublished paper, XXIIIrd Triennial Congress of the International Arthurian Society, University of Bristol, 25–30 July 2011

Bailey, A. E., 'Lamentation Motifs in Medieval Hagiography', *Gender & History* 25.3 (2013), 529–44

Baumgartner, E., 'Le Graal, le temps: les enjeux d'un motif', in *Le Temps, sa mesure et sa perception au Moyen Age*, ed. B. Ribémont (Caen, 1992), pp. 9–17

——, 'Le Choix de la prose', *Cahiers de recherches médiévales et humanistes* 5 (1998), 7–13

Bayer, M., W. Sommer and A. Schacht, 'Emotional Words Impact the Mind but not the Body: Evidence from Pupillary Responses', *Psychophysiology* 48.11 (2011), 1554–62

Bell, C., *Ritual Theory, Ritual Practice* (Oxford, 1992; repr. 2009)
Bennett, M., 'Military Masculinity in England and Northern France c.1050–c.1225', in *Masculinity in Medieval Europe*, ed. D. M. Hadley (London, 1998), pp. 71–88
Benson, C. D., 'The Ending of the *Morte Darthur*', in *A Companion to Malory*, ed. E. Archibald and A. S. G. Edwards (Cambridge, 1998), pp. 221–37
Bergson, H., *Matter and Memory*, trans. N. M. Paul and W. Scott Palmer, Library of Philosophy (London and New York, 1911) [first published as *Matière et Mémoire* (Paris, 1896)]
Blumenberg, H., *The Legitimacy of the Modern Age*, trans. R. M. Wallace (Cambridge, MA, 1983)
de Boer, M. G., 'Talking about Interjections', *Bulletin of The Henry Sweet Society for the History of Linguistic Ideas* 50 (2008), 31–44
— —, 'Tussenwerpseltheorieën', *Voortgang, jaarboek voor de neerlandistiek* 26 (2008), 221–52
den Boon, T., *Van Dale modern uitroepenwoordenboek: van aanvalluh tot Ziezo en 848 andere uitroepen* (Utrecht, 2009)
Boquet, D. and P. Nagy, ed. *Le sujet des émotions au Moyen Âge* (Paris, 2008)
Boquet, D., P. Nagy and L. Moulinier-Brogi, ed. *La chair des émotions*, *Médiévales* 61 (2011)
Bordwell, D., *Narration in the Fiction Film* (Madison, 1985)
Bourdieu, P., 'Authorized Language: The Social Conditions for the Effectiveness of Ritual Discourse', in *Language and Symbolic Power* (Cambridge, 1991), pp. 107–16
Brandsma, F., 'Medieval Equivalents of "Quote-Unquote": The Presentation of Spoken Words in Courtly Romance', in *The Court and Cultural Diversity: Selected Papers from the Eighth Triennial Congress of the International Courtly Literature Society (Belfast, 26 July–1 August 1995)*, ed. E. Mullally and J. Thompson (Cambridge, 1997), pp. 287–96
— —, 'Mirror Characters', in *Courtly Arts and the Art of Courtliness*, ed. K. Busby and C. Kleinhenz (Cambridge, 2006), pp. 275–84
— —, 'Arthurian Emotions', *Actes du 22e Congrès de la Société Internationale Arthurienne* (Rennes, 2008) [http://www.uhb.fr/alc/ias/actes/index.htm, 15 July, session 2 L2: Conte du Graal et emotions]
— —, 'The Court's Emotions', in *Cultures courtoises en mouvement*, ed. I. Arseneau and F. Gingras (Montréal, 2011), pp. 74–82
— —, 'Doing Dialogue: The Middle Dutch Lancelot Translators and Correctors at Work', in *De l'oral à l'écrit: le dialogue à travers les genres romanesques et théâtral*, ed. C. Denoyelle (Orléans, 2013), pp. 69–84
Briggs, C. F., *Giles of Rome's 'De regimine principum': Reading and Writing Politics at Court and University, c. 1275–c. 1525* (Cambridge, 1999)
Bruckner, M. T., 'Redefining the Center: Verse and Prose *Charrette*', in *A Companion to the 'Lancelot-Grail' Cycle*, ed. C. Dover (Cambridge, 2003), pp. 95–105
Bruner, J., *Actual Minds: Possible Worlds* (Cambridge, MA, 1986)
Buridant, C., 'L'interjection: jeux et enjeux', *Langages* 161.1 (2006), 3–9
Burrow, J. A., *Gestures and Looks in Medieval Narrative* (Cambridge, 2002)

——, 'The Fourteenth-Century Arthur', in *The Cambridge Companion to Arthurian Legend*, ed. E. Archibald and A. Putter (Cambridge, 2009), pp. 69–83

Busby, K., 'Diverging Traditions of Gauvain in Some of the Later Old French Verse Romances', in *The Legacy of Chrétien de Troyes*, ed. N. J. Lacy, D. Kelly and K. Busby, 2 vols, (Amsterdam, 1988), II. pp. 93–109

Cameron, M. L., *Anglo-Saxon Medicine*, Cambridge Studies in Anglo-Saxon England 7 (Cambridge, 1993)

Carruthers, M., *The Craft of Thought: Meditation, Rhetoric and the Making of Images, 400–1200*, Cambridge Studies in Medieval Literature 34 (Cambridge, 1998)

——, *The Book of Memory: A Study of Memory in Medieval Culture*, Cambridge Studies in Medieval Literature 10 (Cambridge, 1990; 2nd edn 2008)

——, and J. M. Ziolkowski, ed., *The Medieval Craft of Memory: An Anthology of Texts and Pictures*, Material Texts (Philadelphia, 2002)

Cates, D. F., *Aquinas on the Emotions: A Religious-Ethical Inquiry*, Moral Traditions (Washington, DC, 2009)

Cherewatuk, K., 'Dying in Uncle Arthur's Arms and at His Hands', in *The Arthurian Way of Death: The English Tradition*, ed. K. Cherewatuk and K. S. Whetter (Cambridge, 2009), pp. 50–70

Cheyette, F. L., and H. Chickering, 'Love, Anger, and Peace: Social Practice and Poetic Play in the Ending of *Yvain*', *Speculum* 80.1 (2005), 75–117

Clover, C., 'Hildigunnr's Lament', in *Cold Counsel: Women in Old Norse Literature and Mythology*, ed. S. M. Anderson and K. Swenson (New York, 2002), pp. 15–54

Clunies Ross, M., 'Medieval Iceland and the European Middle Ages', in *International Scandinavian and Medieval Studies in Memory of Gerard Wolfgang Weber*, ed. M. Dallapiazza, O. Hansen, P. M. Sørensen and Y. S. Bonnetain (Trieste, 2000), pp. 111–20

Collette, C., *Species, Phantasms, and Images: Vision and Medieval Psychology in the Canterbury Tales* (Ann Arbor, 2001)

Colm Hogan, P., *What Literature Teaches Us about Emotion* (Cambridge, 2011)

de Combarieu du Grès, M., '"Un cœur gros comme ça" (Le cœur dans le *Lancelot-Graal*)', in *Le 'Cuer' au moyen âge: réalité et 'sénéfiance'*, Sénéfiance 30 (Aix-en-Provence, 1991), pp. 77–105

Combes, A., '*L'Atre périlleux*: cénotaphe d'un héros retrouvé', *Romania* 113 (1992–5), 140–74

——, *Les voies de l'aventure: réécriture et composition romanesque dans le Lancelot en prose* (Paris, 2001)

Cooper, H., *The English Romance in Time: Transforming Motifs from Geoffrey of Monmouth to the Death of Shakespeare* (Oxford, 2004)

Corrigan, J., *Business of the Heart: Religion and Emotion in the Nineteenth Century* (Berkeley, 2002)

Crane, S., *The Performance of Self: Ritual, Clothing, and Identity during the Hundred Years War* (Philadelphia, 2002)

Craun, E. D., *Lies, Slander, and Obscenity in Medieval English Literature: Pastoral Rhetoric and the Deviant Speaker* (Cambridge, 1997)

Damasio, A., *Descartes' Error: Emotion, Reason and the Human Brain* (New York, 1994; repr. London, 2006)
— —, *The Feeling of What Happens: Body, Emotion and the Making of Consciousness* (London, 2000)
— —, *Looking for Spinoza: Joy, Sorrow, and the Feeling Brain* (Orlando, 2003)
Das, S., *Touch and Intimacy in First World War Literature* (Cambridge, 2005)
Deleuze, G. and F. Guattari, *A Thousand Plateaus: Capitalism and Schizophrenia*, trans. B. Massumi, vol. 2 (Minneapolis, 1987) [first published as *Mille plateaux, Capitalisme et schizophrénie*, vol. 2 (Paris, 1980)]
Dennett, D. C., 'Intentional Systems in Cognitive Ethology: The Panglossian Paradigm Defended', *Behavioral and Brain Sciences* 6 (1987), 343–90
Dienstbier, R. A., 'The Role of Emotion in Moral Socialization', in *Emotions, Cognition, and Behavior*, ed. C. E. Izard, J. Kagan and R. B. Zajonc (Cambridge, 1984), pp. 494–514
Diggelmann, L., 'Emotional Excess in Two Twelfth-Century Histories: Wace's *Roman de Brut* and *Roman de Rou*', unpublished paper, 'Emotions in the Medieval and Early Modern World' conference, University of Western Australia, 9–11 June 2011
Donahue, D. P., 'The Darkly Chronicled King: An Interpretation of the Negative Side of Arthur in Lawman's *Brut* and Geoffrey's *Historia*', *Arthuriana* 8.4 (1998), 135–47
Dover, C. R., 'From Non-Cyclic to Cyclic *Lancelot*: Recycling the Heart', in *Transtextualities: Of Cycles and Cyclicity in Medieval French Literature*, ed. S. Sturm-Maddox and D. Maddox (Binghamton, NY, 1996), pp. 53–70
Ekman, P., 'All Emotions Are Basic', in *The Nature of Emotion: Fundamental Questions*, ed. P. Ekman and R. J. Davidson (Oxford, 1994), pp. 15–19
— —, 'Basic Emotions', in *Handbook of Cognition and Emotion*, ed. T. Dalgleish and M. Power (Chichester, 1999), pp. 45–60
— —, and W. V. Friesen, 'Constants across Cultures in the Face and Emotion', *Journal of Personality and Social Psychology* 17.2 (1971), 124–9
Eming, J., 'On Stage: Ritualized Emotions and Theatricality in Isolde's Trial', *Modern Language Notes* 124 (2009), 555–71
Fanger, C., 'Things Done Wisely by a Wise Enchanter: Negotiating the Power of Words in the Thirteenth Century', *Esoterica* 1 (1999), 97–132 [www.esoteric.msu.edu]
Felder, G., *Kommentar zur >Crône< Heinrichs von dem Türlin* (Berlin and New York, 2006)
Fichte, J. O., 'The Figure of Sir Gawain', in *The Alliterative Morte Arthure: A Reassessment of the Poem*, ed. K. H. Göller (Cambridge, 1981), pp. 106–16
Field, P. J. C., *Romance and Chronicle: A Study of Malory's Prose Style* (London, 1971)
Fleischman, S., *Tense and Narrativity: From Medieval Performance to Modern Fiction* (Austin, TX, 1990)
Frank, J., 'Spatial Form in Modern Literature', *Sewanee Review* 53 (1945), 221–40, 433–56, 643–53
— —, *The Idea of Spatial Form* (New Brunswick, 1998)
Frijda, N. H., *The Emotions* (Cambridge, 1986)

——, 'The Laws of Emotion', *American Psychologist* 43 (1988), 349–58; repr. in *Human Emotions*, ed. J. Jenkins, K. Oatley and N. Stein (Oxford, 1998), pp. 270–87

Fuksas, A. P., 'Selezionismo e *conjointure*', *Dal Romanzo alle reti* (Atti del Convegno Soggetti e territori del romanzo Università di Roma La Sapienza. Facoltà di Scienze della Comunicazione, 23–4 May 2002), ed. A. Abruzzese and I. Pezzini (Turin, 2004), pp. 152–84 [updated as A. P. Fuksas, 'Selezionismo e *conjointure*', *Rivista di Filologia Cognitiva* 1 (2003)]

——, 'The Ecology of the Sword Bridge through the Manuscript Textual Tradition of the *Chévalier de la Charrette* by Chrétien de Troyes', *Compar(a)isons* 26.2 (2007), 155–80

——, 'The Embodied Novel: An Ecological Theory of Narrative Reference', *Cognitive Philology* 1 (2008), 1–14

——, 'Characters, Society and Nature in the *Chevalier de la Charrette* (vv. 247–398)', *Critica del Testo* 12.2–3 (2009), 49–77

——, 'Embodied Abstraction and Emotional Resonance in Chrétien's *Chevalier de la Charrette*', *Cognitive Philology* 4 (2011), 1–14

Getz, F., *Medicine in the English Middle Ages* (Princeton, 1998)

Glauser, J. and S. Kramarz-Bein, ed., *Rittersagas: Übersetzung, Überlieferung, Transmission* (Tübingen, 2014)

Glenberg, A. M., B. J. Webster, E. Mouilso, D. Havas and L. M. Lindeman, 'Gender, Emotion, and the Embodiment of Language Comprehension', *Emotion Review* 1.2 (2009), 151–61

——, D. A. Havas, R. Becker and M. Rinck, 'Grounding Language in Bodily States: The Case for Emotion', in *The Grounding of Cognition: The Role of Perception and Action in Memory, Language, and Thinking*, ed. R. Zwaan and D. Pecher (Cambridge, 2005), pp. 115–28

Godden, M. R., 'Anglo-Saxons on the Mind', in *Learning and Literature in Anglo-Saxon England: Studies Presented to Peter Clemoes*, ed. P. Clemoes, M. Lapidge and H. Gneuss (Cambridge, 1985), pp. 271–88

Goldie, P., *The Emotions: A Philosophical Exploration* (Oxford, 2000)

Gowans, L., *Cei and the Arthurian Legend*, Arthurian Studies XVIII (Cambridge, 1988)

Griffiths, P., *What Emotions Really Are: The Problem of Psychological Categories* (Chicago, 1997)

——, 'Is Emotion a Natural Kind?', in *Thinking about Feeling: Contemporary Philosophers on Emotions*. ed. R. C. Solomon (Oxford, 2004), pp. 233–49

Grima, B., *The Performance of Emotion among Paxtun Women* (Austin, TX, 1992)

Harvey, R., *The Inward Wits: Psychological Theory in the Middle Ages and the Renaissance*, Warburg Institute Surveys 6 (London, 1975)

Havas, D. A., A. M. Glenberg and M. Rinck, 'Emotion Simulation during Language Comprehension', *Psychonomic Bulletin & Review* 14.3 (2007), 436–41

Hicks, M.A., *Warwick the Kingmaker* (Oxford, 2002)

Hindley, A., F. W. Langley and B. J. Levy, *Old French–English Dictionary* (Cambridge, 2000)

Hunt, T., *Chrétien de Troyes: Yvain* (London, 1986)

Izzard, C. E., *The Psychology of Emotions* (New York, 1991)
Jaeger, C. S., *The Origins of Courtliness: Civilizing Trends and the Formation of Courtly Ideals, 939–1210* (Philadelphia, 1985)
James, W., 'What is an Emotion?', *Mind* 9 (1884), 188–205
Jay, M., 'Magical Nominalism: Photography and the Re-Enchantment of the World', *Culture, Theory & Critique* 50 (2009), 165–83
Jay, T., 'The Utility and Ubiquity of Taboo Words', *Perspectives on Psychological Science* 4 (2009), 153–61
Jillings, L., *Diu Crone of Heinrich von dem Türlein: The Attempted Emancipation of Secular Narrative* (Göppingen, 1980)
Karnes, M., *Imagination, Meditation and Cognition in the Middle Ages* (Chicago, 2011)
Kay, S., *The Romance of the Rose* (London, 1995)
Kelly, D., 'Two Problems in Chrétien's "Charrette": The Boundary of Gorre and the Use of "Novele"', *Neophilologus* 48 (1964), 115–21
— —, 'Chrétien de Troyes', in *The Arthur of the French: The Arthurian Legend in Medieval French and Occitan Literature*, ed. G. Burgess and K. Pratt (Cardiff, 2006), pp. 135–85
Kemp, S., *Medieval Psychology*, Contributions in Psychology 14 (New York, 1990)
— —, *Cognitive Psychology in the Middle Ages*, International Contributions in Psychology 33 (Westport, CT, 1996)
Kennedy, E., 'The Quest for Identity and the Importance of Lineage in Thirteenth-Century French Prose Romance', in *The Ideals and Practice of Medieval Knighthood, II: Papers from the Third Strawberry Hill Conference*, ed. C. Harper-Bill and R. Harvey (Woodbridge, 1988), pp. 70–86
Kenny, A., *Aquinas on Mind*, Topics in Medieval Philosophy (Oxford and New York, 1993)
Kieckhefer, R., 'The Specific Rationality of Medieval Magic', *American Historical Review* 99 (1994), 813–36
Kinne, E., 'Waiting for Gauvain: Lessons in Courtesy in *L'Âtre périlleux*', *Arthuriana* 18.2 (2008), 55–68
Kinoshita, S., 'Cherchez la femme: Feminist Criticism and Marie de France's *Lai de Lanval*', *Romance Notes* 34 (1993–4), 262–73
Knapp, F. P., *Chevalier errant und fin'amor: das Ritterideal des 13. Jahrhunderts in Nordfrankreich und im deutschsprachigen Südosten* (Passau, 1986)
Knuuttila, S., *Emotions in Ancient and Medieval Philosophy* (Oxford and New York, 2004; repr. 2006)
Köhler, E., *Ideal und Wirklichkeit in der höfischen Epik: Studien zur Form der frühen Artus und Graldichtung* (Tübingen, 1956)
Lacy, N. J., 'Thematic Structure in the "Charrette"', *L'Esprit créateur* 12 (1972), 13–18
— —, 'Spatial Form in Medieval Romance', in *Approaches to Medieval Romance*, ed. P. Haidu, *Yale French Studies* 51 (1975), 160–69
— —, 'The Ambiguous Fortunes of Arthur: The Lancelot-Grail and Beyond', in *The Fortunes of King Arthur*, ed. N. J. Lacy (Cambridge, 2005), pp. 92–103

Lambert, M., *Malory: Style and Vision in 'Le Morte Darthur'* (New Haven and London, 1975)

Larrington, C., 'The Psychology of Emotion and Study of the Medieval Period', *Early Medieval Europe* 10.2 (2001), 251–6

——, *King Arthur's Enchantresses: Morgan and Her Sisters in Medieval Tradition* (London, 2006)

——, '*Sir Gawain and the Green Knight* and English Chivalry', in *The Blackwell Companion to Arthurian Literature*, ed. H. Fulton (Oxford, 2009), pp. 252–64

——, 'The Translated *Lais*', in *The Arthur of the North: The Arthurian Legend in the Norse and Rus´ Realms*, ed. M. Kalinke (Cardiff, 2011), pp. 77–97

——, 'Learning to Feel in the Old Norse Camelot?' *Scandinavian Studies*, special issue on 'Arthur of the North: Histories, Emotions, and Imaginations', ed. B. Bandlien, S. G. Eriksen and S. Rikhardsdottir, 87.1 (2015), 74–94

Le Goff, J. 'Laughter in *Brennu-Njáls saga*', in *From Sagas to Society: Comparative Approaches to Early Iceland*, ed. G. Pálsson (Enfield Lock, 1992), pp. 161–5

McNamer, S., 'Feeling', in *Oxford Twenty-First Century Approaches to Literature: Middle English*, ed. P. Strohm (Oxford, 2007), pp. 241–57

——, *Affective Meditation and the Invention of Medieval Compassion* (Philadelphia, 2009)

Mar, R. A., K. Oatley et al., 'Emotion and Narrative Fiction: Interactive Influence before, during, and after Reading', *Cognition and Emotion* 25 (2011), 818–33

Marnette, S., *Narrateur et point de vue dans la littérature française médiévale: une approche linguistique* (Bern, 1998)

Martín-Loeches, M., A. Fernández, A. Schacht, W. Sommer, P. Casado, L. Jiménez-Ortega and S. Fondevila, 'The Influence of Emotional Words on Sentence Processing: Electrophysiological and Behavioral Evidence', *Neuropsychologia* 50 (2012), 3262–72.

Matthews, D., 'Translation and Ideology: The Case of *Ywain and Gawain*', *Neophilologus* 76 (1992), 452–63

Matthews, W., *The Tragedy of Arthur: A Study of the Alliterative Morte Arthure* (Berkeley and Los Angeles, 1960)

Ménard, P., *Le rire et la sourire dans le roman courtois en France au moyen âge (1150–1250)* (Geneva, 1969)

Mentzel-Reuters, A., *Vröude: Artusbild, Fortuna- und Gralkonzeption in der >Crône< des Heinrich von dem Türlin als Verteidigung des höfischen Lebensideals* (Frankfurt and Berlin, 1989)

Merleau-Ponty, M., *Phenomenology of Perception*, trans. C. Smith (London, 1962)

Metcalf, P., and R. Huntington, *Celebrations of Death: The Anthropology of Mortuary Ritual* (Cambridge, 1980)

Métraux, A., 'Mourning', in *Funk and Wagnalls Standard Dictionary of Folklore, Mythology and Legend*, ed. M. Leach and J. Fried (London, 1949; repr. 1975), pp. 754–5

Meyer, M., *Die Verfügbarkeit der Fiktion: Interpretationen und poetologische Untersuchungen zum Artusroman und zur aventiurehaften Dietrichepik des 13. Jahrhunderts* (Heidelberg, 1994)

— —, 'It's hard to be me, or Walewein/Gawan as Hero', *Arthurian Literature* 17 (1999), 63–78
Miall, D. S., 'Anticipation and Feeling in Literary Response: A Neuropsychological Perspective', *Poetics* 23 (1995), 275–98
— —, and D. Kuiken, 'A Feeling for Fiction: Becoming What We Behold', *Poetics* 30 (2002), 221–41
Miller, W.I., 'Emotions and the Sagas', in *From Sagas to Society: Comparative Approaches to Early Iceland*, ed. G. Pálsson (Enfield Lock, 1992), pp. 89–109
— —, *Humiliation and Other Essays on Honor, Social Discomfort, and Violence* (Ithaca, NY, 1993)
Mizobata, K., *A Concordance to Caxton's 'Morte Darthur'* (Osaka, 2009)
Morin, L., 'Le Soi et le double dans *L'Âtre périlleux*', *Études françaises* 32 (1996), 117–28
Morse, R., 'Temperamental Texts: Medieval Discussions of Character, Emotion, and Motivation', in *Chaucer to Shakespeare: Essays in Honour of Shinsuke Ando* (Cambridge, 1992), pp. 9–24
Mullally, E., 'Registers of Friendship in Layamon's *Brut*', *Modern Philology* 108.4 (2011), 469–87
Nagy, P., and D. Boquet, ed. *Le sujet des émotions au Moyen Âge* (Paris, 2008)
Nievergelt, M., 'Conquest, Crusade and Pilgrimage: The Alliterative *Morte Arthure* in its Late Ricardian Crusading Context', *Arthuriana* 20.2 (2010), 89–116
Nussbaum, M., *Upheavals of Thought: The Intelligence of Emotions* (Cambridge, 2001)
Nykrog, P., *Chrétien de Troyes, romancier discutable* (Geneva, 1995)
Oatley, K., *Best Laid Schemes: The Psychology of the Emotions* (Cambridge, 1992)
— —, 'A Taxonomy of the Emotions of Literary Response and a Theory of Identification in Fictional Narrative', *Poetics* 23 (1994), 53–74
— —, 'Why Fiction May Be Twice as True as Fact: Fiction as Cognitive and Emotional Simulation', *Review of General Psychology* 3 (1999), 101–17
Opperman-Marsaux, E., 'Les interjections en discours direct: comparaison entre fictions romanesques et fictions dramatiques en moyen français', in *De l'oral à l'écrit: le dialogue à travers les genres romanesques et théâtral*, ed. C. Denoyelle (Orléans, 2013), pp. 283–300
Orme, N., 'Gentry Education and Recreation', in *Gentry Culture in Late Medieval England*, ed. R. Radulescu and A. Truelove (Manchester, 2005), pp. 63–83
Paris, G., 'Études sur les romans de la Table Ronde. Lancelot du Lac. II. Le Conte de la Charrette', *Romania* 12 (1883), 459–534
Parkinson, B., 'How Social is the Social Psychology of Emotion?', *British Journal of Social Psychology* 50 (2011), 405–13
Phythian-Adams, C., 'Ritual Constructions of Society', in *A Social History of England 1200–1500*, ed. R. Horrox and W. M. Ormrod (Cambridge, 2006), pp. 369–82
Pollard, A. J., *Warwick the Kingmaker: Politics, Power and Fame during the Wars of the Roses* (London, 2007)

Porter, R., *The Greatest Benefit to Mankind: A Medieval History of Humanity from Antiquity to the Present* (London, 1997)

Pössel, C., 'The Magic of Early Medieval Ritual', *Early Medieval Europe* 17.2 (2009), 111–25

Putter, A., *'Sir Gawain and the Green Knight' and French Arthurian Romance* (Oxford, 1995)

Radulescu, R. L., *The Gentry Context for Malory's 'Morte Darthur'* (Cambridge, 2003)

— —, '*oute of mesure*: Violence and Knighthood in Malory's Morte Darthur', in *Re-viewing 'Le Morte Darthur': Texts and Contexts, Characters and Themes*, ed. K. S. Whetter and R. L. Radulescu (Cambridge, 2005), pp. 119–31

Ratcliffe, M., *Feelings of Being: Phenomenology, Psychiatry and the Sense of Reality* (Oxford, 2008)

Reddy, W., *The Navigation of Feeling: A Framework for the History of Emotions* (Cambridge, 2001)

Reuter, T., 'The Symbolic Language of Medieval Political Action', in *Medieval Polities and Modern Mentalities*, ed. J. L. Nelson (Cambridge, 2006)

Reynolds, S., *Fiefs and Vassals: The Medieval Evidence Reinterpreted* (Oxford, 1994)

Richmond, S., 'Magic in Sartre's Early Philosophy', in *Reading Sartre*, ed. J. Webber (London, 2010), pp. 145–61

Richmond, V. B., *Laments for the Dead in Medieval Narrative* (Pittsburgh, 1966)

Riddy, F., 'Middle English Romance: Family, Marriage, Intimacy', in *The Cambridge Companion to Medieval Romance*, ed. R. L. Krueger (Cambridge, 2000), pp. 235–52

Rikhardsdottir, S., 'Bound by Culture: A Comparative Study of the Old French and Old Norse Versions of *La Chanson de Roland*', *Mediaevalia* 26.2 (2005), 243–65

— —, *Medieval Translations and Cultural Discourse: The Movement of Texts in England, France and Scandinavia* (Cambridge, 2012)

Roberts, R. C., *Emotions: An Essay in Aid of Moral Psychology* (New York, 2003)

Rosenwein, B., ed., *Anger's Past: The Social Uses of an Emotion in the Middle Ages* (Ithaca, NY, and London, 1998)

— —, 'Worrying about Emotions in History', *American Historical Review* 107.3 (2001), 821–45

— —, 'Writing without Fear about Early Medieval Emotions', *Early Medieval Europe* 10.2 (2001), 229–34

— —, *Emotional Communities in the Early Middle Ages* (Ithaca, NY, 2006)

— —, 'Emotion Words', in *Le sujet des émotions au Moyen Âge*, ed. Boquet and Nagy, pp. 93–106

— —, 'Problems and Methods in the History of Emotions', *Passions in Context* 1 (2010), 1–32

Saler, M., 'Modernity and Enchantment: A Historiographic Review', *American Historical Review* 111 (2006), 692–716

Salgaro, M., 'Stories without Words: Narratives of the Brain', *Cognitive Philology* 2 (2009), 1–8

— —, 'The Text as a Manual: Some Reflections on the Concept of Language from a Neuroaesthetic Perspective', *Journal of Literary Theory* 3.1 (2009), 155-66

Sartre, J.-P., *Esquisse d'une théorie des émotions*, 2nd edn (Paris, 1948)

— —, *Sketch for a Theory of the Emotions*, trans. P. Mairet (London, 1962)

Saunders, C., '"The thoghtful maladie": Madness and Vision in Medieval Writing', in *Madness and Creativity in Literature and Culture*, ed. C. Saunders and J. Macnaughton (Basingstoke, 2005), pp. 67-87

— —, 'The Affective Body: Love, Virtue and Vision in Medieval English Literature', in *The Body and the Arts*, ed. C. Saunders, U. Maude and J. Macnaughton (Basingstoke, 2009), pp. 87-102

— —, *Magic and the Supernatural in Medieval English Romance* (Cambridge, 2010)

Le Saux, F. H. M., *A Companion to Wace* (Cambridge, 2005)

Scattergood, J., 'Peter Idley and George Ashby', in *A Companion to Fifteenth-Century English Poetry*, ed. J. Boffey and A. S. G. Edwards (Cambridge, 2013), pp. 113-25

Schacht, A., and W. Sommer, 'Emotions in Word and Face Processing: Early and Late Cortical Responses', *Brain and Cognition* 69 (2009), 538-50.

Scheff, T. J., *Catharsis in Healing, Ritual, and Drama* (Berkeley, 1979)

Schmolke-Hasselman, B., *Der arthurische Versroman von Chrestien bis Froissart: zur Geschichte einer Gattung* (Tübingen, 1980)

— —, *The Evolution of Arthurian Romance: The Verse Tradition from Chrétien to Froissart*, trans. M. and R. Middleton (Cambridge, 1998)

Sedgwick, E. K., and A. Frank, 'Shame in the Cybernetic Fold: Reading Silvan Tomkins', *Critical Inquiry* 21 (1994-5), 496-522

Segre, C., 'Quello che Bachtin non ha detto: le origini medievali del romanzo', *Teatro e romanzo: due tipi di comunicazione letteraria* (Turin, 1984), 61-84

— —, 'What Bachtin Did Not Say: The Medieval Origins of the Novel', *Russian Literature* 41.3 (1997), 385-409

Sheppard, A., 'Of This Is a King's Body Made: Lordship and Succession in Lawman's Arthur and Leir', *Arthuriana* 10.2 (2000), 50-65

Siraisi, N. G., *Medieval and Early Renaissance Medicine: An Introduction to Knowledge and Practice* (Chicago, 1990)

Solomon, R. C., *The Passions: Emotions and the Meaning of Life* (Indianapolis, 1993)

Spearing, A. C., *The Medieval Poet as Voyeur: Looking and Listening in Medieval Love Narratives* (Cambridge, 1993)

Spinoza, B., *Ethics* (1677), Oxford Philosophical Texts, ed. and trans. G. H. R. Parkinson (Oxford, 2000)

Starkey, K., 'Performative Emotion and the Politics of Gender in the *Nibelungenlied*', in *Women and Medieval Epic: Gender, Genre, and the Limits of Epic Masculinity*, ed. S. S. Poor and J. K. Schulman (New York, 2007), pp. 253-71

Stearns, P. N., and C. Z. Stearns, 'Emotionology: Clarifying the History of Emotions and Emotional Standards', *American Historical Review* 90.4 (1985), 813-36

Steiner, C., and P. Perry, *Achieving Emotional Literacy* (London, 1997)

van Sterkenburg, P. G. J., *Woorden van en voor emotie* (Leiden, 2007)

Stock, B., *The Implications of Literacy: Written Language and Models of Interpretation in the Eleventh and Twelfth Centuries* (Princeton, 1983)

Stokes, M., '*Lanval* to *Sir Launfal*: A Story Becomes Popular', in *The Spirit of Medieval English Popular Romance*, ed. A. Putter and J. Gilbert (Harlow, 2000), pp. 56–77

Suerbaum, A., '"Entrelacement?" Narrative Technique in Heinrich von dem Türlîn's *Diu Crône*', *Oxford German Studies* 34.1 (2005), 5–18

Tahkokallio, J., 'Fables of King Arthur: Ælred of Rievaulx and Secular Pastimes', *Mirator* 9.1 (2008), 19–35

Talbot, C. H., *Medicine in Medieval England* (London, 1967)

Tan, E. S.-H., 'Film-Induced Affect as a Witness Emotion', *Poetics* 23 (1994), 7–32

Tasioulas, J., '"Dying of Imagination" in the First Fragment of the *Canterbury Tales*', *Medium Ævum* 82 (2013), 212–35

Terada, R., 'Introduction: Emotion after the "Death of the Subject"', in *Feeling in Theory: Emotion after the 'Death of the Subject'* (Cambridge, MA, 2001), pp. 1–15

Throop, S. A., 'Zeal, Anger and Vengeance: The Emotional Rhetoric of Crusading', in *Vengeance in the Middle Ages: Emotion, Religion and Feud*, ed. S .A. Throop and P. R. Hyams (Aldershot, 2010), pp. 177–202

Tobler, A., and E. Lommatzsch, ed., *Altfranzösisches Wörterbuch* (Berlin and Wiesbaden, 1925–2002)

Tolkien, J. R. R., 'On Fairy Stories', in *Tree and Leaf*, ed. C. Tolkien (London, 1992)

Tolmie, J., and M. J. Toswell, *Laments for the Lost in Medieval Literature* (Turnhout, 2010)

Trachsler, R., 'Brehus sans pitié: portrait-robot du criminel arthurien', in *La Violence dans le monde médiéval*, *Sénéfiance* 36 (Aix-en-Provence, 1994), pp. 525–54

Trigg, S., 'Introduction: Emotional Histories – Beyond the Personalization of the Past and the Abstraction of Affect Theory', *Exemplaria* 26 (2014), 3–15

Tulinius, T. H., 'The Self as Other: Iceland and Christian Europe in the Middle Ages', *Gripla* 20 (2009), 199–215

Turner, V., *The Ritual Process: Structure and Anti-Structure* (New York, 1969; repr. 1995)

Urban, G., 'Ritual Wailing in Amerindian Brazil', *American Anthropologist* 90.2 (1988), 385–400

Veldhuizen, M., 'De ongetemde tong: opvattingen over zondige, onvertogen en misdadige woorden in het Middelnederlands (1300–1550)', dissertation, University of Utrecht, 2013

Vincensini, J.-J., 'Formes et fonctions structurantes: à propos de quelques interjections en ancien et en moyen français', *Langages* 161.1 (2006), 101–11

Vitz, E. B., 'Theatricality and Its Limits: Dialogue and the Art of the Storyteller in the Romances of Chrétien de Troyes', in *De l'oral à l'écrit: le dialogue à travers les genres romanesques et théâtral*, ed. C. Denoyelle (Orléans, 2013), pp. 27–44

Warren, M. R., 'Prose Romance', in *The Cambridge History of French Literature*, ed. W. Burgwinkle, N. Hammond and E. Wilson (Cambridge, 2011), pp. 153–63

White, S. D., 'The Politics of Anger', in *Anger's Past: The Social Uses of an Emotion in the Middle Ages*, ed. B. Rosenwein, pp. 127–52

Wierzbicka, A., 'The "History of Emotions" and the Future of Emotion Research', *Emotion Review* 2.3 (2010), 269–73

Index

Abels, Richard, 51
abstractum agens, 19, 23
Accolon, 43, 140
Achilles, 96
action, 13, 31, 36, 40, 47–63, 69–70
    and affect, 14, 19, 44, 78–80, 84, 167, 179
    military, 89, 99, 104
    political, 117, 176
    ritualistic, 88, 103
    symbolic, 101
Adamic language, 27–8
admiration, 143, 154, 158
adultery, 106, 107–8, 114, 183
Ælred of Rievaulx, *Speculum caritatis*, 8, 138
affect, 13–30, 31–46, 48, 67–85, 123–41, 145, 167
'affective turn', 4, 6–8, 31, 45
Aggravayne, 106–9, 120, 183
Albertus Magnus, 34
Allen, Valerie, 51
Alliterative *Morte Arthure*, 87–104
Amans (the Lover, *Roman de la Rose*), 23
amour lointain, l', 133, 134
Amurfina, 123, 127
Ancrene Wisse, 101
anger (*ire*), 158, 164, 165–6, see also blood, violence
    affect of (*see also under* affect), 34, 49, 71, 94, 132
    Arthur's (*see also under* Arthur, King), 53–6
    cultural rules of, 116
    political, 16, 116–17, 176
    somatic correlates of, 73–8
    symbolic, 120
anguish, 93, 175
anticipation, 139, 141, 169
anxiety, 1, 62, 72, 184
appraisal, 3–4, 55, 69, 72, 116–17, 125, 138–9
apprehension, 16–17, 34
Aquinas, St Thomas, 34–5
Aristotle, 33, 51
'artefact-based' emotions, 124, 134
Arthur, King (Artus), 51–6, 57–63, 87–104, 107–12
    and affect (*see also under* affect), 40, 43, 73–4, 154, 183–4, 186

    emotion of, 20, 52–6, 109, 119
    politics of, 126–7, 184
Arturs doet, 149–53, 156–8
Atanassov, S., 132, 137, 140
Atre Périlleux, L', 123, 131, 135–9
audience (listeners/readers)
    and affect (*see also under* affect), 1, 8–10, 67–85, 156–7
    delivery to, 146–7, 154, 184
    Malory's medieval, 106–8, 113–15, 117, 119–20, 125, 159
    Nordic medieval, 162–3, 168–9, 174, 177–9
    and 'mirror effect', 149
    response, 124, 127, 130, 134–5, 138–41, 152–3, 185
Augustine, St, of Hippo, 32–3
Austria, 123
Avalon, 59
Avicenna, *De anima*, 33–4

Bademagu, King, 75, 82
Balin, 43–4
Bacon, Roger, 34
Ban of Benoïc, 14–15
Barron, W. R. J., 52
'basic emotions', 8, 130, 164 n. 9
battle, *see* war, warfare
behavioural codes, 87, 176
Beheading Game, 134–5
being-in-the-world, 15, 29–30
Bell, Catherine, 103
Benjamin, Walter, 27–8
Benson, Larry, 91
Bergson, Henri, 4
Bertilak, 42
blood, *see also* violence, war, warfare
    and affect (*see also under* affect), 38, 40, 42, 49, 52
    Holy Bloode, the, 44
    symbolic, 89, 95–103
    and violence, 88, 90–1, 94–5, 161, 168–9
Boer, Minne de, 145–6
Bolli Þorleiksson, 169
Bordwell, David, 139
Bors, 21, 42, 61, 186
Brennu-Njáls saga, 100–1, 161–79
Brien, 131–5

Brun (Brehus) sans Pitié, 23–4
Brunhild, 170
Buridant, Claude, 146
Burrow, John, 94

Calogrenant, 164–5
Cartesian dualism, 2, 31
chanson de geste (Old French epic), 7, 16
Chanson de Roland, 92–3, 104
Charlemagne, 92–3
Chaucer, Geoffrey 46, 182–3
    Troilus and Criseyde, 36
Cherewatuk, Karen, 90–1
Chestre, Thomas, *Sir Launfal*, 38–40, 46, 56–9
Chevalier aux Deux Épées, Le, 123
Cheyette, Fredric, 175–6
Chickering, Howell, 175–6
chivalry, 18–19, 29, 60, 135
Chrétien de Troyes, 24, 139, 158
    Le Conte del Graal, 126–8, 147
    Erec et Enide, 56, 87
    Le Chevalier au Lion (Yvain), 36–8, 161–79
    Le Chevalier de la Charrete, 36, 67–85, 152–3
Christ, Jesus, 99, 101–2
Claudas, 14, 21, 29, 30
clergie, 20, 24, 30
Clover, Carol, 177–8
Clunies Ross, Margaret, 163
cognition, cognitive, 3–5, 9–10, 33–6, 40–4, 123–41, 169
cold (*freor*), 49, 72, 146
comedy, 147, 184
complexion (colour), 32, 44, 52, 75–6
consciousness, 2–3, 5, 13–16
Cornwall, 90
corpse, 88, 89, 93–6, 98, 100, 185–7
corrector (in the *Lancelot* Compilation), 148–9
Cortois de Huberlant, 136
courage, 52, 96, 143
court culture, 84, 128, 138–9, 141
Crane, Susan, 172
crying, weeping, 184–5
    audience response to, 137–8, 187
    behavioural, 63, 106, 116, 131, 156, 173
    gendered, 88, 94, 104
    tears, 61, 106, 112, 115, 120
cultural transferability, 182
curiosity, 158–9

Damasio, Antonio, 5, 68, 79
Dame de Beloé, 140
Dame de Malehaut, 24–5
Damoisele du Castiel du Port, 132–3

Dangier (*Roman de la Rose*), 23
Deleuze, Gilles, 4
Descartes, René, *Les passions de l'âme*, 2–4, 5
desire, *see* love
despair, 97, 115, 156, 157
dialogue, 40–1, 42, 146, 147–8, 152–7, 159, 167–8
Dienstbier, Richard A., 176
Dinadan, 184, 186
direct discourse, 144, 147, 156
disenchantment, 25, 30, *see also* enchantment
disguise, 54, 143, 185, 186
distress, 39–40, 49, 94, 126, *see also* affect, anger
Dives and Pauper, 101
dreams, dreaming, 42, 45, 55–6, 148
Duchamp, Marcel, 26

'ecology of emotions', 69
Elaine of Astolat, 44, 187
embodiment, 9, 23, 93, 161–79
embrace, embracing, 58, 93, 96, 102, 129
Eming, Jutta, 173–4
emotionology, 48–9, 62
empathy, 2, 124, 130, 138
enchantment, 8, 21–2, 30, 145, *see also* disenchantment, magic
engin, 20, 24, 30
envy, 120, 183
epic, 7–8, 16, 88, 89, 96, 170
Esclados the Red, 161, 171, 176
Eucharist, Eucharistic, 97–8, 102
evil (*malvaiste*), 71, 74–5
Excalibur, 61, 153–4
exclamation, 143–59

facial expression (*semblant*), 74, 78
faint (*pasmer*), fainting
    in anger, 132
    in grief, 39–40, 43–5, 93–5, 126, 127, 131, 135, 171, 177
    and heart, 15, 129
    seeming, 77
fairy, 57–8, *see also* enchantment, magic, supernatural
false death motif, 140–1
fear (*peor, poor*), 15, 41, 51, 158
    affect of, 41–2, 49, 72, *see also* affect
    and anticipation, 1–2, 62, 72, 135
    somatic correlates of, 73–8, 82
Felder, Gudrun, 128–9, 136, 138
female, feminine, *see* gender
Ferguut, 150, 158
'fiction-based' emotions, 124
fidelity, *see* loyalty

Flosi Þórðarson, 100–1
fornaldarsögur (legendary sagas), 167
France, French culture, 15, 22, 93, 114, 134, 162–4, 177
Frank, Adam, 22
frenzy, 37, 38, 46
Frijda, Nico, 50

Gaheriet, 95, 129
Gaheris, 45, 61, 106, 120, 185
Galahad, 29
Galehaut, 24–5, 28–30
Galen, 32, 49
Gareth, 43, 45, 54, 61–2, 106, 120
Gawain (Gauvain, Walewein, Gawein, Gawan)
    and affect, 40–2, 51, 105–6, *see also* affect
    death of, 90–104, 123–41
    failures of, 1–2, 44–5, 182
    psychology of, 135
gender, 49, 88, 94, 115–17, 158, 163, 176
    female, feminine
        anger, 82
        desire, 145
        grief, 88, 95, 103–4, 161, 171, 173
        intimacy, 92
    male, masculine
        anger, 81, 116
        collective masculinity, 56
        grief, 87, 94, 95, 104
        military ethic, 91, 96, 101
Geoffrey of Monmouth, *Historia Regum Britanniae*, 8, 51–2, 59–60
Gigamec, 123, 125–6, 130
Glenberg, Arthur, 67–8
Glúmr, 168
God of Love (*Roman de la Rose*), 23
Goodman, Nelson, 27
Grail, Holy, 29, 45, 59–60, 98–9
    Grail Quest, 42, 44–5
Green Knight, 1, 40–2, 128
grief (*dolor*), 87–104
    affect of, 37–46, 73, 116, 125, 129, 135, 138, 161, 171–2, 176–7, *see also* affect
    collective, 128, 131
    gendered, 94–5
    mourning, 7, 92, 94–6, 99, 102–4, 123–41, 171–9
    tempered, 178–9
Guattari, Félix, 4
Guðrún Ósvífrsdóttir, 161, 178
Guenevere (Guenièvre, Guinevere, Ginover, Wenhauer), 55–6
    and affect, 25, 43, 82, 184, *see also* affect
    cruelty of, 57, 61

False Guinevere, 19, 29
    relationship with Arthur, 55–6, 183
    relationship with Lancelot, 18, 20, 44–5, 77, 105–7, 113
Guillaume de Lorris, *Le Roman de la Rose*, 23
guilt, 36, 97, 176
Gunther, 170

Hagen, 170
Hákon Hákonarson, king of Norway, 162, *see also* Norway
Hallgerðr Höskuldsdóttir, 161, 168–9
Hamel, Mary, 99
happiness (*joi, leesce*), *see* joy
Hardy, Thomas, 2
hatred, 61, 132
Hautdesert, 41
Havas, David, 67
heart
    and affect, 2, 31, 39–41, 45–6, 54, 71–2, 74, 97–8, *see also* affect
    in medieval medicine, 32–5, 38, 49, 52
    pain of, 15, 129
Heidegger, Martin, 4
Heinrich von dem Türlin, *Diu Crône*, 123–41
Helgi Harðbeinsson, 169
Henryson, Robert, *The Bludy Serk*, 101
heroic tradition, 88, 96, 104
Heytze, Ingmar, 143
Hildigunnr Starkaðardóttir, 100–1
Hippocrates, 32, 167, *see also* humours, theory of
Hoccleve, Thomas, *Complaint* and *Dialogue with a Friend*, 38
Hogan, Patrick Colm, 141
Homer, *Iliad*, 96
Höskuldr Dala-Kolsson, 100–1
Hrútr Herjólfsson, 168
Hugh of St Victor, 34
Hume, David, 3
humours, theory of, 6, 32, 167, *see also* Hippocrates
Huntington, Richard, 173
Husserl, Edmund, 4, 13
hvöt (goading or whetting), 170, 177

Iceland, Icelandic saga, 100, 104, 161–79
illness, 34, 37–8, 44
imagination, 34–5, 42, 54
insults, 146–7
interjections, 149–54
intimacy, 20, 87–104
Ipomadon, 60
irony, 127, 138, 141, 184
Isode, La Beale, 43

Ívens saga (see also Yvain/Ywain), 161–79

Jacob van Maerlant, *Merlijn*, 156–7
Jaeger, C. Stephen, 138
James, William, 3–5
Jay, Martin, 22, 26–8
Jillings, Lewis, 127
John of La Rochelle, 34
joy (*joie*), 54–5, 139, 157–8, see also sorrow
    affect of, 34, 49, 184, see also affect
    collective, 56
    detached, 57
    as positive force, 18, 46, 165
    private, 57
    sexual, 57–9
    somatic, 177, 179

Kay (Keii), 22–3, 126–8, 138, 166, 185
King of the Isles, 132–3
kingship, 87–104
Kinne, Elizabeth, 136
kiss, kissing, 94–5, 106, 127, 129, 139
Knuuttila, Simo, 49
konungasögur (sagas of kings), 167
Kuiken, Don, 124, 139

Lacy, Norris J., 61–2, 81
Laʒamon, *Brut*, 48, 52, 56, 60, 63
Laid Hardi, 137
Lamerok, 185–6
Lanceloet, 149, 150–2, 156, 157–8
Lanceloet en het hert met de witte voet, 157
Lancelot, Launcelot, 105–21, 143
    affect and, 19–20, 28–9, 44–5, 61–3, 71–9, 82, 107, 109–10, 152–3, 156, 183–7, see also affect
    emotion, 19
    loyalty of, 105–21
    madness of, 61
    psychology of, 44
    relationship with Guinevere, 18, 36, 99, 105–7, 113
Lancelot Compilation, 148–9, 152
Lancelot en prose, see Prose *Lancelot*
Langland, William, *Piers Plowman*, 35
language, 8–9, 27, 67–9, 83, 116, 146
Lantsloot vander Haghedochte, 150, 158
Laudine, 161, 163, 171–9
laughing, laughter, 181–8
    affect of, 41–3, 119, 177, see also affect
    defiant, 161, 163, 168–9, 170
    mocking, 126
Launfal, 39–40, 56–9
Laxdæla saga, 161, 169
Le Saux, Françoise, 54

Lionel, 21, 24–5, 155–6
Locke, John, 3
Lodewijk van Velthem, *Merlijncontinuatie*, 144, 150, 158
love
    affect of, 18–20, 36, 45–6, see also affect
    and desire, 41–2, 51
    love of life, 41–2
    love potion, 184
    love sickness, 25–6, 42
    love spell, 144
    psychology, 44
    sexual, 57–9, 132
    and sight, 39, 105
    unrequited, 187
Lucius, 89
Lunete, 172, 174–5

madness, 36–8, 42, 44, 61, 106, 112–13, 171, 176
magic, 10, 13–30, 38, 57, 136–7, 183, see also enchantment, fairy, supernatural
male, masculine, see gender
Malory, Sir Thomas, *Le Morte Darthur*, 42–6, 54, 56, 60–3, 105–21, 129, 140, 181–8
Mandeville, Sir John, *The Travels of Sir John Mandeville*, 7
mania, 34
Marie de France, *Lais* (*Lanval*), 36, 56–9
marvels, marvellous, 41, 46
McNamer, Sarah, 8
melancholy, 34, 38, 157
Meleagant, 73–6, 81–2, 152
memory, 5, 10, 32–5, 38, 41, 45
Mentzel-Reuters, Arno, 128, 130
Mériadeuc, 131–2
Merleau-Ponty, Maurice, 4
Merlin, 43, 144–5, 157, 183, 185
merveilleux, 20–2
Metcalf, Peter, 173
Meyer, Matthias, 127, 135
Miall, D. S., 124, 139
Miller, William Ian, 167, 169
mind-body continuum, 32, 46
mirror character(s), 70, 72, 75, 79, 81, 124, 152, 156, 158–9
mirror effect, see audience
Mitchell, W. J. T., 27
mockery, 166, 182, see also laughter
monologue, 135, 144, 148, 149, 152–7
Mordred, 45, 55–6, 59, 61, 89, 106–10, 120, 140, 183
Morgain/Morgan le Fay, 28, 38, 43, 140, 183
Moriaen, 150, 158
Mort le Roi Artu, La, 60–1, 95
mourning, see grief
Mullally, Erin, 52

INDEX 209

Nagy, Piroska, 6
neuroscience, 4–5, 9, 31, 67, 79
Nibelungenlied, Das, 170
nominalism, 22, 26–7
Norway, Norse culture, 10, 161–79, *see also* Hákon Hákonarson, king of Norway
nostalgia, 141
Nussbaum, Martha, 3–4

Oatley, Keith, 50, 123
Odoric of Pordenone, 7
Oliver, 92–3
Opperman-Marsaux, Evelyne, 147
Orgueilleux Faé, 136

pain (*dolor*), 15, 25, 29, 36, 39, 74–6, 90
Palomides, 43, 182
Parkinson, Brian, 125
passion, passions, 2, 6, 18, 32, 36, 48, 181
Patroclos, 96
Peirce, Charles Sanders, 27
Pelles' daughter, 29–30
perception, 3, 8–9, 17, 33–4, 40–2, 107, 163, 178
Perceval, 136, 156, 186
Perchevael, 149, 150, 158
performance, *see also* audience
 comic, 147, *see also* comedy
 emotional, 10, 125, 129, 131, 140, 161, 173
 and gesture, 104
 literary, 50
 oral, 2, 146–9
 social, 140, 172, 177
phenomenology, 13, 16, 19, 31
philosophy, 2–6, 14
physiology, 37–8, 49, 49
pity, 52, 75, 97, 184
Pössel, Christina, 103
Post-Vulgate *Suite de Merlin*, 140
Priamus, 98
private, *see also* public
 emotions, 3, 5, 60
 grief, 87–9, 102–3, 172–4
 happiness, 57
 social behaviour, 57, 120, 185–6
Prose *Lancelot* (Vulgate cycle), 13–30, 113, 151
prose romance, 13–30
psyche, 16–18, 23, 31, 43
psychology, 2–3, 9, 23, 25, 31–46, 47
 medieval, 32–5
 modern, 50
psychomachia, 23, 35
public, *see also* private
 emotions, 7, 10, 52, 105–6, 114, 167–71
 grief, 102–4, 172–9

honour, 57
intimacy, 93
joy, 54, 61
knowledge, 186
social behaviour, 62, 87–9, 108–11, 116–21, 132–3, 181
sorrow, 131

Queen of the Isles, 131, 133, 136
Queeste vanden Grale, 149, 150, 153, 158
Queste del saint Graal (Vulgate cycle), 29

reader, *see* audience
realism, 25, 27, 39–40, 70
reason, 19, 21, 24, 34, 36
reception studies, *see* audience
recognition, 67, 106, 185–6
Reddy, William, 141
restraint, 54
revenge, 45, 61, 88, 100–4, 110, 120, 168, 178–79
Riddere metter mouwen, 150, 158
Riddy, Felicity, 87, 94
Rinck, Mike, 67
ritual, 7, 9, 10, 88–90, 97–104, 173–5, 177
Roberts, Robert C., 51
Rockwell, P. V., 134
Roland, 92–3
Rome, Roman culture, 53, 55, 89
Rosenwein, Barbara, 6, 15–16, 59, 116, 167
Round Table, 90–1, 99, 111, 120, 134–5, 181
 fall of the, 97, 183

sadness, *see* sorrow
Saler, Michael, 30
Sartre, Jean-Paul, 10
 Esquisse d'une théorie des émotions (*Sketch for a Theory of the Emotions*), 13–26
Schadenfreude, 8, 157
Scheff, T. J., 123, 138
Secreta secretorum, 118–20
Sedgwick, Eve Kosofsky, 22
Segre, Cesare, 81
senses, 3, 5, 31–46, 48–9, 72, 84
Sgoidamur, 127
shaking (*trambler*), 71–2
shame (*honte*), 7–8, 40, 42–3, 52–3, 74, 78, 108, 174, 176
shivering (*fremir*), 72
sight, 44, 90–1
silence, 103, 112, 183–4
simulated emotions, 78–9
sin, sinners, 33, 49, 51, 97–9, 146, 187
Sir Gawain and the Green Knight, 1–2, 40–2, 46, 128, 134, 182–3
Skarpheðinn Njálsson, 100

smile, smiling, 136, 161, 169–71, 177–9, 181–8
somatic correlates, 67–85
somatic response, 8, 10, 72, 171–2
sorrow (*poinne*), 54–5, 157–8, *see also* crying, weeping, grief, joy
    affect of, 37–40, 56, 73–5, 90, 97–8, 119, 131, 138, 161, 171, 177, *see also* affect
    and audience, 152, *see also* audience
    hidden, 177–9
    language of, 113
    paternal, 29
    public/private, 87–8, 173, 175
    somatic correlates, 73–8, *see also* somatic correlates
    and suffering, 55
Spinoza, Baruch, 3–4
spirit(s), animal, 33
Starkey, Kathryn, 170
Suerbaum, Almut, 130
suicide, 136–7
Suite-Vulgate du Merlin, La, 143–4
supernatural, 40, 46, 136, *see also* divine, fairy, magic
surprise, 57
suspense, 1, 137, 157, *see also* audience
swoon, swooning, *see* faint, fainting

Tan, Ed, 123
tears, *see* crying, weeping
theatricality, 146–7
theory of mind, 80
Tolkien, J. R. R., 139
Torec, 150, 158
transference, 149, 156, 158–9, 170, 177–8, 181–2
Tristan-*qui-jamais-ne-rit*, 136
Tristram, 42–4, 184–6
Troilus, 182–3, 185
Tryamour (Triamour), 39–40, 57, 59
Tulinius, Torfi, 163
Turner, Victor, 114

universals, 26
unrequited love, *see* love
Urry, 45, 184
Uther Pendragon, 42, 52

Veldhuizen, Martine, 146
vengeance, *see* revenge
verse romance, 25, 30, 67, 78–85, 140, 149
vice, vices, 49, 181, *see also* sin, sinners
Vincensini, Jean-Jacques, 146
Vincent of Beauvais, 7
violence, 23, 53, 89, 95, 100–4, 105, 117, *see also* anger, blood, war, warfare
virtue, virtues, 29, 40, 43, 46, 49, 95, 127
Vitz, Evelyn Birge, 147
vocalisation, 93, 161–79

Wace, *Roman de Brut*, 52, 54, 55, 91
Walewein, 135, 150, 158
Walewein ende Keye, 150, 158
war, warfare, 51, 53–4, 60–1, 89–92, 96, 109–10, *see also* violence
    battle, 43, 53, 71, 73–4, 91–102, 104
    battlefield, 88–98, 102, 104
    war counsel, 53
    war horse, 59, *see also under* Blanchard
    Wars of the Roses, 115
    war token, 101–2
weeping, *see* crying
Weinburg, S. C., 52
White, T. H., *The Once and Future King*, 143
wickedness, *see* evil
Wrake van Ragisel, Die, 150, 151, 158
wringing of hands, 94, 127, 172, 187

Ygrainne, 42
Yvain li Avoutres, 29
Yvain/Ywain, 36–8, 161–79
Ywain and Gawain, 37–40, 46

Þjóstólfr Bjarnason, 168

ARTHURIAN STUDIES

- I   ASPECTS OF MALORY, *edited by Toshiyuki Takamiya and Derek Brewer*
- II   THE ALLITERATIVE *MORTE ARTHURE*: A Reassessment of the Poem, *edited by Karl Heinz Göller*
- III   THE ARTHURIAN BIBLIOGRAPHY, I: Author Listing, *edited by C. E. Pickford and R. W. Last*
- IV   THE CHARACTER OF KING ARTHUR IN MEDIEVAL LITERATURE, *Rosemary Morris*
- V   PERCEVAL: The Story of the Grail, by Chrétien de Troyes, *translated by Nigel Bryant*
- VI   THE ARTHURIAN BIBLIOGRAPHY, II: Subject Index, *edited by C. E. Pickford and R. W. Last*
- VII   THE LEGEND OF ARTHUR IN THE MIDDLE AGES, *edited by P. B. Grout, R. A. Lodge, C. E. Pickford and E. K. C. Varty*
- VIII   THE ROMANCE OF YDER, *edited and translated by Alison Adams*
- IX   THE RETURN OF KING ARTHUR, *Beverly Taylor and Elisabeth Brewer*
- X   ARTHUR'S KINGDOM OF ADVENTURE: The World of Malory's *Morte Darthur*, *Muriel Whitaker*
- XI   KNIGHTHOOD IN THE *MORTE DARTHUR*, *Beverly Kennedy*
- XII   LE ROMAN DE TRISTAN EN PROSE, tome I, *edited by Renée L. Curtis*
- XIII   LE ROMAN DE TRISTAN EN PROSE, tome II, *edited by Renée L. Curtis*
- XIV   LE ROMAN DE TRISTAN EN PROSE, tome III, *edited by Renée L. Curtis*
- XV   LOVE'S MASKS: Identity, Intertextuality, and Meaning in the Old French Tristan Poems, *Merritt R. Blakeslee*
- XVI   THE CHANGING FACE OF ARTHURIAN ROMANCE: Essays on Arthurian Prose Romances in memory of Cedric E. Pickford, *edited by Alison Adams, Armel H. Diverres, Karen Stern and Kenneth Varty*
- XVII   REWARDS AND PUNISHMENTS IN THE ARTHURIAN ROMANCES AND LYRIC POETRY OF MEDIEVAL FRANCE: Essays presented to Kenneth Varty on the occasion of his sixtieth birthday, *edited by Peter V. Davies and Angus J. Kennedy*
- XVIII   CEI AND THE ARTHURIAN LEGEND, *Linda Gowans*
- XIX   LA3AMON'S *BRUT*: The Poem and its Sources, *Françoise H. M. Le Saux*
- XX   READING THE *MORTE DARTHUR*, Terence McCarthy, reprinted as AN INTRODUCTION TO MALORY
- XXI   CAMELOT REGAINED: The Arthurian Revival and Tennyson, 1800–1849, *Roger Simpson*
- XXII   THE LEGENDS OF KING ARTHUR IN ART, *Muriel Whitaker*
- XXIII   GOTTFRIED VON STRASSBURG AND THE MEDIEVAL TRISTAN LEGEND: Papers from an Anglo-North American symposium, *edited with an introduction by Adrian Stevens and Roy Wisbey*
- XXIV   ARTHURIAN POETS: CHARLES WILLIAMS, *edited and introduced by David Llewellyn Dodds*
- XXV   AN INDEX OF THEMES AND MOTIFS IN TWELFTH-CENTURY FRENCH ARTHURIAN POETRY, *E. H. Ruck*
- XXVI   CHRÉTIEN DE TROYES AND THE GERMAN MIDDLE AGES: Papers from an international symposium, *edited with an introduction by Martin H. Jones and Roy Wisbey*

XXVII   SIR GAWAIN AND THE GREEN KNIGHT: Sources and Analogues, *compiled by Elisabeth Brewer*
XXVIII   CLIGÉS by Chrétien de Troyes, *edited by Stewart Gregory and Claude Luttrell*
XXIX   THE LIFE AND TIMES OF SIR THOMAS MALORY, *P. J. C. Field*
XXX   T. H. WHITE'S *THE ONCE AND FUTURE KING*, *Elisabeth Brewer*
XXXI   ARTHURIAN BIBLIOGRAPHY, III: 1978–1992, Author Listing and Subject Index, *compiled by Caroline Palmer*
XXXII   ARTHURIAN POETS: JOHN MASEFIELD, *edited and introduced by David Llewellyn Dodds*
XXXIII   THE TEXT AND TRADITION OF LAƷAMON'S *BRUT*, *edited by Françoise Le Saux*
XXXIV   CHIVALRY IN TWELFTH-CENTURY GERMANY: The Works of Hartmann von Aue, *W. H. Jackson*
XXXV   THE TWO VERSIONS OF MALORY'S *MORTE DARTHUR*: Multiple Negation and the Editing of the Text, *Ingrid Tieken-Boon van Ostade*
XXXVI   RECONSTRUCTING CAMELOT: French Romantic Medievalism and the Arthurian Tradition, *Michael Glencross*
XXXVII   A COMPANION TO MALORY, *edited by Elizabeth Archibald and A. S. G. Edwards*
XXXVIII   A COMPANION TO THE *GAWAIN*-POET, *edited by Derek Brewer and Jonathan Gibson*
XXXIX   MALORY'S BOOK OF ARMS: The Narrative of Combat in *Le Morte Darthur*, *Andrew Lynch*
XL   MALORY: TEXTS AND SOURCES, *P. J. C. Field*
XLI   KING ARTHUR IN AMERICA, *Alan Lupack and Barbara Tepa Lupack*
XLII   THE SOCIAL AND LITERARY CONTEXTS OF MALORY'S *MORTE DARTHUR*, *edited by D. Thomas Hanks Jr*
XLIII   THE GENESIS OF NARRATIVE IN MALORY'S *MORTE DARTHUR*, *Elizabeth Edwards*
XLIV   GLASTONBURY ABBEY AND THE ARTHURIAN TRADITION, *edited by James P. Carley*
XLV   THE KNIGHT WITHOUT THE SWORD: A Social Landscape of Malorian Chivalry, *Hyonjin Kim*
XLVI   ULRICH VON ZATZIKHOVEN'S *LANZELET*: Narrative Style and Entertainment, *Nicola McLelland*
XLVII   THE MALORY DEBATE: Essays on the Texts of *Le Morte Darthur*, *edited by Bonnie Wheeler, Robert L. Kindrick and Michael N. Salda*
XLVIII   MERLIN AND THE GRAIL: *Joseph of Arimathea, Merlin, Perceval*: The Trilogy of Arthurian romances attributed to Robert de Boron, *translated by Nigel Bryant*
XLIX   ARTHURIAN BIBLIOGRAPHY IV: 1993–1998, Author Listing and Subject Index, *compiled by Elaine Barber*
L   *DIU CRÔNE* AND THE MEDIEVAL ARTHURIAN CYCLE, *Neil Thomas*
LII   KING ARTHUR IN MUSIC, *edited by Richard Barber*
LIII   THE BOOK OF LANCELOT: The Middle Dutch *Lancelot* Compilation and the Medieval Tradition of Narrative Cycles, *Bart Besamusca*
LIV   A COMPANION TO THE *LANCELOT-GRAIL* CYCLE, *edited by Carol Dover*
LV   THE GENTRY CONTEXT FOR MALORY'S *MORTE DARTHUR*, *Raluca L. Radulescu*

LVI	PARZIVAL: With *Titurel* and the *Love Lyrics*, by Wolfram von Eschenbach, *translated by Cyril Edwards*
LVII	ARTHURIAN STUDIES IN HONOUR OF P. J. C. FIELD, *edited by Bonnie Wheeler*
LVIII	THE LEGEND OF THE GRAIL, *translated by Nigel Bryant*
LIX	THE GRAIL LEGEND IN MODERN LITERATURE, *John B. Marino*
LX	RE-VIEWING *LE MORTE DARTHUR*: Texts and Contexts, Characters and Themes, *edited by K. S. Whetter and Raluca L. Radulescu*
LXI	THE SCOTS AND MEDIEVAL ARTHURIAN LEGEND, *edited by Rhiannon Purdie and Nicola Royan*
LXII	WIRNT VON GRAVENBERG'S *WIGALOIS*: Intertextuality and Interpretation, *Neil Thomas*
LXIII	COMPANION TO CHRÉTIEN DE TROYES, *edited by Norris J. Lacy and Joan Tasker Grimbert*
LXIV	THE FORTUNES OF KING ARTHUR, *edited by Norris J. Lacy*
LXV	A HISTORY OF ARTHURIAN SCHOLARSHIP, *edited by Norris J. Lacy*
LXVI	MALORY'S CONTEMPORARY AUDIENCE: The Social Reading of Romance in Late Medieval England, *Thomas H. Crofts*
LXVII	MARRIAGE, ADULTERY AND INHERITANCE IN MALORY'S *MORTE DARTHUR*, *Karen Cherewatuk*
LXVIII	EDWARD III'S ROUND TABLE AT WINDSOR: The House of the Round Table and the Windsor Festival of 1344, *Julian Munby, Richard Barber and Richard Brown*
LXIX	GEOFFREY OF MONMOUTH, THE HISTORY OF THE KINGS OF BRITAIN: An edition and translation of the *De gestis Britonum* [*Historia Regum Britanniae*], *edited by Michael D. Reeve, translated by Neil Wright*
LXX	RADIO CAMELOT: Arthurian Legends on the BBC, 1922–2005, *Roger Simpson*
LXXI	MALORY'S LIBRARY: The Sources of the *Morte Darthur*, *Ralph Norris*
LXXII	THE GRAIL, THE QUEST, AND THE WORLD OF ARTHUR, *edited by Norris J. Lacy*
LXXIII	ILLUSTRATING CAMELOT, *Barbara Tepa Lupack with Alan Lupack*
LXXIV	THE ARTHURIAN WAY OF DEATH: The English Tradition, *edited by Karen Cherewatuk and K. S. Whetter*
LXXV	VISION AND GENDER IN MALORY'S *MORTE DARTHUR*, *Molly Martin*
LXXVI	THE INTERLACE STRUCTURE OF THE THIRD PART OF THE *PROSE LANCELOT*, *Frank Brandsma*
LXXVII	*PERCEFOREST*: The Prehistory of King Arthur's Britain, *translated by Nigel Bryant*
LXXVIII	CHRÉTIEN DE TROYES IN PROSE: The Burgundian *Erec* and *Cligés*, *translated by Joan Tasker Grimbert and Carol J. Chase*
LXXIX	THE *CONTINUATIONS* OF CHRÉTIEN'S *PERCEVAL*: Content and Construction, Extension and Ending, *Leah Tether*
LXXX	SIR THOMAS MALORY: *Le Morte Darthur*, *edited by P. J. C. Field*
LXXXI	MALORY AND HIS EUROPEAN CONTEMPORARIES: Adapting Late Medieval Arthurian Romance Collections, *Miriam Edlich-Muth*
LXXXII	THE COMPLETE STORY OF THE GRAIL: Chrétien de Troyes' Perceval and its continuations, *translated by Nigel Bryant*
LXXXIII	EMOTIONS IN MEDIEVAL ARTHURIAN LITERATURE: Body, Mind, Voice, *edited by Frank Brandsma, Carolyne Larrington and Corinne Saunders*

LXXXIV THE MANUSCRIPT AND MEANING OF MALORY'S *MORTE DARTHUR:* Rubrication, Commemoration, Memorialisation, *K. S. Whetter*
LXXXV PUBLISHING THE GRAIL IN MEDIEVAL AND EARLY RENAISSANCE FRANCE, *Leah Tether*

www.ingramcontent.com/pod-product-compliance
Lightning Source LLC
Chambersburg PA
CBHW070804230426
43665CB00017B/2480